The Talyllyn Railway

The
Talyllyn
Railway

DAVID POTTER

Abergynolwyn · block post ·

DAVID ST JOHN THOMAS
DAVID & CHARLES

British Library Cataloguing in Publication Data

Potter, David
  The Talyllyn Railway.
  Gwynedd. Meirionnydd (District). Narrow gauge railway
  services: Talyllyn Railway, history
  I. Title
  385.520942929

  ISBN 0–946537–50–X

Printed in Great Britain
by Redwood Burn Ltd   Trowbridge
Published by David St John Thomas and
distributed by David & Charles Publishers plc
Brunel House   Newton Abbot   Devon

Distributed in the United States of America
by David & Charles Inc
North Pomfret   Vermont 05053   USA

Contents

Foreword

This is the story of a Welsh railway. Of how, owned by a family company, it remained almost unchanged for nearly a century. Of how it was taken over by a small group of enthusiastic volunteers and became a pioneer of railway preservation. Of how this captured the imagination of a country experiencing its first real bout of socialism and nationalisation. Of how these few brave individuals, standing out against the mindless uniformity and greyness of bureaucracy, re-built their railway. Of what in effect became a 'workers co-operative' – although never acknowledged as such – with almost all the 'workers' unpaid, freely giving their labour in return for the privilege of controlling and operating their own railway.

This account of how a derelict railway was resurrected, virtually from the grave, represents a triumph of the human spirit. Of how men and women of very diverse backgrounds worked together irrespective of class, education, and wealth, united in a common purpose, almost all of them paying for the pleasure of so doing. Of how a handful of men and women, by their dedication and enthusiasm, without initially any governmental financial assistance, preserved the past for the enjoyment not only of themselves, but of the community at large. Of how they turned the company into a viable on-going concern: even to the extent of providing permanent jobs in an area of high-unemployment.

For the first four years after the take-over, the Talyllyn Railway was unique, the only preserved private railway in Britain: now there are over eighty. The Talyllyn and its preservation society pioneered much of what is today taken for granted.

This is not just an account of yet another railway. It tells of the constructive conflict of strong personalities: of the evolution of the idea that work can be part of leisure: of the change in attitude to our environmental and historical heritage: and of a living memorial to a prophet before his time. Tom Rolt, engineer and author, saw long before most other people, that unrestricted technological development could destroy the human environment. As such the Tallylyn story should prove of interest to a wide readership.

Quarry Siding · block post ·

CHAPTER 1

The First Eighty-five Years

In 1911 Henry Haydn Jones bought the Talyllyn Railway Company from the McConnels. Haydn Jones was the newly elected Liberal Member of Parliament for the Welsh county of Merioneth, where he was also a solicitor, a land agent, a property owner and a retailer in the small coastal resort of Tywyn. He was destined to remain the local MP for the next thirty five years, and to own the Talyllyn Railway until his death in 1950.

The McConnels were a mill-owning family from Manchester who had made a fortune spinning cotton from the southern states of the USA. When civil war broke out in that country in 1861 they felt it was time to diversify their investment. With the rapid growth of the industrial towns, there was an increasing demand for roofing materials, notably slate. The best slate veins were located in Wales, the finest of these being in the north around Snowdonia. But these had already been snapped up, and were no longer in the market. However there appeared good prospects further south in the hills overlooking the ancient settlement of Tywyn. Indeed there was already a slate quarry at Bryneglwys, above the gorge at Nant Gwernol, and had been since 1844. The slates were loaded on to pack-mules and carried four and a half miles over the mountains to wharves along the Dyfi estuary.

But the McConnels had other plans. They knew of a far more efficient and much cheaper way of getting the slates to the wharves. This was to build a railway. They were aware that already slates were being carried the fourteen miles from the mighty quarries at Blaenau Ffestiniog to the harbour at Porthmadog by means of a narrow-gauge railway, on rails half an inch less than two feet apart. The man who had built the line had since died, so

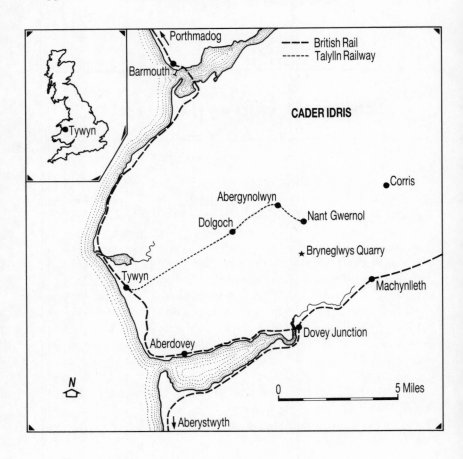

the McConnels hired one of his sons, James Swinton Spooner, to build them a railway too. But theirs was to be built to a gauge of two feet three inches, probably because that was the width of the tramways already in use in the quarry at Bryneglwys, and they wished to use the wagons that were already there.

They wanted a railway with the latest technology. So they decided to use steam locomotives to pull their slate wagons. James's younger brother, Charles, who had succeeded his father as engineer to the Festiniog Railway, had just confounded the experts, who had said it was impossible to design a steam engine to work successfully on such a narrow gauge, by doing just that. Previously horses had been used to pull the empty slate wagons up to Blaenau, with the full ones coming down by gravity – so well had father Spooner surveyed and built the line. The horses rode in their own special trucks! The first locomotive Charles designed, the world's original narrow-gauge steam engine, *Prince*, began hauling trains between Porthmadog and Blaenau in 1863, and still does so today!

But the McConnels wanted to carry passengers as well as slate. So besides ordering two new narrow-gauge locomotives of the latest model – they had to be, as there was only one other in the world, namely *Prince* – they decided to buy four passenger coaches, and a brake-van.

But even in free-market Victorian days it was necessary to have Parliamentary approval for a public railway. So a Parliamentary Bill was drawn up, and the Tal-y-llyn Railway Act, 1865 (28 and 29 Vict,cap cccxv) enabled the Company to run passenger trains as far as Abergynolwyn, six and a half miles from the terminus at Tywyn. The Company obviously regarded the three quarters of a mile of track beyond Abergynolwyn to the foot of the first incline up to the quarry as a private mineral line, for Spooner's plans for this section, 'The Extension of the Talyllyn Railway', were not submitted to Parliament for its approval. The plans actually passed by Parliament did however include a 'Line No 2', never built, which would have provided direct narrow-gauge access, by means of a spur and reversal, from the other terminus at Wharf to the standard-gauge Cambrian (now BR) main-line station at Tywyn.

The Victorians did not believe in hanging about. The Aberdovey Slate Company was registered on 23 January 1864, and took over the quarry on March 25. But according to the *Caernarvon & Denbigh Herald* of 30 January, James Spooner was already surveying the line. Whilst the railway was being built the slates were loaded into sledges, which were then lowered down the side of the mountain. At the bottom the slates were packed into carts and taken along the valley road to Tywyn,

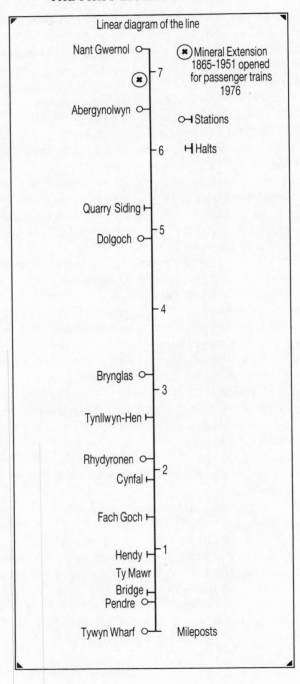

Linear diagram of the line

Nant Gwernol

⊛ Mineral Extension
1865-1951 opened
for passenger trains
1976

⊙⊣ Stations

⊣ Halts

Abergynolwyn

Quarry Siding

Dolgoch

Brynglas

Tynllwyn-Hen

Rhydyronen

Cynfal

Fach Goch

Hendy

Ty Mawr

Bridge

Pendre

Tywyn Wharf   Mileposts

where they could be loaded on to the newly-arrived railway for the four-mile journey to the port of Aberdovey. Carts could carry about ten times the load of a pack-horse, thus compensating for the extra mileage of going down the valley and along the coast instead of straight over the hills. But the carts made an awful mess of the turnpike road, and there were bitter complaints in the local Press; the Victorian version of today's opposition to heavy lorries on narrow roads. Indeed the McConnels told the Trustees of the turnpike road that they would pay them £10 for every £50 spent on it.

Although the standard-gauge railway had arrived in Tywyn in November 1863, the track only went as far as Aberdovey harbour, four miles to the south. This was because the original plan was that it should connect with the Crewe-Whitchurch-Aberystwyth line at Borth, crossing the mouth of the Dovey Estuary on a long bridge similar to that over the Mawddach estuary at Barmouth. But it never happened as the engineers could find no firm rock on which to place their piers: and the Victorians knew their bibles too well to build on sand!

Tywyn was not connected to the national railway system until 1867, when the highly picturesque, but very expensive link, connecting Aberdovey to the main Aberystwyth line at Dovey junction was opened. The single-line runs along a narrow ledge etched out of steep cliffs. It commands magnificent views south across the broad tidal sands of the wide Dyfi estuary, the home of myriads of sea-birds, to the mountains beyond.

Even after the connection to the national rail network was established, most of the slates brought down the narrow-gauge company line to Tywyn for transfer to the Cambrian railway, were still being taken only as far as the port of Aberdovey. There they were loaded on to schooners, coastal sailing ships, which did the jobs lorries and freight trains do today. The McConnels actually owned one of these ships, the locally built *Seven Brothers*, from 1870 to 1878. These schooners took the slates to ports all round the coasts of Britain and Ireland.

Thus the Talyllyn railway was established. It remained virtually unaltered through the rest of the reign of Queen Victoria, the reigns of her son Edward VII and grandson

George V, and of the latter's sons, Edward VIII and George VI.

At the outbreak of World War II in 1939 the Talyllyn was much as it had been from its beginning, sixty three years earlier. Its motive power and stock still consisted of the two original locomotives and the five carriages, which the McConnels had bought seventy three years before, the original track, and an assortment of slate wagons and associated equipment.

In 1939 Hugh Jones, then aged thirty-five, was employed as a fireman on the railway. When there were no trains running he worked in the yard at Wharf station loading slate on to main-line railway wagons, or on to Jos Humphrey's lorries if the slate was to go out by road. Hugh was born in 1904 in the cottage in which he still lived, *Plas Goch*, by Rhydyronen Station, two and a half miles up the line. The cottage went with the job, for his father – like his uncle – was also employed by the quarry company of which the railway was an integral part. In 1918 Hugh had been apprenticed to the slate quarry to work the machines which trimmed the slate. But over the years the dust had got to his lungs and he had begun to suffer badly. His mother did the washing for Sir Haydn, and one day, taking courage in both hands, she told him that her son Hugh was not at all well, was having to take more and more time off work, and could he have a change of job to get him away from the worst of the dust. So he was moved down to Wharf to load slates and gradually began to spend more time on the engines. Passenger trains, by the late 1930s, ran only on Mondays, Wednesdays and Fridays, due to increasing competition from buses. But there were occasional freight trains on other days, depending on the availability of a locomotive, and the demand for slates.

Nor had the cottage *Plas Goch* changed much by 1939. It still had no running water, no electricity and no gas. Cooking was done on a coal-fired range, black-leaded each day, and heating was from open coal fires. Oil lamps provided illumination, and it was years later before Hugh was able to convert one of the three small bedrooms into a bathroom. Until then bathing took place in a large zinc tub before the kitchen fire. As for even more basic requirements these were met by means of a 'thunder-box'.

But this was no ordinary single, but a double, with two holes side-by-side in the wooden top, each with its own bucket beneath, thus facilitating connubial bliss and family cohesion.

Each morning Hugh let himself out of the front door of the cottage and crossed the road to join the railway track by Rhydyronen station. Not infrequently the rain would be coming down in that clinging penetrating drizzle so much a feature of the climate of the western coasts of Britain. He picked his way along the lineside, under the dripping trees, between the sodden hedgerows, past the still quiet farmsteads, the silence only disturbed by the crowing of dawn-aware cockerels. After he had walked a good two miles, he came to the white crossing gates at Pendre, and knew from the smoke spiralling up from the chimney of *Railway View*, the cottage that shared the same roof as the locomotive shed, that Peter Williams, engine driver and platelayer, or more likely Mrs Williams, was already up and about.

The two pairs of gates protected an unmetalled farm track. They were rather battered and distinctly off-white: hardly surprising, as they had already been swinging there for over seventy years. (And it was to be nearly another fifty before they were replaced.) Hugh stepped out into the lane, carefully closing the gate behind him, and crossed over to a wicket gate leading on to the platform of Pendre station. This was the passenger terminus of the railway throughout the nineteenth century, and indeed for most journeys, for the first two decades of the twentieth. In the

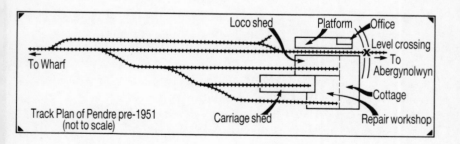

Track Plan of Pendre pre-1951 (not to scale)

centre of the low platform, constructed of slabs of slate, stood a
wooden shelter, largely open to the elements, just like those on
seaside promenades. One end had however been boxed in to form
a tiny booking office, rarely used since the turn of the century
when it had become the practice at all the stations, except Wharf,
to issue tickets from a booking office in the guard's van. But it
still possessed the diminutive scuttle (as it does today) through
which intending passengers once obtained their tickets.

Having recrossed the line, Hugh opened up the main doors of
the engine shed. He lit a candle standing on an old saucer on a
ledge just inside the entrance, as it was still almost pitch black
in there, for the sun had not yet risen high enough in the east
to clear the surrounding mountains. The Pendre cottage and its
contiguous workshop and loco shed had once been lit by gas:
but after a sharp disagreement between Sir Haydn and the gas
company, the supply had been cut off.

By the light of the flickering candle Hugh could just make
out the features of the dark shades before him. The one nearest
to him was called *Talyllyn* and its neighbour further up the shed
was *Dolgoch*. These two steam engines represented the sole motive power of the Talyllyn Railway. Like most of the rest of the
railway these were originals, virtually unchanged since they first
ran on the line back in 1865.

Holding the candle before him, Hugh climbed up into the
cab of *Talyllyn*. 'Climbed up' is somewhat of an exaggeration:
'stepped-up into' would be more accurate, as the footplate is
only about two feet off the ground. He then put some dry wood,
taken from a pile stacked at the side of the shed, into the firebox,
together with some paper and a drop of oil to get the fire going.
Making a taper from some more waste paper, he lit it from the
candle and dropped the flaming torch through the firebox door.
This he quickly closed till the fire caught up. He then gradually
put on pieces of coal from the bunker on the cab side until the
fire was established and could be left for a while. Once there
was enough steam pressure to move the engine, Hugh backed
it a few yards to the hose near the door,for it was now time
to water the loco. Steam locomotives of course work on the
principle of turning water into steam by means of fire. So it is

vitally important if the locomotive is to continue doing its job, and is not to be damaged, that there is enough coal for the fire, and water for the boiler. Otherwise it is very embarrassing, to say the least, for the loco crew, and annoying and expensive for everyone else, and an error not soon forgotten, if the engine fails to move when required.

So Hugh climbed up the side of *Talyllyn*, opened the lid of her water tank, and pulled a length of hose, apparently out of the ceiling. Pushing the hose well down into the interior of the engine he stretched up, pulled on a long metal handle and water came pouring down out of a tank perched precariously on the roof beams above him. Some years later the handle of this tank came adrift and caught Hugh's son, Herbert, by then also working on the railway, a nasty crack on the temple. The story goes that the Talyllyn Railway received all its water from the mains completely free for many a long year, indeed right up to the 1950s. This was because when the town supply was being installed the water company needed to take its pipes under the railway. As a condition of granting them a wayleave to do this, Sir Haydn demanded, and got, a free supply of water for Pendre, both for the cottage and the railway.

Whilst cleaning and oiling the engine Hugh found he needed a spanner to effect a minor repair. So he nipped through the doorway in the solid slate wall into the adjoining workshop to get one. This workshop was a rather larger shed with a line of rails over against the far wall so that carriages, engines and wagons could be brought in for repair. The equipment available was very limited, and mostly dated from the earliest days of the railway.

Hugh, whilst he still had the spanner, took the opportunity of tightening the nuts holding the hinges of a home-made wooden door fixed across the entrance to the loco cab on the driver's, the right-hand, side. This door gave some protection from the prevailing south-westerly winds which swept down the mountain sides driving rain on to the footplate. But neither locomotive had even a cab when first delivered, leaving the crew fully exposed to the elements. So one of the earliest tasks carried out at the Pendre works was the construction of a cab for each engine. These were extremely cramped, just covering the footplate, with very little headroom. Later users commented that they must have been built for Welsh 'midgets'. Indeed most of the doorways on the railway, to carriages and buildings, as well as locomotives, were equally low, and humility – the bending of heads – is required of more recent, and generally taller, generations.

Hugh then checked the fire, and built it up with discretely placed shovefuls of good Welsh steam-coal. Most of the coal came from pits in South Wales, through the Ocean Coal Co. Building up the fire had to be done carefully so that it would have the correct shape to give maximum heat for minimum fuel consumption. The shape of the fire is not only peculiar to each individual steam engine, but changes with a loco's work-load. So considerable skill is required, not only to drive, but also to fire a steam-locomotive.

The next task was to get the carriages ready, so Hugh left the gloom of the engine shed, and emerged into the now much brighter light of day. Already the sun's rays were illuminating the still damp roof of the open-sided hay-barn across the tracks to the north of the yard. This barn was used to store hay made from grass cut from the lineside. The hay was consumed by the pony which drew the family trap or governess dog-cart, until the day Sir Haydn acquired a motor-car. From then on it was sold to local farmers. Hugh walked the length of the long wooden shed housing the five vehicles that formed the whole of the Talyllyn Railway's passenger stock. This had remained unchanged since 1867 when a straight-sided carriage had arrived from its makers, the Lancaster Wagon Co. The three other carriages and the brake-van, built by Brown Marshalls & Co of Birmingham, with curved sides reminiscent of the old stage-coaches, had arrived earlier, the first of them in January 1866. They were very solidly built with bodies of oak and mahogany, proved by the fact that they have been in continuous use ever since. This probably makes them the oldest railway carriages in the world still in regular service.

Hugh pulled aside a rough wooden slatted gate, which to-gether with a wire fence along the lower part of the open-sided shed, served to keep out children and any wandering animals. He picked up a rather moth-eaten broom from several propped up against the wire and began sweeping out the carriages and the brake van. Usually only one or two coaches and the brake-van, which also acted as a mobile booking office, were required to make up the train, but in the height of summer all the stock was brought into use.

Having finished the carriage cleaning, Hugh returned to the engine shed to find his driver, Peter Williams, had come through from the adjoining cottage. Peter had worked on the railway for many years. On the days when there were no trains he either worked on the line as a platelayer, keeping the track fit for use, or in the workshop on the locomotives or stock. This was quite a task as Sir Haydn spent as little as possible on repairs and maintenance, most probably because he lacked the wherewithal to do so. The main reason for the McConnels selling the quarry and railway was its lack of commercial success and poor outlook as tiles took the place of slates on the roofs of Britain. Things had not improved since 1910, and the whole outfit was run very much on a hand-to-mouth basis.

Peter checked the steam pressure. This had risen to over 50 lbs a square inch, according to the indicator in the cab, well on the way to the 70 lbs that was the then working pressure. The fire was drawing well, so Peter and Hugh left the shed and strolled back along the line through Pendre station to the cottage at the other end of the building. They knocked on the already open door, for it was now a fine warm sunny morning. Mrs Williams almost immediately appeared with two cups of tea, on saucers. Things were done properly in those far-off days before World War II. They drank their tea outside in the little garden, before returning to their duties.

It was now half past eight and they still had to get their train assembled and down to Wharf Station for the first service of the day, the 9.25 am. Returning to the shed they stepped aboard No 1 *Talyllyn*. Peter the driver backed the loco very gently out into the sunlit yard.

Hugh meanwhile had put a few more shovelfuls of coal on the fire, and checked that the water levels were satisfactory. The pressure was now up over the 70 lbs mark and some of the excess steam was lifting the safety valve on top of the engine. This is just like the valve on a pressure cooker. When the steam pressure is too high it lifts the springs and the steam escapes by blowing off.

As soon as the loco had cleared the first set of points, still open to the shed road since the last trip, Hugh dropped to the ground, ambled back to the point and held the lever down whilst Peter brought the engine forwards towards the carriage shed. Talyllyn locomotives traditionally face up the line towards the hills for the main pulling power is required on the upward gradient, and some drivers claim they work better that way round. The engine came to a halt as its buffers gently kissed those of the nearest carriage, the brake van. After Hugh had coupled up the loco to the brake van, and climbed into it, Peter reversed the engine pulling the whole rake of carriages back up the yard on to the main line, and the train headed sedately down the cutting towards Wharf station.

As the train drew close to Wharf yard, Hugh began to apply the brake in the guard's van, fully winding it home as the engine came to rest beneath the road bridge. He then got down from the van and undid the coupling in front of the engine. Whilst he held over the point lever, Peter drew the engine forward into the siding in front of the station building, the one leading to the weighbridge. Hugh made sure the points were set for the second siding before returning to the van. He then slowly unwound the

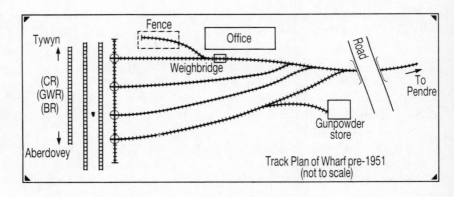

Track Plan of Wharf pre-1951
(not to scale)

brake, allowing the rake of carriages to roll gently all by itself into the yard. He then held the point over again whilst Peter took *Talyllyn* up the line, before reversing gently onto the carriages in the second 'road' where Hugh again coupled up. The train was now ready to leave, with the engine at the front of the train, facing up the line. This was correct, for it is an operating rule for all railways, at least in the United Kingdom, that an engine is not allowed to propel carriages containing passengers, save in exceptional circumstances, unless it is specifically fitted out for doing so, like the Gatwick express from London Victoria, the Glasgow-Edinburgh push-pull, and an increasing number of other main-line services.

Whilst all this was going on Mr Edward Thomas, the railway's manager, would have been standing at the door of his office. With him might have been the great man himself, Sir Henry Haydn Jones MP, owner of the railway, the slate quarry and much else besides. In appearance the two men accurately reflected their individual characters, and their respective stations in life. Sir Haydn was a tall, broad man with a little moustache. He was always well-dressed in a pin-striped suit, a smart trilby hat, and looked very neat and tidy, unlike his office which was the just the opposite. But that is another story. As a leading figure in both the town and the surrounding County of Merioneth, MP and County Councillor for decades – he was to be knighted in 1937 – and a pillar of the local Methodist church, he was much respected if little loved. First elected to parliament in the election of January 1910, when he defeated his Conservative opponent, he was returned unopposed the following December, and was to remain the Liberal MP for Merioneth until his retirement in 1945. A solicitor and the major private employer, he knew everyone's business. Like a spider at the centre of a web, he manipulated the local people, flies caught in the gossamer threads of his long and intimate knowledge of their backgrounds, deeds and misdeeds, and their past history and secrets. Some escaped, but most were trapped by his influence on employment, local government, the magistracy and thus the police, the chapel: in fact on all the centres of local power and control. It was no use writing to the local MP, for whom should that be, but Sir Henry Haydn Jones himself. He was 'tight' with money, probably because he did not have much. In many ways, with the exception of extra-marital relationships, and in addressing the mother of Parliaments – not once did he do so in his thirty five years in the House of Commons – he resembled his long-time party leader, the 'Welsh Wizard', David Lloyd-George.

If Sir Haydn was the 'Wizard', then Edward Thomas was his 'Grand Vizier'. A short, thin little man, he always wore greeny flecked tweed suits, and shiny black boots of patent leather coming up over his ankles. Like Sir Henry he wore a trilby hat and was neat and fastidious in his dress. He was a quietly spoken, gentle man, loved by all who were fortunate enough to know him. He was always polite, but could be firm if necessary. He acted as 'Agent' for Sir Haydn. He collected the rents from the tenants of the railway and quarry cottages, and of the other properties Sir Haydn owned. He dealt with the staff, passed on their requests to the great man, and relayed back the response. He kept the books of the railway company and quarry, and recorded the movements of the slate. He issued invoices, collected debts, paid off creditors, operated the Avery weighbridge, issued tickets for the trains, and then locking up his office, became guard, ticket collector and booking clerk on the train itself. Very much a 'General Factotum'.

Although neat and tidy in appearance like Sir Haydn, his office too was just the opposite. Situated at the foot of a slight slope leading down from the Tywyn-Aberdovey Road, the original office, built to cover the trans-shipment of goods to and from the adjacent main line, was the only brick-built building on the railway, all the others being constructed of slate blocks. This was because it was erected before the line reached the quarry, and thus there was no slate waste available. This is no doubt the reason for the bridges and Dolgoch viaduct also being constructed of brick, whereas the other station buildings and the works at Pendre are built largely of slate waste.

The office at Wharf had two rooms, each with its own fire place. The main room had a long wooden counter, at which the tickets were sold and customers attended to. Beneath the counter were cupboards stuffed full of old papers. On the wall were racks full of old books and more papers. In the inner office were more shelves filled with still more papers, stretching back over decades. The filing system appeared to be one of piling any new papers on top of the old, so when years later the office was eventually tidied up, the original plans of the railway were found at the bottom of the heap.

The passenger trains used the second of the four tracks into which the single line from Pendre divided. At the end of each track was a very small turn-table, about five feet in diameter, just sufficient to accommodate a single slate or coal wagon. Along the end of the yard was a continuous line of rail, into which these turntables were set, on the edge of a platform, or wharf, which served a siding of the standard-gauge Great Western Railway. The slate wagons were stored on one of the tracks, pushed forward individually on to the turn-table, turned through ninety degrees, and then pushed along the platform until opposite the main-line truck into which the slate was to be hand-loaded. The trucks were moved around by manual pushing; indeed on many occasions the coaches were also shunted by hand.

The track nearest the office building was not used for passenger trains. It was kept as free as possible as it contained the weigh-bridge on which the wagon loads could be weighed. The weight of the empty wagon was known, and this, subtracted from the gross weight of the loaded wagon, gave the weight of the cargo, such as coal or flour coming in, slate or scrap going out. The tracks were used for storing loaded wagons until they could be emptied, and for collecting together empties, prior to their either being re-filled with supplies for the quarry or settlements up the line, or simply being returned empty to the quarry.

When a down goods train was approaching Wharf, it first stopped on the cutting. The brakes were then applied on each wagon. The engine pulled clear, and the wagons were released one by one and allowed to run by gravity into the siding desired. Particular care had to be taken with the special gunpowder wagons. The explosive, used for blasting in the quarry, was stored in a small shed with its own access siding in the far corner of the yard. Other wagons, with valuable loads waiting to be taken up the line, were locked into a walled yard beyond the weighbridge, served

TAL-Y-LLYN RAILWAY.

TIME TABLE

FOR

AUGUST 1ST, 1867,

And until further Notice.

Passengers to ensure being booked should be at the Station five minutes before the time fixed for the departure of the Trains. The times shown on this Bill are the times at which the Trains are intended to leave and arrive at the several Stations, but the Company cannot guarantee these times being kept under any circumstances, nor will they be responsible for delay.

PASSENGERS' LUGGAGE.—The Company are not responsible unless it is booked and paid for according to its value. Each Passenger is allowed 60lbs weight of personal Luggage free of charge, the same not being Merchandise. Any excess above this weight will be charged.

For the protection of their Luggage in the Van, Passengers are requested to have their names and destinations clearly stated upon, and properly fastened to each article.

The Company will not be responsible for any articles left in any of their offices for the convenience of Owners, unless deposited in the Booking Office, and the fixed charge of 2d. per Package paid.

It is requested that all Goods and Parcels be delivered at King's Station, Towyn, (and not at Pendre Station), at least half an hour before the time fixed for starting, so that they may be Booked and Signed for.

UP TRAINS.	a.m.	a.m.	p.m.		DOWN TRAINS.		Except on Saturday.	Saturdays only.	
	a.m.	a.m.	p.m.			a.m.	p.m.	p.m.	p.m.
Towyn (Pendre Station)..leave	8.0	11.0	3.45		Abergynolwyn..........leave	9.30	12.30	1.30	5.10
Rhydyronen	8.10	11.10	3.55		Dolgoch	9.43	12.45	1.45	5.25
Dolgoch	8.25	11.25	4.10		Rhydyronen	10.0	1.0	2.0	5.40
Abergynolwyn......arrive	8.40	11.40	4.25		Towyn ....arrive	10.10	1.10	2.10	5.50

☞ TAL-Y-LLYN RAILWAY.—This Railway runs up a narrow valley east of Towyn to Abergynolwyn, the privacy of which has been seldom intruded upon, and the inhabitants left unmolested to pursue the noiseless tenor of their way, until the Iron Horse with breath of Steam and Smoke startled with its echoes the quiet ravines. The scenery is all that can be desired, the mountains on both sides are majestically grand. The Waterfall and Railway Bridge at Dolgoch are to be seen to advantage, and are objects of romantic beauty which require the Painter or the Poet's touch to vividly portray. Reaching Abergynolwyn, the Visitor can either pursue his journey to Tal-y-llyn Lake or Casterbiniae Castle, called in history Castell y Bere. The latter is most interesting to archaeologists, and its architectural features surpass any of the old Welsh Castles, as many fragments have been found amongst the ruins, which have been carefully preserved. Tal-y-llyn Lake is about two miles distant from Abergynolwyn, and is celebrated for its Trout fishing. The lake is 1¼ mile in length, ¼ mile in breadth, and 5 miles in circumference. This Lake fills the head of the Valley, with the exception of a road on each side. The Scenery from its position at the Southern base of Cader Idris is strikingly romantic, at the upper end the hills almost meet, and present a rugged aspect, and are broken into numberless crags, of which some are vertical and sharply pointed, but the greater part project horizontally and impend with threatening gloom over the vale beneath. Cader Idris can easily be ascended from Tal-y-llyn, and the neighbourhood abounds with rich and numberless objects of romantic beauty, including mountains of different forms and elevations, valleys, lakes, &c., which combined form a picturesque and diversified landscape, rarely excelled for richness and variety.

N.B.—Trains do not run on Sunday.

BY ORDER.

PRINTED BY D. EDWARDS, "ST. CADVAN'S OFFICE," CORBET SQUARE, TOWYN.

by a small siding. These goods included regular consignments of fish from Grimsby, beer from Wolverhampton, and less regularly, boots from Northampton, all consigned as through freight to Abergynolwyn on transhipment from the GWR, together with household furniture and all manner of personal goods and mail orders, the smaller parcels being retained in the office until the next available train.

For years the scheduled departure time of the morning train was 9.25. Some passengers came by bus or car, and a few on the morning school trains, the 8.20 am from Barmouth Junction, and the 8.49 from Aberdovey: for the Tywyn GWR (BR) station is only 300 yards from the Wharf terminus of the Talyllyn Railway. But most had walked from their boarding house or hotel in Tywyn itself. For Tywyn, spelt Towyn until 1972 when the Welsh spelling was re-adopted, had pretensions as a holiday resort. In the late nineties a Thomas Corbett, made rich by the salt mines he owned in the Droitwich area of Worcestershire, had erected a long promenade along the sea front at Tywyn. He and one or two other misguided entrepreneurs went on to build boarding houses and hotels in a vain attempt to turn Tywyn into a major seaside resort. But like a similar grandiose scheme by Midland businessmen in the nineteen-sixties, the investment came to nought, being scuppered by the local weather, which tends to be somewhat damp. Today all that remains of Corbett's venture is the main hotel in the town which carries his name, the old grammar school, and a plaque at the end of his promenade.

There were no platforms at Wharf station. The terminus for passengers had been built at Pendre, and it was not until 1904 that passenger services were first reported to be running from Wharf. An article in the October edition of *The Railway Magazine* for that year stated: 'The Wharf Station is used for goods traffic but passengers are permitted to join the train here on the up journey, obtaining their tickets at the Pendre station . . . On the down journey, obtaining their tickets at Pendre.' This they apparently continued to do for another twenty years. Things change slowly on the Talyllyn railway. The terminus at Wharf was known as 'King's' station throughout the nineteenth century, and even as such on the 1901 25in Ordnance Survey map. This

TAL·Y·LLYN RAILWAY.

(NARROW GAUGE, 2ft. 3in.)

Time Table, Oct., 192   , and until further notice.

THE terminus of the Railway, Abergynolwyn, forms a convenient starting-point for the ascent of Cader Idris, and is only 3½ miles from Tynycornel Hotel and Penybont Hotel, Talyllyn Lake, thus bringing the visitor a mile nearer than any other route.

Other objects of interest in the immediate neighbourhood:—The Bryneglwys Slate Quarries, the village of Llanfihangel-y-Pennant, most picturesque in its antiquity, with the celebrated Bird Rock and the ancient Castell-y-Bere (Bere Castle) close by. Conveyances for Talyllyn Lake can be hired at Abergynolwyn. .

The times shown on this bill are the times at which the trains are intended to leave and arrive at the several stations, but the Company cannot guarantee these times being kept under any circumstances, nor will they be responsible for delay.

PASSENGERS' LUGGAGE.—The Company are not responsible unless it is booked and paid for according to its value. Each passenger is allowed 60 lbs. weight of personal luggage free of charge, the same not being merchandise. Any excess above this weight will be charged.

The Company will not be responsible for any articles left in any of their offices for the convenience of owners, unless deposited in the Booking-office and the fixed charge of 2d. per package paid.

It is requested that all Goods and Parcels be delivered at the Wharf Station, Towyn.

UP TRAINS.	† Mondays only.	Daily.	Every other Sat. starting Oct.	Daily.	Fridays only	DOWN TRAINS.	† Mondays only.	Daily.	Daily.	† Fridays only.	Every other Sat. starting Oct.
	a.m.	a.m.	p.m.	p.m.	p.m.		a.m.	a.m.	p.m.	p.m.	p.m.
Towyn (Wharf) dep.		9-25		3-15		Abergynolwyn dep.	7-0	11-20	4-35	6-45	1-5
„ (Pendref) ...	6-15	9-30	12-20	3-20	6-0	Dolgoch ...	7-15	11-35	4-50	7-0	1-20
Rhydyronen ...	6-25	9-40	12-30	3-30	6-10	Brynglas ...	7-25	11-45	5-0	7-10	1-25
Brynglas ...	6-30	9-45	12-35	3-35	6-15	Rhydyronen ...	7-30	11-50	5-5	7-15	1-30
Dolgoch ...	6-40	9-55	12-45	3-45	6-25	Towyn (Pendre) ...	7-40	12-0	5-15	7-25	1-40
Abergynolwyn arr.	6-55	10-10	1-0	4-0	6-40	„ (Wharf) arr.		12-5	5-20	7-30	

†These trains will not run when any stoppage occurs at Bryneglwys Quarries.
The 6-15 a.m. and 6-0 p.m. trains from Towyn start from Pendre and not from the Wharf.

N.B.--NO SUNDAY TRAINS.

H. HAYDN JONES,
General Manager.

J. Wynn Williams, Printer, Towyn.

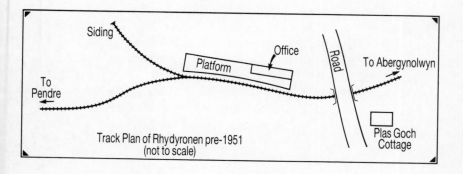

Track Plan of Rhydyronen pre-1951
(not to scale)

was not because of any royal connection, but because the land was originally owned by a man called King. 'Towyn (Wharf)' appeared as such in the 'Tayl-y-llyn' table for the first time in the April 1914 edition of *Bradshaw*, but only with a line of dots, all services being shown as departing from 'Towyn (Pendre)'. In the April 1910 edition a footnote to the table states 'Trains leave Slate Wharf Station 5 minutes before leaving Towyn (Pendre station).' Whilst the station was officially being called Wharf in 1904, no doubt because it had been called the 'slate wharf' (platform) for years unofficially, it was still named 'King's' on an official map published by the Railway Clearing House in 1926.

The railway also provided a local delivery service. The butcher's boy, the baker's boy and the grocer's boy would be at Pendre when the up train arrived from Wharf, with parcels to be dropped off at the various farm halts and stations up the line. The number of passengers had begun to decline, especially from stations towards the top end of the line where they are nearer the main road, after a bus service started to operate between Corris and Tywyn via Abergynolwyn in 1927. The buses were originally run by the Corris Railway Company, in which the Bristol Tramways and Carriage Company had a major interest. The Corris Railway, just a few miles away over the mountains, was the only other line in Britain operating to a 2ft 3in gauge. In 1930 it was taken over by the GWR as part of a complex deal. The buses went back to Bristol, and after a short delay the routes went to the Crosville Motor Company of Chester, in which the main-line railways had a minority interest.

One reason for the railway keeping the local delivery trade long after the arrival of the buses may have been that Crosville did not give extended credit if needed. For many years the Talyllyn Railway served the Royal Mail. From at least 1871 to 1905, the railway had carried the post up from Pendre. It was brought by hand-cart from the main Tywyn Post Office to the station and there delivered into the care of the guard, for many years one Jacob Rowlands. On 15 October 1896 the *Towyn-on-Sea and Merioneth County Times* reported: 'On Monday morning an accident occurred to one of the engines of the Talyllyn Railway which caused some inconvenience and necessitated the conveyance of mails to Abergynolwyn by road.' At Abergynolwyn 'Willy Post', one William Rowlands, would have been waiting to collect the post bags, and take them to the sub-post office in the village for sorting and delivery. In the afternoon the process would have been reversed.

At that time the language of the railway was Welsh, at least amongst its workforce. Some English people when first visiting the railway thought its employees were a bit dim because they were so slow in replying to questions put to them. They did not realise that first the question was being translated into Welsh, the answer formed in Welsh, and then translated back into English for the reply to be understood.

Slate was not only brought down from the quarry, Bryneglwys, at the end of the line, but also for a time from another quarry half a mile up the road from Rhydyronen station, where a small siding left the running line just before the platform. The slates were stored in a small yard behind the station, prior to loading. But that business had ceased in the early years of the century and by 1939 the area was just a pleasant wooded glade. At one time there had been talk of developing Rhydyronen as a spa, for there are chalybeate springs nearby, and for a time it was possible to buy bottles of Rhydyronen mineral water. But as so often seems to happen in mid-Wales, nothing came of it.

Whilst the railway belonged to Haydn Jones, picnic parties, usually family groups, were allowed to hire slate wagons and come down the line after the last train had gone. This was the 4 pm from Abergynolwyn, except in the high season, when there was a third, later train at 6.25 pm. But in the long summer evenings some parties preferred to stay up the line even longer, or perhaps arrive later if they had been climbing Cader Idris or walking in the hills. They would have arranged in advance with Edward Thomas for a slate wagon equipped with brake, and fitted out with rough seats, to be left at Abergynolwyn. It must have been quite a thrilling ride down the line, and indeed somewhat hazardous, considering the poor state of the track. But no serious injuries have been recorded, although there must have been several instances where these 'passenger' wagons came off the track. The regular trains certainly did. If it was a quarryman's train the workmen buckled to and lifted the carriages or trucks back on the line. So did the paying passengers, if the alternative was a long walk back home. None of the accidents was serious, largely because of the slow speed at which the trains travelled. The only accident that could have been serious was in the 1890s when the early morning quarrymen's train ran off the line and down an embankment because the flangeways at the level crossing had become blocked. No one was going to tell the Railway Inspectorate, for if the line was closed, so would be the quarry, and everyone would be out of work. Sir Haydn did not consider liability, or indeed any other insurance necessary, and no doubt did not have the money to pay for it. No local was likely to take

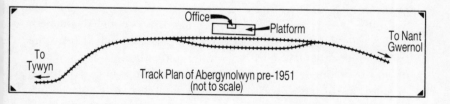

Office   ←Platform

To Tywyn

To Nant Gwernol

Track Plan of Abergynolwyn pre-1951
(not to scale)

on the all-powerful local solicitor, the redoubtable Sir Haydn, and any holidaymaker who pushed it, was simply to go ahead and sue, as the Company had no money anyway!

Abergynolwyn station, six and a half miles from Wharf, was the upper terminus for passenger trains, being the end of the line approved by Parliament for a public transport service. It was the only station besides Pendre to have a loop, thus enabling the engine to run round its train. The railway itself went on for another three-quarters of a mile, but that section of the line was only for slate wagons and locomotives.

The Talyllyn had one branch line, which left the 'main line' about half a mile beyond Abergynolwyn station. However branch lines on the Talyllyn were not as on most other railways. This one went off at a right angle straight down the steep mountain side, and disappeared into the village below. It was known as the 'Abergynolwyn Incline'. At its top was a small turn-table, just like the ones in the yard at Wharf, sited on the main running line, which ran straight through the winding-house. This building housed the large wooden drum around which were wrapped the ropes that controlled the movement of the wagons up and down the slope. There was an avoiding loop round the back of the winding-house. The incline was self-acting, which meant that loaded wagons going down one line of track pulled up less heavily loaded wagons coming up the other. The rope linking the two sets passed round the winding drum, which was fitted with a friction brake to regulate its speed. The tracks went across the main street, past the Railway Hotel, down between two rows of houses and ended up by a chapel on the banks of the Afon Dysynni right at the other end of the village. There were sidings into other streets and alleys, along which trucks could be pushed. The system was that the loaded wagons were detached from the train, man-handled one by one on to the turntable, and then sent down the incline with the rope attached in groups of two or three, or singly if the cargo was particularly valuable or fragile. Down the slope went coal and other merchandise, but what came up? The surprising answer is, in the days before septic tanks and more sophisticated methods of waste disposal, the village sewage. The lines ran along the backs of the houses where the outside privies were located. The 'loo' buckets were emptied directly into the wagons on the rails outside the back gate, pushed along to the foot of the incline, and hauled away up the slope for disposal. This was effected by taking the wagons down the line and disposing of the contents west of Dolgoch, or on occasions west of Brynglas. A very simple and effective method of disposal.

The end of the line for locomotives, but not for the wagons, was at Nant Gwernol, three-quarters of a mile on from Abergynolwyn station. Above a deep ravine a shelf had been blasted out wide enough to take three rail tracks. These served as sidings on which the wagons were parked before being hauled up the inclines to the quarry far above, or loaded with slate, assembled into train loads for the locomotives to take down to Wharf for onward transhipment to the great world outside. This was as far was the locomotives came. The three lines coalesced into one leading up the Alltwyllt (Wild Hill) incline. This was the first of three inclines carrying the tramway to the quarry, eight hundred feet higher up the mountain. In between each incline were stretches of relatively level tramway. These like the main line were located on a ledge cut out of the valley side. But on these stretches high up the mountainside, the wagons were pulled by a horse. Just as on the village incline to Abergynolwyn, the wagons were hauled up the three quarry inclines by other wagons descending, to which they were joined by a rope wound round a large drum in a winding house at the top of each slope, and controlled by rather crude brakes. As could be observed by glancing into the valley below, accidents did happen. Jammed between the trees, by the stream edge, could be seen the remains of wagons which had hurtled down the incline when the restraining rope had snapped, and shot off into space; on one or two unfortunate occasions together with the quarrymen who, contrary to regulations, had been riding them.

CHAPTER 2

Sir Haydn and Industrial Relations

The quarry at Bryneglwys was the main business; the railway being merely a means of transporting the slate. If the quarry closed so did the railway: a not unlikely prospect on several occasions during the hundred or so years the quarry was open, for the Company's financial position for most of that period was by no means secure.

When Sir Haydn purchased the quarry in January 1911, together with the railway and Abergynolwyn village, he was a reluctant buyer. He bought it, he claimed, in order to preserve local employment when no other purchaser could be found. He took a considerable financial risk in borrowing capital to buy the plant and machinery, and in forming a company, the Abergynolwyn Slate and Slab Co Ltd of which he was the sole director. Because of poor demand for slate, and competition from other roofing materials, lack of capital for development, and technical difficulties, the quarry was barely able to keep viable. Sir Haydn simply could not match the level of wages the more economic quarries to the north. This led to some interesting and revealing exhanges with the North Wales' Quarrymen's Union.

Haydn Jones was not a member of the North Wales Slate Quarry Proprietors Association. He could not afford to be, and in any case he regarded himself as a benefactor in providing work for his constituents. In September 1918, in a confidential letter to the North Wales Quarrymen's Union, replying to a demand for higher wages, and also for an extension to the existing 5-day week to include Saturday morning!, he wrote:

My position is a simple one. I restarted the quarry to provide work for men who were unemployed. I have paid them as you know a minimum wage all along, when other quarries did nothing of the kind, and if I could I would, without being asked, gladly increase the minimum because I believe the best work is to be got from men who are decently paid.

I have carried the place entirely on borrowed capital and in the interests of the men, and by doing so have increased my overdraft by several thousands of £s. This increase is the loss I have sustained in trying to keep the men employed and an industry alive.

And what is the position today? The army has taken the young men. Men who went on their knees to ask me to reopen the quarry have left for temporary employment at ridiculous wages in the timber trade, and I have been left with a little over forty men, mostly old, infirm and long past their best, and a few young lads over 14.

And now you come along and ask me to do the impossible. I have lost thousands of £2 already and as I explained to the men a few months ago I can make a pile of money now by scrapping the machinery and especially the railway.

No business can be run for long except at a profit. I have run the quarry for 7 years at a big loss in the hope of getting it refunded if better times come. But to carry it on and pay what you suggest, much as I would like to do so, is simply impossible and I write quite frankly to say that if your letter is seriously meant, I shall at once take steps to close down and realise my losses by scrapping the railway while it is still possible to get big prices for the rails. Or in the alternative I am quite willing to sell the whole concern at a valuation to anyone who can carry the old place on and pay the wages your Union demands.

I hope you understand the position. If the place could be made to pay the wages you set forth, I would be the first man to agree to do so – indeed you should never have had an opportunity of asking me to do it – I would have have done it of my own accord. I have Old Age Pensioners at work here – who in the name of fortune could make enough money to pay those 6/3 per day?

Quite recently I had an interview with a number of

quarrymen, I showed them my bank account from the outset. They saw how my overdrafts had increased by thousands and I gave them the option of continuing or closing down the place. I do not feel justified in completely ruining my circumstances in the interests of other people and I shall be glad to learn of anyone who has sacrificed more for others. If you seriously mean to ask me to do the impossible I shall have no alternative but to close down and that of course would be by far the best course for me.

R.T. Jones, the union secretary, asked for a reply he could lay before his executive, but Sir Haydn insisted his letter must remain confidential; presumably not to alarm his creditors.

The union negotiated a settlement with the Proprietors Association in October 1918. Sir Haydn again pointed out he could not afford to pay the level of wages agreed. Indeed he had been forced to sell timber to maintain the existing guaranteed wages. He had offered the men the choice of closing down so that they could accept better paid work locally. The union replied that he should be able to afford to pay higher wages because he was not doing development work in a quarry he claimed to be exhausted. In addition he was selling slates at a lower price than that on the authorised price list produced by the Proprietors Association – a cartel – and this was at the expense of his employees and the rest of the industry. They also asked that the union be allowed to put in a qualified person to examine the company's books.

This caused Haydn Jones to see red. He said it was untrue he was trying to put the blame for stopping the quarry on the union. Months before the men, two-thirds of them, had joined the union he had shown them the books. He had offered to close the quarry so that they could go timber felling at higher wages, and to reopen it when the war was over and this temporary work had ceased. His letter of 10 December continued

The exhaustion of the quarry is not due to lack of development. As a practical quarryman you must know that there are quarries which no amount of expenditure will make successful. I was well aware of this at Abergynolwyn and it was at the urgent appeal of the men that I undertook to reopen the quarry for the sole purpose of providing work for the men at a time of great depression, guaranteeing a minimum wage and as a result I have incurred a serious loss to myself.

The suggestion that the slates are sold under the market value is absolutely puerile. Do you allege that I am stupid enough to sell the produce at a lower price than it will command?

Haydn Jones told the union he had lent the quarry several thousand pounds of private capital on 'which not a penny interest has been paid', and that the rents of the houses at Abergynolwyn, as well as the two to three thousand pounds resulting from the sale of the estate timber had also 'been thrown in . . . to carry the place on'. He categorically refused to let an outsider see his books, although he was prepared to allow the union secretary and local organiser sight of his bank book. This offer was taken up and these two men discussed the books with the company's manager, David Jones.

Full, or at least sufficient, information was given to the union for it to be well aware that the position was indeed as Haydn Jones had indicated, and that they had no realistic option but to hold back. So R.T. Jones, the union secretary, wrote to Haydn Jones on 17 February 1919 saying 'I am instructed to state that the application forwarded by us shall not be pressed until such time as we feel the state of affairs will improve'.

Trade did pick up a few months later and the Company advanced its wage rates, without of course any reference to the union. However the rest of the industry had agreed even higher rates. So the union came back in a huff because it had not been consulted about the increased rate of wages, thereby giving the impression union membership was not of much value to the men. The union said 'it now remains for the men to decide'. There was considerable tension as some felt Haydn Jones might well cut his losses, and close the quarry and railway down completely. Others took a more militant stance, possibly with the aim of embarrassing Haydn Jones politically, as he was still the local MP. R. T. Jones in a further letter to Haydn Jones accused him of penalising the local secretary for being a union member. The manager had stopped the work in a part of the quarry where the secretary of the local union lodge was working, and the latter claimed it was because of his union activities that he had been suspended. He claimed he had been told that he would only be signed on again if he agreed not to mention the union whilst at work. The manager obviously hoped the union man would be forced to find work elsewhere. In a letter to the union's secretary, R.T. Jones, the suspended man wrote: 'The quarryman's union is too weak to defend the workers who have to work for five days a week for seven shillings wages.'

A further letter from the union made Haydn Jones even angrier:

> The increase (in wages) was paid not as a result of representations by your Union, but by better working results and prices. I simply paid them a higher rate the moment I was able to do so. If you suggest that I must do nothing directly with those whom I employ – many of whom are not members of your union – I am afraid I shall never agree to such a proposal. You say that "you trust no further action will be necessary". If that is intended to intimidate me, and it can have no other meaning, you have for once committed a grievous mistake. You cannot intimidate a man who has sacrificed so much for the men and who is quite prepared to close down any moment the men think fit to say so.

The acrimonious correspondence continued. The manager refused to see the local organiser to discuss the suspension. In January 1920 Haydn Jones said he would give the men a fortnight to decide whether they wished to carry on working or whether he could close the quarry. The union replied that the local Lodge had met and 'considering that Mr Haydn Jones was intent on closing the quarry, and saying absolutely positively that he was going to, it was unanimously passed that it would be unwise to push things that far'. This was signed by three local officials and the original resolution was in Welsh. The resolution was presumably as unclear in Welsh as in the English translation. In any case it did not satisfy Haydn Jones and he closed the quarry on 31 January.

No move was made to dispose of the machinery or to sell off the rails at an advantageous price. In reports in the local paper it was suggested that the troubles had been fomented to embarrass the sitting MP politically. But Haydn Jones held all the cards. The union executive could hardly ask for the quarry to be re-opened on the same terms as before, although they may have gone along with wages below the norm whilst the quarry was still working. R.T. Jones had merely passed on the resolution of the local Lodge. He pointedly omitted to state whether or not it had the support of his executive. After a month without income, and fearing the machinery might soon be sold off, some of the older men persuaded the lodge to ask R.T. Jones to resume negotiations with Haydn Jones. But R.T. Jones replied that he could hardly do this as his executive would not allow him to discuss re-opening the quarry on the same terms as before, which were worse than in any other quarry. Some members had wanted the union to call them out on strike. This would however have required a ballot with three-quarters in favour, and it was because there was no alternative work available at Abergynolwyn that he (R.T. Jones) had previously persuaded his executive to overlook the longer hours and lower wages at Bryneglwys.

By the time the union reply reached the Lodge at Abergynolwyn, the quarry had re-opened. Nothing more was heard of unions, at least at a national level.

The passenger trains often had a few empty wagons attached on the up journeys, loaded ones on the down. So an hour or so was allowed at the top end of the line for the locomotive to take empty wagons up to Nant Gwernol, collect loaded ones, and get back to Abergynolwyn in time for the down passenger train scheduled for an 11.20 am departure. On the down journey several local passengers would join the train, due in Pendre at noon. This gave ample time for the shoppers to make their way down Tywyn's long main street to Wharf station ready for the 2.15 pm home. It also gave time for the crew to water the engine at Pendre, and to place the loaded slate waggons in the loop, ready to be taken down to Wharf later, and have a quick bite of lunch themselves; Peter Williams no doubt having his at home.

Due at Abergynolwyn at 3pm, an hour was allowed to proceed

to Nant Gwernol and shunt the wagons. Leaving Abergynolwyn at 4.0 pm the train arrived back at Wharf at 4.45 pm. The empty passenger stock was then propelled back up the cutting to Pendre. The coaches were safely lodged in the carriage shed, and the locomotive in the engine shed. Only in the summer season, for six weeks from late July, was this routine disturbed, when an evening train was run from Pendre at 5.40 pm. It was scheduled to return from Abergynolwyn at 6.25 pm, giving only five minutes for the engine to run-round its train, too short a time for most of today's drivers! This service was intended for those picknickers and walkers who could not afford, or did not fancy, a gravity ride down the line in their own hired slate-wagon.

The time-table had changed little since the previous century, although there were three trains a day in 1867. In 1898 there were up services leaving Towyn at 9.30 am and 3.20 pm, returning from Abergynolwyn at 11 am and 4.35 pm. There was an additional departure at 6.30 pm daily, except Fridays, in August, and up to 18 September and on Saturdays only in July, returning from Abergynolwyn at 7.15 pm, giving again only five minutes for the run round. In addition there was a Mondays only 6 am service, returning at 7 am; and a Fridays only service leaving Towyn (Pendre) at 5.40 pm returning from Abergynolwyn at 6.30 pm. These were for the quarrymen going up the valley to work, and the children from all the surrounding farms and hamlets as far as Corris coming down the valley to school at Towyn, where they were weekly boarders. The quarrymen spent the week up at Bryneglwys where they lived in barracks, and had a five-day week, even in the nineteenth century. It is clear from the time-table that the coaching stock did not go beyond Abergynolwyn, so presumably the quarrymen had to walk down to the station to board their train, rather than have a ride on the wagons. It is interesting that the timetable allowed forty minutes between Towyn, Pendre and Abergynolwyn, and vice-versa, one minute less than the 1988 timetable. Even running times are preserved on the Talyllyn!

Hugh's elder son, Dai, recalled as a young boy how on coming out of Bryncrug school at about half past three, he would catch a glimpse of steam above the trees up the valley beyond Brynglas, and then run up the lane as fast as his little legs would carry him to watch the train pass through Rhydyronen station. His father would give him a wave from the footplate, and young Dai vowed then, like almost every other boy of his age at that time, that he too would one day drive a steam engine. But unlike most of them his chances of doing so were pretty good, and he knew it. His father, grandfather, and uncle had all worked, or were still working, on the railway.

Only one engine at a time was then fit for use so he never saw a double-headed train, although his father claimed to recall seeing one in the dim and distant past, perhaps in 1918 when the Armistice after the Great War to end all wars was celebrated. The trains usually consisted of two coaches and the van, more than ample for the relatively few passengers, although all four coaches would be brought into service for the peak season. There were nearly always a few slate wagons tacked on behind. At that time there were some days when there were trains consisting wholly of about a dozen or more slate wagons, but these grew more infrequent as the slate trade declined. There were special trains for the fair at Easter, and for the singing festival at Whitsun. These would go up the line about 8 am to bring the people from Abergynolwyn and along the valley down to Tywyn, and at 6 pm another special would take them home. But then came the 'charabang', with its solid tyres, based at the garage at Bryncrug, later bought out by Crosville, who established a small depot there; and that was the end of these particular specials.

Even as a boy Dai could tell all was not right with the railway. Sir Haydn would spend nothing on repairs and maintenance, other than that essential to keep the railway running. As for replacements, they were out of the question. Dai could see the railway was run down as the slate wagons kept coming off the rails at Rhydyronen, where the inside rail had gone at the junction point to the siding. It was eventually replaced by a bit of rail taken from somewhere else on the line. The number of derailments gradually increased. Men would have to be brought from the quarry to get the wagons and loco back on the line. The condition of the track and the locomotives continued to deteriorate. On one occasion, probably in the late forties, when a local firm had hired a train to provide an outing for its employees, the owner complained when they reached Brynglas that the train was going too slowly. So he persuaded the driver to open the regulator, much against his will. The train accelerated and then crunch, the engine came off the track, and finished up in the bank. Edward Thomas had to get the Royal Engineers from Morfa Camp, on the outskirts of Tywyn, to come up and lever the loco back on to the rails, with sleepers and spare rails as tools. Dai recalled how when he first started with father as his fireman, he was always being told 'you are going too fast', or 'you're going to slow'. He was always 'on pins' that they were going to come off, or that the engine would fail. Things got so bad in the end that they were trying to make sleepers out of oak trees from the woods above Abergynolwyn. These were taken to the sawmill in the village - also owned by Sir Haydn -driven by his hydro-electric power, and cut up to sleeper size. Cutting was not possible on Tuesdays or Thursdays because these were the days that the village ladies did their ironing, and the electric power from the turbine was insufficient to allow both activities to take place simultaneously. In fact when the lights went out at night, the men in the pub had to tumble out into the darkness, and climb part way up the hill to where the turbine was located to free the intake from the leaves clogging it up. The oak sleepers of course split when the spikes were driven in, but it was a last expedient.

Dai remembered that when he was a child his father would often not be home until after 10 pm, worn out from working by candlelight on the loco trying to get it back to running order ready for the service the next morning. On occasions the children would hardly see their father for weeks on end, as Dai, Herbert and their sister Violet, would be in bed by the time he came home, and still in bed when he went out to work early next morning. His father had learned about fitting from his uncle Hugh Jones from whom he sought advice if he got stuck. If things got really bad they had to call in an old fitter named Roberts from the Britannia foundry at Porthmadog. He used to be all right until he said he would have to nip off for some lunch. They got to know the signs, for he liked his beer, and if he once got away from them, that was him, and the work, finished for the day.

In the 1940s Hugh and the other railway staff had to get up to all sorts of tricks to keep the railway going, with at least one loco in service. Dai recalled going with father up the line to get some blue-clay from a place called 'Caerffynon' to push into the cracks to seal the bottom of the smoke-box to make it air-tight. They also used cement and bricks for this purpose. Another dodge, although it only worked for a short time, was to put oatmeal in the water. This then swelled and sealed up the cracks: rather like Radweld in a car radiator. The locomotive smelt of porridge for the rest of the day!

Driving the locos in those days required even greater skills than were needed later. The locos at times had no brakes at all, nor, unless the brake van was on the train, did the stock. The method of stopping was by playing with the reverse lever. It is amazing there were no serious accidents.

By the time Sir Haydn died in July 1950 the railway was fit for little more than to be sold as scrap. But occasionally miracles happen.

Pendre Loco Works.

CHAPTER 3

L. T. C. Rolt

Hugh Jones being older, and with vivid memories of the unemployment and misery of the great depression of the early thirties, was far more worried about the future of the railway than his sons. Dai remembered him constantly saying 'What is to become of the railway?' They knew deep down that when Sir Haydn died the railway was likely to die with him. The old man finally passed away in July 1950. Mr Edward Thomas told them that the company could carry on to the end of that season, as Lady Haydn Jones, Sir Henry's widow, had guaranteed all their wages from the estate. There had been rumours of some Englishmen coming to see Sir Haydn about the future, but as employees they knew no detail. They had no dealings with Sir Haydn. Edward Thomas was their boss, and all orders from, and requests to, the management were channelled through him. Dai recalled that he had never actually spoken to Sir Haydn, and indeed rarely seen him.

The first he knew about the possibility of the railway carrying on, was in October 1950 when Edward Thomas went off to Birmingham, to attend a meeting called by three men, who were apparently interested in seeing if the railway could be saved. These men were called Rolt, Trinder and Russell; Rolt apparently being the moving spirit. Edward Thomas came back saying something might come of it, but he was not very hopeful. On the last Friday of that month they ran what they thought was very likely to be their last passenger train. It consisted of No 2 *Dolgoch* with one carriage and the brake van.

But it was not the last train run by the old Company. A few weeks later in November a special train hauled by *Dolgoch* was

laid on for some of the men interested in saving the line, including John Wilkins, owner of the Fairbourne railway, a 15-inch
gauge line just up the coast from Tywyn. He had been asked to
inspect the track, and report on the state of the railway. It was
not a very successful trip, for on the way back *Dolgoch* came off
the line on the sharp curve half a mile above Brynglas, and the
party had to walk back to Tywyn. It was in February 1951, Dai
recalled, that he first met one of the men who were trying to save
the railway, a Mr Trinder, who was looking round Pendre. This
gentleman told him that he, a Mr Rolt, a Mr Whitehouse, and an
accountant, a Mr Garland, were on their way to Machynlleth to
meet Lady Haydn Jones and her solicitor, Mr Arthur. He hoped
that as a result of this meeting they might be able to keep the
railway going. Dai and his father were pleased that there now
seemed a distinct possibility that someone was going to try and
keep the railway running.

Dai recalled that whilst Bill Trinder was a pleasant man of
medium height, rather pedantic in his ways, he was not the sort
to fire great enthusiasm. Certainly not the sort with the drive,
the determination and the charisma required to launch and carry
through an entirely new approach to the running of a statutory
railway. For this was what these people had in mind: to rebuild,
mainly by voluntary effort, a long-established commercial company still providing a public passenger service, and acting as a
common carrier.

The driving force behind this idea of preserving that part of the
national heritage represented by the Talyllyn railway was Tom
Rolt, a man who was to have an enormous beneficial influence
on the lives, not only of the Jones family, but also on the lives
of hundreds, indeed thousands. Yet he was, and is, largely unknown, except to those interested in the archeology and history
of industry and transport.

Tom Rolt has been described as resembling the typical image of a First World War Army officer in 'civvies'. He was tall
and slender, with a neat tooth-brush moustache, and dark hair
brushed back. He spoke with a clear upper-class accent. But
appearances were deceptive. He was a radical who reached his
own conclusions. He was a pioneer and independent thinker, very

much his own man. He could be rather unsociable, as he himself admitted in his deeply moving first volume of autobiography, *Landscape and Machines*. He was rather reticent, not a good mixer. 'You couldn't imagine him slapping anyone on the back.' Yet he could be charming, as even those bluff, self-made Black Country businessmen, with whom he often clashed, admitted. 'As soon as he opened his mouth you knew he was someone special.' And yet he was not smooth. He admired craftsmen and the effort put into a job, and he himself was often covered in grease and oil.

He was born in 1910. His father was a man of independent means, most of whose fortune evaporated in 1920 as a result of bad investment advice. Ever thereafter the family, and Tom in particular, could be described as living in 'genteel poverty'. Young Tom was sent off to be a boarder at a public school at the age of ten. He was unhappy at Cheltenham, making only two friends in the six years he spent there. When he was sixteen he persuaded his father to take him away, and he started work in an engineering workshop near Evesham. For someone brought up in a completely non-mechanical, rural environment, this was a strange choice. But he was influenced by an uncle, Kyrle Willans, who was chief development engineer with Kerr, Stuart & Co, of Stoke-on-Trent, builders of steam locomotives. Two years later, at the age of eighteen, Tom started a three year apprenticeship with Kerr, Stuart. At week-ends he would escape into the countryside on his motorcycle, away from the grime of the 'Five Towns', made famous by the novels of Arnold Bennett. He usually made for the west, where he explored the canals and the numerous branch line railways along the Welsh borders.

He would often stay at his uncle's house near Melverley in Shropshire. It was there that he first came into contact with *Cressy*, a former Shropshire Union canal narrow-boat that was to play such a large part in his life. His uncle had bought the horse-drawn craft, fitted it out as a cruising 'house-boat', and equipped it with a power-unit in the shape of a small vertical compound steam engine taken from a naval pinnace. His plan of spending the family holidays touring the country's canals by boat was, at the time, a new and revolutionary concept. Tom joined his uncle on *Cressy's* first steam-trial on the Llangollen

Canal, and later assisted in the voyage which took the narrow boat to his uncle's new home at Barlaston on the edge of the Potteries. This voyage had a great effect on Tom. It showed how he could combine his love of things mechanical with his love of the natural world; in the simplicity of a rural Britain he sought to preserve, not only for himself, but also for others.

But it was several years before he realised his dream. Late in 1930 Kerr, Stuart & Co went into receivership and Tom and his uncle were out of a job. *Cressy* had to be sold. Tom finished out the remaining year of his apprenticeship with the petrol and diesel company, R.A. Lister & Co, at Dursley in Gloucestershire, and was then unemployed. He had short spells of work as a motor mechanic, with longer periods at home. He became interested in vintage sports cars, and acquired and sold several. He took part in the veteran run to Brighton. In 1934, with money borrowed from his father, he went into partnership with a friend, and bought a garage at Hartley Wintney in Hampshire. He then set up the Vintage Sports Car Club, and bought a 1924 12/50 Alvis two-seater 'duck's back', which remained with him for the rest of his life, and later became a very familiar sight along the line of the Talyllyn.

In 1936 *Cressy* re-entered his life. His uncle had bought the boat back, so off they went on more cruises, now propelled by a Model T Ford petrol engine in place of the old steamer. At the end of the season the boat was laid-up for the winter in Tooley's yard at Banbury, another fateful decision.

In 1937 Tom's 'design for living' took on a new dimension when a white Alfa Romeo, obviously in deep trouble, staggered on to the forecourt of the Hartley Wintney garage. It was not the car however that took Tom's eye, but the driver, a young blonde in a white sweater. Angela Orred, then twenty two years of age, lived in a small private apartment in South Kensington on an allowance from her wealthy father, an ex-Army major, who had twenty servants. Angela was well-connected. She was descended from King William IV through his mistress, the actress Mrs Jordan. Tom talked to her of canals. She shared his interest in racing cars, and indeed herself drove in speed trials. But canals were something new.

So in the spring of 1938 they had a trial run. There were then no boats for hire on the canals, only on the Thames and Norfolk Broads; but they managed to find a converted lifeboat. Tom and Angela were not conventional. It was certainly not the done thing then for a bachelor and spinster to holiday together in the close propinquity of a small boat. Angela liked canals. So when the garage business collapsed, with war threatening, Angela and Tom decided to get married and go and make their home on a canal boat. Not any old canal boat, but *Cressy*, which Tom had persuaded his uncle to sell to him for £100: quite a large sum in those days, and an enormous one for Tom, as it was almost all he possessed. The Major did not approve at all of his daughter marrying an impoverished professional engineer, becoming a sort of vagrant water gypsy and threatened to cut her off without a penny if she married Tom. But they were married at Caxton Hall on 11 July 1939. Tom was twenty nine and Angela twenty four.

They set off from Banbury on a most leisurely cruise, immortalised in Tom's best selling book *Narrow Boat*, which was to have such an influence on the future development of Britain's inland waterways. The intention was to reach the Llangollen Canal on the Welsh border. But it was not to be. War intervened. Tom, despite his military appearance, was not a warlike man. His father, no doubt with the senseless carnage of the 1914-18 war in mind, had written to him begging him not to volunteer. In any case, there was none of the jingoism in 1939 that there was in 1914. Tom, as a professional engineer, knew he would have to do something to help the war effort. So they took *Cressy* to as near the Rolls Royce works at Crewe as they could, and Tom went in daily by motor bike to work on a production line making bits for the Merlin engine for the Spitfire. The mindless, tedious work nearly drove him mad, but he was saved by the offer of a job in a machinery foundry in Berkshire. They only managed to get *Cressy* as far as Banbury, before she was frozen in by the severe winter of 1940-41. They eventually reached Hungerford at the end of April 1941. It was there Tom finished his book on their voyages in *Cressy*. He called it *A Painted Ship*, a quotation from *The Ancient Mariner*. It was rejected by almost every publisher in

London, bar two. One offered to publish it at Tom's expense, and the other offered £75 for the full rights. Although Tom was almost broke at the time, he had the courage and, as it turned out, the sense to refuse. So the, by then, somewhat battered copy was put away for the next two and a half years.

The new job was badly paid, and even with Angela's small allowance, ends would not meet. So Tom became a civil servant, a technical assistant monitoring supplies to works in the Birmingham area. They first sailed *Cressy* back to what Tom now regarded as her 'home' port, Tooley's yard at Banbury. During a week's leave they took their floating home to Tardebigge, by Bromsgrove. Angela cycled off every day to the nearby Dixon's fruit farm, where she hoed and dug, picked fruit and harvested. Tom started writing again at week-ends, mostly for magazines, and mainly on the theme of the clash between modern technology and economics, and world ecology: a man before his time. This brought him into contact with the well-known writer on countryside matters, H.L. Massingham, who learned of his interest in canals and asked him why he did not write a book about them. Tom replied that he had. Massingham asked to see it, sent it to a leading firm of publishers, Eyre & Spottiswood, and the book appeared on the bookstalls in December 1944, retitled *Narrow Boat*, at a price of 12s 6d (63p) in hardback. It was a great success, well reviewed, and within two years had sold 35,000 copies.

The book was well-timed. It satisfied a public longing, and aroused considerable public interest in the canals as a part of the nation's heritage which seemed about to disappear. Many people wrote to Tom, but two in particular seemed to want to do something positive about it. One was Charles Hadfield, who, after a career in publishing, as a member of the wartime River Fire Service had become interested in the history of canals, and had himself written the only other canal book at the time. He described *Narrow Boats* as 'one of the great books – to my mind, the best canal book ever written'.

The other was Robert Aickman, a literary agent. He and his wife went to see Angela and Tom at Tardebigge, an event commemorated by a bronze plaque on the canal bank. It reads 'At this spot in 1946 on board *Cressy* Tom and Angela Rolt first

met Robert Aickman and decided to found the Inland Waterways Association'.

At the first meeting of the Association Robert became chairman,
Charles vice-chairman, and Tom, honorary secretary. Tom wrote
the constitution and rules, and an introductory booklet *The Future of the Waterways*, illustrated with Angela's photographs. With
direct mail approaches and newspaper publicity, the Association
was soon well established. Within six months Charles Hadfield
had resigned, ostensibly because he had accepted a senior post in
the civil service as director of publications at the Central Office
of Information, but mainly because he had quickly recognised
that he would be unable to work with the emotional Robert.
He also realised, long before Tom did, that the founders did not
agree on the objects of the Association. Charles wanted to see the
growth of large economic waterways with, where practicable, the
narrow boats used for pleasure cruising. As a pragmatist, he saw
no future for the working boat community on the narrow boats.
Robert wanted to preserve everything and even bring back into
use long closed waterways. Tom was a romantic. He wished
to perpetuate the life of the working boatman as something
set apart from the modern world. In *Landscape with Canals* he
summed up his views:

> What chiefly appealed to me about the canal system was its
> indigenous working life. On the narrow boats this meant the
> working narrow boats, and their crews which were so essential
> a part of them. These working boaters, so many of whom I
> knew and admired, unconsciously supplied the subtle tradi-
> tional patina of constant use – the worn and dusty towpath,
> the polish that generations of 'uphill or downhill straps' had
> given to the bollards of cast-iron or grainy oak at the locks;
> it was an essential part of that blend of utility and beauty
> which used to compound the particular magic of canals. This
> was something that some members in the IWA could never
> fully appreciate.

Later, after he had been kicked out of the IWA, he found
something similarly worth preserving in the Talyllyn Railway,

and again met that self-same conflict between preservation and pure utility, endemic in all such undertakings.

Before the differences came to a head, the IWA attracted considerable publicity. The British have always had a soft spot for those who cock a snook at the faceless bureaucrats of government and large organisations and the IWA made the authorities re-open statutory canals they were trying to close. They recruited some big names to their cause such as Sir Alan Herbert, Sir Peter Scott and his then wife Elizabeth Jane Howard, the Earl of Portsmouth, Lord Methuen and Lord Lucan, father of the one who disappeared.

Tom and Angela continued to cruise, although *Cressy* was now getting old and suffering from creeping wood-rot. Tom had intended to sell her and get a shorter boat suitable for cruising the narrow canals of the north, for which *Cressy* was too long. But he never did. It was on one of those cruises in 1947 that they met up with George and Sonia Smith. Sonia had been educated at a public school and become an actress. During the war, when women were conscripted, she was one of a small band of women who had responded to an appeal to work the narrow boats. Some of them became hooked, and Sonia went further than most by marrying into one of the well-known boating families, the Smiths; in the shape of a handsome, extremely 'macho', working boatman, who could neither read nor write. For years they operated their working boats, *Cairo* and *Warwick*. Sonia was a fiery personality and served on the Council of the IWA, representing the real professionals. These regarded the Rolts with their bath and comfortable furnishings in *Cressy*, and Angela with her fine jewellery, as mere drones. Actually Sonia had first met Tom and Angela in Birmingham at the 1945 film premiere of *Painted Boats*, the Ealing Studio classic about canal life. Tom, as the most articulate and knowledgeable expert on canals, had been the film's technical consultant. Sonia felt that Tom was someone who did not say much, but what he did say was always worth hearing. He hated idle chatter at parties, and stiffened up. But he gave the impression of some one on whom one could rely, a man of wisdom from which emanated a sort of power.

In 1950 Tom resigned from the post of honorary secretary

of the IWA. He had done four years, and with Robert had made the IWA a very successful campaigning body. But the Association took up too much of his time and tied him down. He wanted to write and go cruising, the former financing the latter. Sadly, however, the parting became acrimonious. Tom believed the Association should concentrate on saving the major canals, and not dissipate scarce resources on fringe waterways. Robert considered he had to keep his finger in the dyke, on the premise that if even one waterway went, they would all go. The dispute became personal. Tom and Angela organised a boat rally at Market Harborough. Robert wanted an arts festival as an added attraction. Tom was violently opposed to the idea. Robert, a very powerful character, who liked his own way, felt Tom was being disloyal. Tom thought Robert was autocratic and dictatorial. Mr and Mrs Rolt were called upon to resign from the IWA committee by eleven votes to three, which they did; and not to attend the rally they had done so much to arrange, a request they ignored. Whilst the rally was a huge public success it heralded a disastrous winter for the Rolts. Tom was depressed at what he saw as wasted years on the canals, by the discovery that *Cressy* was rotten beyond repair, and because his marriage with Angela was breaking up. Then he, perhaps unwisely, signed a memorandum against Robert's autocratic role, and was expelled from the IWA along with about thirty others.

Later, much later, Robert was to comment that in the evolution of societies such as the IWA (and the Talyllyn Railway Preservation Society?) the first stage called for 'grass root prophets' like Tom Rolt, the second stage for organising and militant idealists like himself, and then at the third stage, for 'realists' and 'consolidators'.

Tom was getting interested in the Talyllyn Railway, and in 1951 accepted the post of its general manager. Angela was not interested in railways, and wanted a nomadic life. So one morning she loaded her belongings in the Morris Oxford she had bought for £10, and drove off to join Billy Smart's Circus. Tom watched her go from the deck of *Cressy*. He was not to see her again for twenty years. He took *Cressy* north to Stone in Staffordshire where he failed to sell her. Eventually she was broken up, and apart from a few painted panels and doors, burned. But the Ford model T engine was retrieved by Tom to power an inspection trolley on his new love, the Talyllyn Railway.

When Tom received his letter of expulsion from the IWA in July 1951, he was busy issuing tickets to passengers on the Talyllyn. He was now much too fully absorbed in this new challenge to get angry with the IWA. He was thinking of getting married to Sonia with whom he was living in a caravan at Dolgoch. This was somewhat to the disquiet of Lady Haydn Jones, who was heard to ask of Edward Thomas if it was true that the lady Mr Rolt was living with was not his wife. Marriages between those born in a boat cabin and those 'off the bank' rarely worked, and Sonia's was no exception. Tom wrote of her that 'though she was highly intelligent and much better read than I was, she was by no means the rather frightening left-wing blue stocking I had supposed her to be at first sight'.

Tom and Sonia married and had two sons, Richard and Timothy. In 1974 Tom died of cancer at the age of sixty four in the family home at Stanley Pontlarge in Gloucestershire, where Sonia continued to live. She could not but be proud of a man whose vision led not only to the preservation of canals, but also of hosts of private railways, whose drive, industry and dedication had brought happiness and contentment to thousands. His memorial was not just the simple unmarked mound in the churchyard at Stanley Pontlarge, nor the tablet at Tardebigge, nor the institution of the Rolt Memorial Research Fellowships at the University of Bath, but the hundreds of miles of preserved canal and railway, now appreciated and enjoyed by millions of men and women: 'Si monumentum requiris, circumspice' (If you would see his monument, look around), to quote Sir Christopher Wren and St Pauls.

CHAPTER 4

How The Railway Was Saved

Tom Rolt had become aware of the Talyllyn during the war, as he so graphically describes in the second chapter of his classic book, *Railway Adventure*. His attempt to take the Wednesday train – they also ran on Mondays and Fridays – was thwarted. 'NO TRAINS TODAY' said a handwritten notice on a board by the gate at Wharf station. So there being no one about, he walked up the line and fell in love with it. He ignored two men banging at a locomotive by the light of a candle in a shed at Pendre, and shouting at one another in Welsh, or perhaps at the broken-down loco – obviously the reason for the cancellation of that day's rail service. He did not think they would relish being interrupted. He also failed to make contact with two old men, very slowly but deliberately doing something to the line at Rhydyronen, as they obviously had no English – or if they had, were not letting on to this rather upper-crust Englishman.

As Tom Rolt had been interested in canals for most of his life, it was in that connection that he was examining the text of the 1947 Transport Bill, when he discovered that the Talyllyn Railway Company was not listed amongst those due to be nationalised. The Talyllyn was totally independent. It was not connected with any other concern. It paid no dividends, and apparently no taxes. It probably just got overlooked.

Nearly every day in the winter of the 1947, Tom used to stroll up the narrow lane from the boatyard to collect Bill Trinder from his radio and electrical shop at 84 High Street, Banbury. They would then adjourn to a cafe close by for coffee and a chat. Bill Trinder recalled that one day they were discussing the forthcoming nationalisation of the railways, and generally deploring the demise of the great and small railway companies, and everything coming under a single bureaucratic control, when Tom told him that as far as he could tell there was just one statutory railway that was not going to be nationalised. 'Which would that be?' asked Bill. Tom replied, 'The Talyllyn in Central Wales, in Merioneth.' 'Never heard of it,' was Bill's response, and nor had most other people at that time.

In March 1948 Tom suggested to Bill that they get in the car and go and have a look at this railway. It had been a cold winter, and the idea of getting away for a couple of days with spring at hand, was very appealing. So on the thirteenth he and Tom and Jim Russell, who was a photographer in Banbury and a long-time friend of Bill's, set off. They had a look at the Lickey incline south of Birmingham, and then went on through Cleobury Mortimer to Ditton Priors where they chatted to the old signalman in his box. Then over Clee Hill, with another stop at Craven Arms for a look round. In the valley beyond they kept their eyes skinned for traces of the remote Bishops Castle line, long since gone. After leaving Welshpool, they were lucky enough to see the *Countess* hauling a goods train on the narrow-gauge Welshpool & Llanfair Caereinion branch of the Great Western Railway nationalised only a couple of months earlier. They also saw, in what must have been the last few weeks before its closure, locos still working on the Corris Railway, another GWR narrow-gauge outpost which ran from Aberllefeni quarry via Corris village to the main line at Machynlleth. The Corris had lost its passenger services in 1930 when the GWR, coveting its bus network, took it over.

By the time they had finished prowling around the Corris Railway, the light had gone. It was pitch dark when Tom turned the car into the narrow little lane which dropped down on to the road past Talyllyn Lake. Not that they could see anything of the lake in the blackness of the night, with the wind howling and the rain pouring down. Eventually they came to the Tyn-y-Cornel hotel at the other end of the lake where they booked themselves in with Mr Hunter, the owner. They stayed there two nights, and Bill Trinder recalled 'They did us well. We had a good dinner and sat and yarned away – ghost stories and that sort of thing – until well into the night. And the doors and that were rattling in the wind, and I had very little sleep that night.'

The next morning was glorious. The full beauty of the glaciated valley, rising up to the surrounding peaks, with Cader Idris towering above, was revealed by the bright sunshine of that fine spring morning. They took the car to the foot of the Abergynolwyn incline, and Tom and Bill scrambled up it and then up three further inclines to the quarry in the hills above. Jim Russell went off on his own to do some photography. On arriving at the quarry they found two men there waiting – waiting to send off the last two wagon-loads of slate before the quarry closed for ever. It was Tuesday and *Dolgoch* was coming up next morning to take them down to Wharf. They spent some time talking to the pair, and looking round the office, workshop and manager's house, before setting off back down the line.

It was still a glorious day. They ate their sandwiches sitting on the platform of Dolgoch station, and then walked down to Tywyn Wharf. Although many of the sleepers were split and rotten and the rails cracked, most of them hardly visible in the long grass, Bill recalled having remarked to Tom that the line itself was so well engineered he was sure it could be saved, and they had better see what could be done about it. There was nobody about. But when they reached Wharf station they found Edward Thomas and introduced themselves. This first meeting was the beginning of a long friendship. Edward Thomas wanted them, if it was possible, to do something about keeping the line open. It was a major part of his life and that of the town and its neighbourhood. But as he said to Trinder, 'It's all very sentimental, isn't it? He [Sir Haydn] will keep it going until he dies, if possible at all. But he's losing money on it, so how long he can manage to do it, I don't know.'

Bill Trinder became hooked on the line, and went down to Tywyn several more times in 1948 and 1949, by car with Tom, or by train on his own, or with his son Peter. Tom had a very busy life at that time. He was all over England with *Cressy*. He would keep Bill informed of where he might be, and Bill would go, usually by train, to see him. Bill had been a Methodist local preacher for fifty years, and as his friendship with Edward

Thomas grew, so the latter persuaded Bill to preach for him on a few summer Sundays at the English Presbyterian Chapel in the High Street in Tywyn. Sir Haydn, also a keen churchman, would have thus probably known of Mr Trinder even before they actually met.

Bill Trinder, whilst on an Easter family holiday at Tywyn in 1949, staying at the Corbett Hotel, after discussions with Edward Thomas, called on a Mr Jonathan, the owner of the Cambrian Stores, just across the road from Sir Haydn's office. Edward Thomas had told him Jonathan was chairman of the local Urban District Council, a member of the Merioneth County Council and, not least, another Methodist. Bill Trinder asked Mr Jonathan, 'Would you be kind enough to introduce me and a colleague to Sir Haydn Jones?'. 'H'm, h'm, I don't know' was the reply from a now very nervous Mr Jonathan. 'You know he is a very, very difficult man to get on with; almost unapproachable. None of us dare go near him for anything. We'd rather keep away from him altogether. So I would rather not, if you don't mind. If you'll excuse me, I'd rather not.' Bill pointed out that although he was a stranger, with only the introduction from Edward Thomas, he was a Methodist and had only the best of good intentions. He reiterated that he would be glad if Mr Jonathan would help, even if it meant sinking any differences he might have with Sir Haydn. 'All right' Jonathan replied, 'I will'. It was agreed that they would meet at 2 pm in Jonathan's shop during the Whitsun holidays, when Trinder would next be in Tywyn, and Jonathan would take him across to meet Sir Haydn.

So one day in the late spring of 1949 Bill Trinder set off from his home at seven in the morning, accompanied by his son Peter and a couple of local friends. He was to pick up Tom Rolt, as already arranged, at Diglis Basin at Worcester, where *Cressy* was then moored. Arriving at Worcester just a few minutes before eight o'clock, he parked the car near the basin, telling his friends to wait, as he would only be a few minutes collecting Tom. He walked across two or three other boats, knocked on the hull of *Cressy*, and Angela's head came round the living quarters at the back. 'Hallo Bill,' she said. 'Is Tom ready?,' asked Trinder. 'He's not very well,' replied Angela. 'Does that mean he's not able to come?' 'No, he won't be able to come. You'd better come in and speak to him.' Trinder suspected there had been some domestic friction, as there had been from time to time. He found Tom in bed, and when Tom said he would not be able to come, Bill told him he had made this firm appointment with Mr Jonathan to take them across to see Sir Hadyn. Although he did not want to leave Tom behind, he intended to carry on. He felt he must go. He promised to let Tom have a full report of what happened.

Bill Trinder duly arrived in Mr Jonathan's shop at five minutes to two, after a good lunch in the Corbett Arms hotel. Jonathan told Trinder he 'would be out on his ear' in a matter of minutes. Trinder replied 'We shall see'. At two o'clock they went across the road, and walked into the ironmongers and Jonathan asked the two fellows who were always hanging on the counter there if Sir Haydn was in. On learning that he was, Jonathan and Trinder made their way up the stairs, along the corridor and Jonathan knocked on the office door. A stern voice said 'Who is it?'

'I've brought a Mr Trinder to see you, Sir, about the little railway.'

'Then you'd better come in.' At that Jonathan turned on his heel and fled. 'He never even saw me in, face-to-face with Sir Haydn,' Trinder recalled.

He was then in the 'Lion's Den'. Trinder said he let Sir Haydn do the talking. They had much in common. Sir Haydn was 'the biggest man' in the local Methodist church, and Trinder was a Methodist local preacher. Haydn Jones had served in the Yeomanry with Lord Saye and Seale, whose family tree stretched back to Norman times, and who lived at Broughton Castle, a stately home near Daventry. Bill Trinder claimed the noble Lord had been a generous friend to him in numerous ways, and that he had often been to the Castle for coffee to talk about 'many things'. As Liberal Organiser for Banbury, he had been in contact with Sir George Schuster, who lived nearby. A director of the Southern Railway, prior to nationalisation, and a former financial adviser to the Government of India, Sir George had sat in the Commons as a National Liberal, where of course he knew Sir Haydn Jones. Trinder himself had been for a time a member of the Liberal Party's National Executive Committee. He recalled that he let

Sir Haydn ramble on, occasionally interjecting to ask what was to happen to the railway. This went on for three-quarters of an hour, and Trinder felt he must not overdo it. He contented himself with asking Sir Haydn if he could bring his colleague, Mr Rolt, an author, and a 'very responsible sort of chap' to see him, so they could talk things over. Sir Haydn replied 'Trinder, you keep in touch with me, and if you've got some scheme in the back of your mind between you that you think might save the railway, I'll give you every sympathy, and all the help I can.'

That, Trinder claimed, was the first positive thing that had happened, and when he told Edward Thomas 'his eyes lit up, and he was as thrilled as I was'. Bill telephoned Tom and said they must go down as soon as convenient. They laid their plans and went down together. Trinder was upset later when he read page 41 of Rolt's book *Railway Adventure* which seemed to him to imply that Rolt's meeting with Sir Haydn was the first contact. But Rolt does not say that. He says 'I shall not forget my first and only meeting with Sir Hadyn', and in the previous paragraph wrote, 'So there began a series of visits to Towyn in which we made the acquaintance of Sir Haydn Jones, his second in command Mr Edward Thomas, and various other interested local people'.

Trinder at that first meeting was obviously being tested by Sir Hadyn in the classic manner, as to whom he knew, so he could be placed in the 'correct' social context. Arranging the introduction must be Bill Trinder's greatest contribution to the saving of the Talyllyn. On the second visit with Tom, he knew his way round, and they were given a warm welcome. Trinder described Sir Haydn as being very kind to him 'like a Dutch uncle': not at all the unapproachable figure he was usually made out to be.

The second meeting was obviously much more business like, and once the pleasantries were over, Rolt seems to have taken the lead. He records that Sir Haydn, even in his mid-eighties, had all his wits about him. He made it clear he would run a summer service as long as he lived, even though he was losing money on it. Whilst he would welcome any ideas on how the line could be kept alive, it would need a large sum spent on it without any foreseeable return on the investment.

Then the search for a way of keeping the railway alive began.

Trinder had an idea that Sir George Schuster, after nationalisation no longer a director of the Southern Railway, might, as a possible railway enthusiast, get together with half a dozen other rich men and buy out the Talyllyn and rebuild it. Tom's response to this was that he would rather have hundreds of railway enthusiasts making a small contribution of a few pound than tapping half a dozen wealthy men to take it over. The idea of having a preservation society seems to have come from Owen Prosser, at that time a junior civil servant, who immediately after the war had become very interested in transport matters, and in particular with the retention of the railway system. Already, as nationalisation loomed with the 1947 Transport Act, the future of small branch lines looked precarious. Prosser became especially interested in the Talyllyn from 1947, but realised nothing much could be done whilst Sir Haydn was still in control. He began to think matters were starting to come to a head in the autumn of 1949, when on 5 September an anonymous article 'From a correspondent' appeared in the *Birmingham Post*, under the headline 'Breakdown on Talyllyn Railway'. It described the railway as 'one of the last privately owned lines in Wales,' in imminent danger of closing, and concluded 'Will not the government or British Railways do something?' No one has discovered who this correspondent was, but his article, and particularly the final question, stung Tom Rolt to reply. He wrote in a letter to the *Post* published on 9 September, 'It is a sorry symptom of the decline of individual initiative at the present time that we so often grumble and say "Why don't they do something about it?" And so seldom pause to consider whether we might not be doing something about it ourselves.'

Bill Trinder thought the idea of a preservation society first came from Tom Rolt, but Owen Prosser had a letter from Tom Rolt dated 22 September 1950 in which he wrote 'Regarding your suggestion of a Talyllyn Railway Preservation Society, I certainly had not envisaged such a body: but it would be for the meeting to decide how the railway could be administered.' Owen Prosser had admitted that he got the idea from a letter in the January 1941 issue of *The Modern Tramway*, the journal of the Light Railway Transport League, from a Mr Arthur E. Rimmer. He had proposed that clubs and societies supporting the revival of the Welsh Highland Railway, closed to passengers in 1936, should take over its operation.

Tom Rolt made several more visits to the railway, on one occasion taking along his friend David Curwen, a locomotive engineer. Tom records that he checked with the appropriate authorities whether there was any chance of the quarry being re-opened, and received a very negative response. The idea of relaying the Talyllyn at 10¼ or 15 inches gauge was examined as being a much cheaper proposition, with track 2 feet 3 inches wide being retained only between Wharf and Pendre, so the original historic locos and stock could still be run.

Owen Prosser in thinking about how the Talyllyn could survive had written to Rolt pointing out that the 15-in gauge would only be viable if there was quarry traffic, and if not, 10¼ in was sufficient for holiday traffic, although he himself did not favour either gauge. Prosser suggested using *Tattoo* from the Corris Railway for holiday traffic in a relatively short season. He had a holding reply from Rolt from *Cressy* dated 19 September 1949, and on 13 December 1949 Rolt sent Owen Prosser a letter giving full details and estimates of a possible miniature railway. Trinder and Rolt had met a Mr Fuller of Bassett-Lowke's in an accountant's office at Banbury and had gone into it thoroughly, as a Mr Wilkins had taken over the 15-in line, at Fairbourne. However Trinder reckoned that he personally was never very enthusiastic: it seemed to him more like a toy.

In November 1949 an illustrated feature article on the Talyllyn Railway appeared in *Picture Post*, the news magazine, with an enormous circulation in the days before television. This led to a sharp rise in the number of passengers the next season to over five thousand, more than the railway could cope with, so many were disappointed.

Sir Haydn Jones died on 9 July 1950, and this precipitated action. Tom Rolt and Bill Trinder set out for Wharf to see Edward Thomas as soon as they could after getting the news. He suggested they go off to Machynlleth and see Mr H.M. Arthur, the Haydn Jones' solicitor, 'because Lady Haydn has got copies of all the correspondence you have had with Sir Haydn, and I know, because she has told me, that she is as anxious to save the railway as much as he was, and that she wants to put the railway in as her contribution'. So they went off that morning and saw Mr Arthur in his office, and told him that they would discuss what should be done, and would be writing to him. They now had something more definite to go on: that there was a very likely prospect they would get the railway, provided they could keep it running; a tall order indeed in view of its utterly run-down condition.

Tom had received a fair number of supportive replies to his letter published in the *Birmingham Post* of 9 September 1949. Owen Prosser had also publicised the position of the Talyllyn in *Modern Tramway* in November 1949, and had received replies which he subsequently passed on to Tom Rolt.

Owen Prosser also took action on hearing of Sir Haydn's death. Taking a few day's leave from his Birmingham office he went down to Towyn and had an interview with Edward Thomas in Abergynolwyn station on 24 July 1950. Prosser had some thoughts of buying the railway himself, and was therefore anxious to know its financial position. He recorded verbatim Edward Thomas' replies to some of his questions. On the question of disposal Edward Thomas said:

> The railway is wholly private property, which now vests in the widow of Sir Hadyn Jones, who died about three weeks ago. In my opinion, in view of the condition of the undertaking and the financial results of operating in recent years she is lucky to receive any offer at all for it, and I think it is very likely to go very cheaply indeed. I do not think any scrap merchant would look at it. If Lady Jones knows any one intends to operate it, she might treat that person more favourably than anyone who was interested in it merely as scrap. This would be a token of respect for her late husband's memory.

On the financial position:

> The annual loss in recent years has been in the region of £300. The wages bill covers a weekly wage of £4 per week to the driver and £4.10s. to the fireman.

Mr Thomas explained that this apparent anomaly is caused by the driver's having been willing to accept the sum he had always received, whilst the fireman, his son, on returning from National Service, had insisted on the increase.

I should mention that in addition to my work on the railway, I am employed in the late Sir Haydn's ironmongery. Only £2.10s. of my salary is in respect of my duties on the Tal y llyn. What will be my position in the new scheme?

Owen Prosser recorded that he answered that he would be happy to retain the services of anyone with lengthy experience of the line at the rates mentioned by Mr Thomas, if the receipts allowed him to do so. He explained that although he might have enough money to buy the line, it would be essential to make a slight profit or at least cover expenses. This matter of covering expenses led to him asking: 'Why are trains now run on only three days per week – is it because it is considered such a service taps all the available potential holiday traffic, or is there some other reason?' Mr Thomas replied:

I certainly do not think the existing service is adequate, and I believe that if we ran three trains per day for each day of the week, we should still get them well filled. The reason we do not do so is because we have only one engine [*Dolgoch*, 84 years old] and to use it to any greater extent than at present would throw so heavy a strain upon it that it might break down suddenly. If this happened at the height of the season, it would mean a serious loss of revenue for each day that it remained out of use. The absence of a spare engine is, in fact, one of the most serious problems with which we are now faced. I have thought of obtaining the Corris engines and have had them inspected. The judgement upon them was that both boilers were so far gone that it would be equally advisable to repair the boiler of *Tal y llyn*. (sic) I have thought of buying a diesel tractor as a cheap form of spare motive power but am not attracted by the idea. So many people are eager to see the complete train in its original form. The use of a diesel would mean coupling something new to something old.

Prosser noticed on the day of his visit that the train was well filled and somewhat more accommodation would have enabled passengers to spread themselves out in greater comfort. He therefore asked 'Why are the slate trucks which were formerly pressed into service at busy times no longer used?' Replied Mr Thomas: 'The trucks are not sprung and so would give an uncomfortable ride with the track as it is.'

Owen Prosser's plans to buy the line were overtaken by other developments. Rolt and Trinder decided a public meeting should be called, and steps were taken to arrange one. Bill Trinder, who had business contacts with the Imperial Hotel in Temple Street in Birmingham, hired a room for 11 October 1950. Tom Rolt drafted a circular to be sent to all who had expressed an interest, and there was a small news item in the *Birmingham Post*, actually on 11 October itself, illustrated with a picture of *Dolgoch* and train taken the previous July by Owen Prosser. Rolt had meanwhile written to Mr Arthur asking him to obtain the reactions of the executors of Sir Haydn's estate, actually Lady Haydn and Arthur himself, to the idea of the railway being run by a voluntary society on a non-profit making basis. The new Society would assist the Railway Company with inputs of cash from subscriptions, and of labour from its members. Just how the Company would be controlled was a matter for further discussion.

Other people had by now become involved. Jim Russell was a client of a Birmingham accountant called Patrick Garland, also a railway buff, who was at the time chairman of the Midland branch of the Stephenson Locomotive Society, and therefore had fairly wide-reaching contacts amongst railway enthusiasts. They both shared a love of the GWR, Jim Russell modelling it on the 4mm scale. Garland became honorary treasurer of the TRPS at its first meeting and remained so until 1965 when he was succeeded by Colin Roobottom. Pat then became a director of the Railway Company, and was president of the Society from 1975 to 1988. In that year he was not as in previous years re-nominated owing to his having upset many of the Society's members by criticising (see *Talyllyn News* December 1987) its failure to re-elect one of its Council members. In 1989 he was elected a vice-president.

Another person destined for a long association with the TRPS was Pat Whitehouse, later a very well-known railway writer, who was honorary secretary from the first meeting until 1966, when he was succeeded by Richard Hope, editor of *Railway Gazette International*, the trade 'paper'. Pat had known the Talyllyn Railway before the war, making good use of a run-about ticket when on family holidays at Barmouth to travel on all the local railways, including the Talyllyn and the Festiniog. He had seen the item in the *Birmingham Post*, and went along to the meeting with Pat Garland. He said most of the people there knew one another, as they were mostly members of the SLS or the Birmingham Model Railway Club who had nothing better to do that particular evening. He vaguely remembered having been introduced to Rolt and Trinder at the Model Railway Exhibition in London in 1947 when the idea of a miniature railway, which he considered ludicrous, had been mentioned.

Impressions of that first meeting vary somewhat. Trinder reckoned hardly anybody much came, a dozen to fifteen people and a dozen members of the Press, including some from the nationals, such as the *News Chronicle* and *Daily Telegraph*, as well as from the local papers. Trinder recalled: 'It was just at that psychological moment when the railways had all been nationalised, and here was something that had a bit of go about it.' Rolt thought the meeting 'a great success with the large room they had hired full of people.' Pat Garland has said that it was very well attended, considering there had been little chance for much publicity. Owen Prosser, in his meticulous way, actually counted the number present, and made it thirty-six. Pat Whitehouse recalled that Tom Rolt definitely came across as a leader, and also someone with a strong artistic bent. He did not think much would come of the meeting, but agreed to be on the committee.

Bill Trinder was chairman, supported on the platform by Tom Rolt, Jim Russell, and Edward Thomas, who having hardly stirred out of Wales all his life, came up and stayed the night in a room booked for him at the Imperial Hotel. Mrs Mathias, the only daughter of Sir Haydn, was also present. Rolt said he hoped that the meeting would lead to the formation of a strong working committee to investigate two possible lines of approach: acquisition and the formation of a supporting Society which would keep the railway running under its present ownership. The committee should have two practical priorities, track improvement, and provision of additional loco power, so that the railway could operate six days a week. He suggested they obtained rails from the nearby closed Corris Railway and lay them with voluntary labour. Mr Edward Thomas gave an excellent speech pointing out that the railway was likely to fold up unless something was done quickly. Their only working loco was not in good shape and was not strong enough to run every day, so they only operated Mondays, Wednesdays and Fridays. The track was bad but they had bought ten tons of ex-Corris rail, now in stock, together with four hundred sleepers, most of which were already laid. The past year, 1950, had been a record season with 5,235 passengers generating receipts of £400/8/-: and there would have been 8,000 passengers had they not had to leave the rest behind.

Very persistent questioning came from A.F. Fuller who pointed out that they had no information on the railway's financial position. Trinder and Rolt replied that up to that moment as private persons they had no 'locus' to investigate the Company's financial affairs. If a committee was formed this would be one of its first tasks. But at the moment the object was to see if there was enough enthusiasm to form a committee. When Fuller did not seem satisfied with the explanation that they were doing it for the love of saving a railway, Jim Russell stood up and said: 'You needn't think anyone's getting a gold brick out of this.'

A Mr Gray suggested leasing the line for a season or two at a nominal figure, as a trial, guaranteeing the owners against any deficit. On three occasions in the last season he had been forced to struggle for a seat, and he thought the commercial possibilities were greater than had been imagined. Mr R.K.Cope offered to contribute to keep the line open for a year. The question was asked: if a private individual bought the line would the committee give its support? The chairman replied that not only would the person have the whole-hearted approval of the committee, but that of all railway enthusiasts. Mr Oliver, who said he lived in Tywyn, reported the sleepers were bad, there was a lack of ballast, and there were even worse faults in the rails themselves. He suggested ballast could be obtained from an adjacent quarry and reasonably good rails could be reclaimed from the funiculars on the inclines.

It was agreed that the launch of a publicity drive and the collection of funds should be delayed awaiting the results of the financial investigations. Mr Garland said that there must be many enthusiasts who would be prepared to do something practical to assist in the maintenance and repair of the line in their spare time. The meeting carried unanimously a formal motion that a committee be set up, proposed by Ron Oakley, a distinguished canal enthusiast and a friend of Tom Rolt's,. The following were elected to the committee, or perhaps more accurately, all the railway enthusiasts present who did not actually decline, were appointed: Messrs Clifford, Cope, Fuller, Garland, Gray, Oliver, Prosser, Rolt, Russell, Smith, Tonks, Tippetts, Trinder, Walker, and Whitehouse. Mr Wilkins was co-opted for the first committee meeting.

The committee met on 23 October 1950 in Pat Garland's office at 36 Waterloo Street, Birmingham, which was to be their regular meeting place until 1966. They elected Trinder as chairman, Whitehouse as secretary, Garland as treasurer and Rolt as public relations officer. Mr Trinder said £5 had been donated by a Mr Gerrard. The committee agreed the organisation should be called 'The Tal-y-Llyn Railway Preservation Society'. A copy of the original Railway Act should be obtained, together with details of who owned the shares and loan capital, and a copy of the balance sheet up to the latest possible date, 30 September. The committee gratefully accepted an offer by Mr Wilkins, who owned the Fairbourne miniature railway to send his manager over to vet the track and give an estimate of the cost of urgent repairs, and also investigate the state of No 1 locomotive, *Talyllyn*.

Pat Garland recalled that an ad-hoc committee under Trinder's chairmanship was set up to liaise with Lady Haydn Jones, her solicitor, and Edward Thomas, and see what they could do. Rolt came up with the idea of opening up the society to anyone interested and willing to pay a £1 subscription, with free travel for members. This proved to be a very successful formula. No money was taken, although it was offered, because no one was sure anything concrete would come of their efforts. Owen Prosser reckoned a letter of support enclosing a pound note was received from John Betjeman, one of a number of distinguished people whom Tom had interested in the Society and the railway. Pat Garland did not want to send it back and hung on to it until it was decided to take in subscriptions, and so Sir John Betjeman became TRPS member No 1. Bill Trinder had a different story. He claimed No 1 membership card of the TRPS was issued to him by order of the Council (sic) because of his work. But he was perturbed because John Betjeman had it, and the plaque on the outside wall of Wharf station commemorating the Society take-over of the railway mentions this. He recalled that when John Betjeman was there giving his speech and saying how proud he was to have the first membership card one of Trinder's brothers piped up saying 'that's not true' and was told to shut up. Trinder felt slighted by the need to award it to someone more prestigous.

Much later, in 1981, the year after Bill Trinder died, Pat Garland wrote that 'with the benefit of hindsight Tom Rolt or Bill Trinder should have been designated No 1 but the fact is that John Betjeman is the first name in my cash book, the money having been handed to me by Tom Rolt who received it as a spontaneous response to his discussion with our Poet Laureate'.

Pat Garland also remembered that he took some persuading to become honorary treasurer. 'The only reason that I accepted the invitation was I really thought the whole scheme as put forward of taking a statutory railway in a derelict condition and trying to restore it with volunteer labour was very unlikely to succeed. Consequently, and before very long, they would need someone who knew how to wind the thing up to be on hand. It was perhaps not a bad idea for me to be honorary treasurer, as I would know how to perform the last rites, which as far as I was concerned were inevitable. How wrong I was!'

CHAPTER 5

The Agreement and
The Preservation Society

There were major clashes of temperament in the committee. Tom Rolt was a very different character from the cautious businessmen who very quickly took over the reins of power. Men who knew about the perils of business, of legal and insurance requirements, of public liability and about the need to watch the cash flow. Men like John Wilkins, a successful manufacturer, who a few years earlier had bought the Fairbourne Railway and so had practical experience of running a private, albeit miniature line in Wales; and Ken Cope, who was by then deputy traffic manager of the Midland Red bus company. He, after a good education, being unemployed in the 1920s, won a Midland Red competition to travel the most mileage in twenty four hours. Asked what he would like as a prize, he replied 'a job', and although eventually they could give him one as a conductor he achieved a senior position. A good administrator, thorough and knowledgeable with facts, files and statistics at his finger tips, he became one of the original three Society directors of the railway Company; the others being John Wilkins and Bill Trinder; the latter was elected board chairman. It has been said that Ken Cope ran the traffic side of the railway from Birmingham for years, with David Woodhouse, later general manager of the Talyllyn, but then a young volunteer and a very junior employee of the Midland Red, doing all the work.

Pat Whitehouse considered subsequently that none of them, except John Wilkins, had really any idea of what they were up against. Wilkins pointed out that it would cost them five thousand pounds alone to relay the track, and where were they going to get that kind of money? If it had not been for the enthusiasm shown by Rolt and Trinder, it would probably have been left to die. Pat Garland remembered there was much goodwill. Many people, especially but by no means exclusively railway enthusiasts, resented the nationalisation of the railways, the stamping out of individuality. The engine driver in almost every boy and man at that time disliked the thought of politicians tampering with our 'lovely' railways. So when people heard there was a little minnow of a railway which had escaped the drag-net of nationalisation but was in danger of dying, they enthusiastically rushed to its assistance. There was spontaneous support, even from people who had little or no interest in railways as such.

It was still somewhat speculative whether they would actually get the railway for nothing. The idea at the beginning, Pat Garland recollected, was for the Society to produce the labour for restoration, but not necessarily to own the railway. But until the Society knew where it stood vis-a-vis the existing, if almost moribund, Company, nothing practical could be done. Negotiations, with Pat Garland more closely involved, came to a head on 8 February 1951 when a Memorandum of Agreement was drawn up and signed by Lady Haydn Jones on behalf of the executors, and Bill Trinder on behalf of the TRPS. Also present were Pat Garland, Pat Whitehouse and Tom Rolt from the Society, and Mr H.M. Arthur and Edward Thomas from the Company and the executors. The day before Pat Garland had visited the railway for the first time, and walking up the track had found red and white marks on the rails and evidence of some tidying up, showing that some reclamation work had already started.

He has described in some detail that first momentous trip to the railway, a trip that changed his life and that of hundreds of others. Tom Rolt came up to Henley-in-Arden where Garland then lived. First they called in at his office in Waterloo Street where letters and money were arriving by every post. He mentioned one letter written in a very round hand enclosed their largest donation to date, a cheque for £50, signed by E.B. Gibbons. He wondered if it might be a joke from a schoolboy and that the cheque would bounce when presented. Little did he know that Eric Gibbons was to become one of the railway's greatest benefactors, rebuilding locomotives in his firm's works, expanding greatly the turnover of the railway's shop, and serving as the Company's first commercial manager. He also had a spell as chairman of the Society and later of the board.

Pat and Tom stopped off at the Atlas Foundry Works at Shrewsbury, as No 2 *Dolgoch* had been sent there for repairs as recently as 1947. Tom was very anxious to find out from the firm what the locomotive's future was likely to be, bearing in mind that the railway's only other engine had been derelict for years, and was currently functioning as a hen-coop. Motoring on, the rain grew heavier, and darkness had fallen by the time they reached the Tyn-y-Cornel Hotel by Talyllyn Lake where they were warmly welcomed by Mr and Mrs Hunter. Pat described the hotel, much smaller then, where it being out of season they and Tom were the only guests. They had a thoroughly enjoyable meal and next morning the mist across the lake, framed by the mountains beyond, presented enchantment.

Repeating Bill Trinder's experience of three years earlier, the morning mist gave way to a glorious sunny day, and whilst they did not climb up to the quarry, they left their car at Abergynolwyn and walked down the railway to Wharf. The weather was so warm, even though it was early February, that they had to take off their jackets and roll up their sleeves. Garland, seeing the line for the first time, was staggered at its appalling condition. It was unbelievable how any trains were run on it. Many of the rails were loose, only kept in gauge by the earth and grass. He had never seen such a run down thing in his life.

The following day negotiations began at Machynlleth. Pat Garland recalled how the participants just sat down and looked at each other. He remembered saying to himself: 'Nothing ventured. Nothing won! Let us ask if we can have the railway in exchange for an undertaking to keep it alive'. That was really the gist of the matter. He explained to Lady Haydn Jones and Mr Arthur that the Society had no money and the prospect of being able to buy it was out of the question. But if she would give it to them, they would undertake to maintain it and keep it running as far as it was possible. The Korean conflict was raging, and nobody knew what the future held. A value had to be placed on the

C O P Y

MEMORANDUM OF AGREEMENT between Lady Haydn Jones and Talyllyn Railway Preservation Society.

1. Lady Haydn Jones agrees to transfer all the shares in the Talyllyn Railway Company to a new holding Company (known as Talyllyn Holdings Limited).

2. The Talyllyn Railway Preservation Society agrees to raise funds by subscription to carry on the operations of the Talyllyn Railway

3. The Directors of the Talyllyn Holdings Limited and of the Talyllyn Railway Co. shall be nominated as to two by Lady Haydn Jones and two by the Talyllyn Railway Preservation Society together with the Chariman to be nominated by the Talyllyn Railway Preservation Society

4. The present value of the Railway should be determined and the value so arrived at should be taken into account as Lady Haydn's share in the event of the Railway ceasing to operate and in the event of disposal

5. The house at Fendre and the cottage Plascoch Rhydyronen shall remain the property of the Railway Company and the present value shall be taken into account when assessing Lady Haydn Jones' share as set out in paragraph 4 and the net rents from these properties shall be paid to Lady Haydn Jones quarterly.

6. The house Llechfan shall be conveyed to Lady Haydn Jones

7. Letters to be sent to the tenants of the houses at Fendre and Plascoch intimating conditions of tenancy as service tenancies.

Dated this 8th day of February, 1951

G. Haydn Jones
w. G. Trinder.

railway as it stood. If the line subsequently had to be closed down, the value attributed to it then would subsequently be paid to Lady Haydn Jones and the balance distributed to those who had chipped money into its restoration. Fortunately it never came to this. The value of the line prior to the TRPS taking over was agreed at £1350. There is a typewritten copy of the Memorandum of Agreement in the Talyllyn railway documents deposited at the County Council archives at Dolgellau, but the original document has disappeared.

What did Lady Haydn Jones think about all this? It must have seemed most extraordinary to her. Why was she so generous? Or was she? Garland recollected that she was by then a fairly old lady, she really did not react one way or the other. She was brought to the meeting, and was content to listen and agree with anything her solicitor said. If he nodded his head then that was good enough for her. The TRPS representatives were able to convince Mr Arthur they were in earnest. It is always possible that Mr Arthur (or possibly Sir Haydn himself, who was after all also a solicitor) had looked into the matter carefully, and already discovered, or at least suspected, what the Festiniog found out the hard way several months later.

In 1952 the Festiniog (like the Talyllyn) was probably worth more as scrap than as a going concern. At an extraordinary Company meeting held in November 1950, the Festiniog decided to seek an Abandonment Order, presumably to be able to sell the railway to the scrap dealers who were badgering them. But the reply from the Ministry of Transport stated it had no powers to grant such an order. The railway had been established by an Act of Parliament, and once it had been opened for public traffic only another Act of Parliament could disband it.

Some credence to the suspicion that Sir Haydn may have had an inkling of the difficulties of disposing of a Statutory Railway is given by a story that he tried to sell his to the Towyn Urban District Council for £6000. If the rumour is correct (no written evidence has come to light), the offer was probably made in 1946 or thereabouts, on the closure of the quarry – although it could have been made as long ago as 1911 just after it came into his possession.

Pat Garland and most of the other people involved, including Lady Jones, had a great affection for the railway, if only because Sir Haydn had kept it going for so many years after it ceased to be financially viable. In 1950 total receipts were just over £400 and there were 5235 passengers. Even in 1951, the first year under society auspices, the railway took in £650.

Mr Arthur no doubt thought the Society's request to be given the line somewhat unusual, but at the same time he was impressed by the *bona fides* of those wishing to preserve it. Trinder was a man of whose sincerity one could not help but be convinced. Rolt was another, and there was the enthusiasm shown by many other people. Of course, the alternatives facing Mr Arthur and Lady Haydn Jones were none too attractive. To close a statutory railway is not an easy proposition as British Rail have found to their cost on several occasions, and the solicitor may have known, or at least suspected, that an Act of Parliament might be required. Almost certainly he thought that at the very least he would need to get an Abandonment Order. In the context of the family businesses making up the estate, such as the slate company, Daniels' hardware, the farm and so on, the railway was probably pretty small beer. It was in desperate need of a lot of money being spent on it, and this the executors were not prepared, or even able, to contemplate.

Garland remembered they were very limited in their expressions one way or the other. He felt they were a bit overwhelmed with the proposition, and the persuasive way it was put forward. There had no doubt been earlier discussions, some with Edward Thomas. They knew what Sir Haydn wanted, and had probably agreed amongst themselves to accept the offer before the meeting ever took place. Pat Garland has stated that it was probably the easiest agreement with which he had been associated throughout his career. It was drawn up in the course of the morning, probably typed out there and then, as it is only 223 words long, and quickly signed on the spot. It may have been signed later, but there is a typing error in the third paragraph, and it is highly unlikely this would have been allowed to stand if the typing and signing had not been done quickly. Typing in those days, especially in small town solicitor's offices, was meticulously checked, and such an error would have been picked up if there had been time to peruse the document carefully. But no doubt the slip was overlooked in the shock or euphoria of the moment. Even if it was noticed, it would probably have been ignored in the desire to get the other party to sign before they started to have second thoughts.

There is little doubt that the Society's representatives were euphoric. They had actually achieved ownership of a railway they could run themselves. They knew that they could now really get started working on the railway, and that the fact of the Society's ownership would release enormous enthusiasm and dedication. A few years later the Festiniog's preservation did not really get off the ground whilst potential volunteers considered it was owned by Alan Pegler; it first had to be made into a Trust.

The business of tracing all the shares and of arranging for their transfer to a new Company set up to hold them, Talyllyn Holdings Ltd, took a lot longer than expected. Instructions were given to a firm of solicitors in West Bromwich. The firm was selected because it was known that one of the younger partners was a railway enthusiast, and the hope was that the work would be done without charge. This became the usual Talyllyn approach. The committee deliberately made it its business to enlist the sympathy and practical help of leaders of industry and other influential people who could assist.

There was no precedent for a Company limited by guarantee without share capital taking over and holding the issued shares of a Company incorporated by Act of Parliament. The new Company was finally incorporated on 3 October 1952, eighteen months after signing the Memorandum of Agreement. The Talyllyn Railway Company Limited had issued 750 shares of £15 each. Lady Jones could only produce 585, and much research and effort took place to get the rest. This detective work was mainly undertaken by the society and Company's honorary solicitor, George Tibbetts. On his death in 1968 Jeremy Wilkinson took over, and eventually the task was completed when the final twenty shares were handed over by the executors of an old farmer who had been given them by Sir Haydn, and who had hung on to them maybe in the hope that they would some day be of value.

So in the first two seasons of the Society operating, the railway was still actually owned by Lady Haydn Jones. The Society paid the staff from February 1951, but handed over the rents received from cottages and other property to Lady Haydn until her death in 1960. From October 1950 until February 1951, the wages had still been paid by the 'old' Company, in effect by Lady Haydn, and in the early years of preservation the sum was carried on the balance sheets as a contingent liability. The only employees at the time were Hugh Jones, his son Dai, and Edward Thomas, who took official retirement when the Society took over running the railway and its future seemed more secure. Tom Rolt became the Society's first general manager, moving to Wales in April 1951 and remaining there until October, living in a caravan at Dolgoch. As already stated, Angela did not come, the lady who shared his living accommodation and helped him enormously on the railway being his second wife, Sonia. In 1952 Tom was again there from April to October. In 1951 Tom had his friend David Curwen with him, keeping No 2 locomotive going (No 1 was beyond immediate repair) so that it could manage a couple of trains up the line and back five days a week. He also had the task of getting two former Corris engines acquired from British Rail into running order. He was greatly assisted by two volunteers, engineers on British Rail, Bill Harvey from the Norwich shed, and Alan Garraway soon to become general manager of the Festiniog Railway, but then also employed on BR's Eastern Region.

Bill Harvey took the trouble to go to Birmingham for the sole purpose of inspecting P.B. Whitehouse, the honorary secretary, and P.J. Garland to form an opinion as to their credibility. Though he was clearly perplexed about the Society's ambitions, and doubtful about the eventual outcome, the two Pats presumably acquitted themselves well for Bill threw his whole weight into maintaining the engines and getting them going. It is, and was then, no mean journey from Norwich to Tywyn, and showed the extent of his and Alan's dedication. Bill the 'doyen of steam railway engineers', followed Alan to the Festiniog in 1954, and did not pay another working visit to the Talyllyn until October 1986.

The committee soon made a shopping list of the items needed to put the railway in working order. Requests used to appear in *Talyllyn News* asking if any member knew where a certain spare part (or certain lengths of a particular steel) might be found. Undoubtedly the finest scrounger the railway ever had was Bill Faulkner. He was in 1951 the works manager of Tearne Ltd, a Birmingham firm that made transfers. He seemed to know everyone who mattered in business in the West Midlands. Each week-end, having despatched his wife Peggy and the children in her small van ahead, he would load up the boot and much of the interior of his Jaguar with bits and pieces 'acquired'. The Faulkner family spent almost every week-end that first season in their caravan parked by the line at Brynglas station. In 1964 Bill and Peggy moved to Tywyn and bought a cafe and residence in the High Street, Bill then acting as unpaid relief driver and deputy general manager until 1965 when he became managing director. In 1967 he gave this up on becoming general manager of the Dart Valley Railway in Devon. In 1970 he resigned this post and the family moved to Aberdovey, Bill again becoming unpaid managing director of the Talyllyn in 1973 and remaining so until his death in 1982. Pat Whitehouse is doubtful if the railway would have got off the ground but for Bill Faulkner, who 'gave it his whole life'.

Pat Garland recalled that in those early years the committee included several business men who were chairmen and managing directors of Companies, usually family concerns. Pat Whitehouse described the Birmingham area manufacturing sector at that time as a kind of tribal society with lots of small independent engineering firms, run by tough minded, opinionated and often abrasive men who made their own decisions. They did not have to ask a committee or their board for permission to give things to the Talyllyn or do work at cost only. Fortunately many of these men were interested in railways, certainly in helping an independent one. According to Whitehouse 'half the firms didn't have any books – didn't know what they were!' Business was done by word of mouth. These men had no time for bureaucracy but ample sympathy for the Talyllyn.

These 'captains' of industry were asked to serve on the committee for the practical help they could give. Major Walker, a timber merchant from Gloucester, provided a considerable quantity of timber without charge: albeit some of rather poor quality and mostly used for telephone poles. Other notable members of this type were Tom Noble of Turner Asbestos, Eric Gibbons of Gibbons Bros, Ken Cope of Midland Red, and Jimmy Boyd the proprietor of a clothing firm. Pat Whitehouse owned a building firm.

Enormous help with the locomotives came from firms such as Hunt Bros of Oldbury, while Tommy Hunt (a friend of Tom Rolt's), overhauled and converted to 2ft 3in gauge a locomotive given by Abelson & Co (Engineers) in 1953. This became No 6 *Douglas* because it was a condition of the gift that it should be named after the firm's chairman, Douglas Abelson. The gift resulted from an appeal sent out in 1952 by Lord Northesk, then president, to over four hundred firms appearing in trade directories. Hunt's also did a fair amount of work on No 2 *Dolgoch*, later finished off by Gibbons Bros. Gibbons also rebuilt No 1 *Talyllyn*, a massive undertaking. The Hunslet Engine Co Ltd of Leeds, successors to Kerr, Stuart, the original builders of No 4 *Edward Thomas* overhauled it very quickly in 1952, so the TR would have at least one reliable engine available for service. When the bill for this job came, it was in the form of a fully itemised invoice setting out the work done, totalling £650, then a sizeable sum, but for amount claimed, 'SAY NIL'. The gentleman most closely involved was another of Rolt's friends, John Alcock, Hunslet's managing director and later chairman. His firm also supplied a new boiler for No 4 in 1964. The Hunslet company over the years was not only most generous to the TR, but produced work of the highest standard.

The Talyllyn also owes a very great deal to John Wilkins, co-opted on to the first committee and one of the three original Society-appointed directors. Another typical Black country business man, he was a real leader of industry, chairman of Wilkins & Mitchell, who made a lot of money out of Servis washing machines (advertised in many of the early editions of *Talyllyn News*) and, as already mentioned, owned the Fairbourne Railway. His help was especially valuable in the first season when the Society had to gain credibility as well as cash, running a regular service.

Loco No 2 would just work, but must have rails to run on. Most of the existing ones were no longer really fit, a few positively unsafe.

Rails were thus the number one priority. The only rail available, apart from a small quantity to be recovered from the abandoned inclines, was that lifted from the Corris Railway, which had been sold by British Rail to W.O. Williams, a scrap dealer of Harlech. He was persuaded to sell the rail to the Fairbourne Railway as the Talyllyn had no money! The Fairbourne then sold it to the Talyllyn and collected their money when it became available. For many years the Fairbourne was one of the TR's largest creditors. It only rendered accounts once a year, the Talyllyn paying a lump sum when it could. Not only was rail supplied on this basis but coal and other supplies. Moreover, the Fairbourne also supplied people to lay the rails during those crucially important first weeks in early 1951. Most important was Mr Vaughton, its permanent way-foreman, who supervised his own men and volunteers on a more or less open commitment to do what he could for the TR's track; certainly to get it open as far as Rhydyronen. The Talyllyn owes the Fairbourne, under its former ownership, a considerable debt.

The committee appointed a very different type of man to themselves as the Society's first president; one of the genuine landed gentry, related to the Queen Mother, a man whose family tree could be traced for generations through the pages of Debrett. On the wall of the 'Master Builder' inn, Bucklers Hard, a lovely old preserved village on the right bank of the Beulieu River in Hampshire, where Nelson's ships were built, is a poster inviting 'all good men and true' to join the crew of one Captain the Earl of Northesk. It was a descendant of that same captain, David Northesk, who became president in 1952, and later chairman of both Society and Company when Bill Trinder resigned in May 1954. A true aristocrat sure of his position, David Northesk had no 'side' on him. A friend to all, he will be best remembered as a volunteer fireman. As Tom Rolt wrote 'For how could we ever forget that burly, bear-like, unmistakeable figure in fireman's overalls and cap, striding across Pendre yard in his heavy boots or beaming with pleasure from the cab of No 4. He was never happier than when he was on the footplate of a locomotive. He not only looked the part but acted it so well that a tip from a satisfied customer was not unknown. He has been described as the spitting image of that well-known actress of yesteryear, Margaret Rutherford, both in appearance and unmitigated energy and enthusiasm, particularly for the TR, for which he was an excellent ambassador.

John Snell, who later became managing director of the Romney, Hythe & Dymchurch Railway in Kent, wrote to Tom Rolt offering his services while waiting to go up to Oxford. He recalled this his first job in April 1951 was helping chief engineer David Curwen in re-laying track on Cynfal Bank. Because No 2 *Dolgoch*, the only locomotive, was under repair, they had to push the loaded wagons up the line. Later that month No 2 was steamed for the first time under the Society's auspices, having passed a boiler test. Her first job was to haul the two ex-Corris locos which had been standing for some weeks on the siding at Wharf, together with twelve slate wagons full of coal up to Pendre. After taking some rails and sleepers up to the track gang at Rhydyronen that evening, it was decided that *Dolgoch* should make a foray up the line together with an ex-Corris van, the first 'new' vehicle to go up the line for eighty years. They proceeded safely through a flooded cutting above Brynglas, disturbing millions of tadpoles; thereafter known as 'Tadpole Cutting'. Arriving at Dolgoch station it was discovered to the train crew's horror that the water tank was dry. They then drove the engine back to Pendre at what must have been the fastest pace for years. The locomotive soon exhausted its remaining supply of water, so they had to let the fire out. With only ten pounds of pressure on the gauge the engine stuck on four months of accumulated gravel on Pendre level crossing – in the middle of the road. It was not until 10 pm that they succeeded in 'pinch-barring' her to one side, edging forward inch by inch with the toe of a long crowbar.

Before the actual first 'official' Society train was run as far as Rhydyronen on Whit Monday, 14 May 1951, *Dolgoch* made one or two more trips up the line with track materials. On the Saturday before Whit Monday a special train went to Abergynolwyn and back. On the following Monday five return trips were made to Rhydyronen, and the rails shone for the first time in years!

In June 1951 John Snell was taken on to the paid staff as a general assistant, mainly to carry on helping David Curwen but also to work as guard and booking clerk when Tom Rolt (on his own that first season) needed a hand. Tom had agreed on a monthly salary of £30. Absolutely dedicated, he requested no more. He used his talents wisely in putting the story of the venture into his best-selling book *Railway Adventure*, reprinted for another twenty five years. In those early days, and indeed for the first couple of years or so until more trained voluntary help became available, it was the practice to pay for tasks long since normally carried out by volunteers. Not that at a time of high employment the Talyllyn could afford to employ good local people. When an effort to find a fireman failed. John Snell was left to do most of the firing in June and July. When another lad was taken on as fireman John resumed duty as guard, but four days later was back on the footplate since the new recruit had gone. Then a better if less orthodox choice was made: a local schoolboy, Gareth Jones, whom John Snell had noticed constantly watching the train as it left Wharf. Although only thirteen, Gareth was an immediate success and so John resumed guarding, and on Thursday 9 August recorded his train as carrying a record 121 passengers. Gareth was paid 2s 6d (12½p) for each train he fired. He probably got 2s 6d because that was the amount he earned at The Star grocery where he was a delivery boy. He went on to become a fireman on British Rail at Machynlleth, eventually advancing to senior driver and instructor on the West Coast main line out of Euston. But in 1954 when the railway was very short of drivers, the TR persuaded the BR supervisor at Machynlleth to arrange young Gareth's shifts so that he would be able to pay working visits to the Talyllyn. Gareth was one of the very few Tywyn residents to give practical help at that time. Not perhaps surprising, as to the local people the railway was a business which like any other should pay properly.

Peter Williams who lived in Railway View in the same building as the engine shed and workshops at Pendre, was paid £1 for lighting up the loco's fire on eight mornings. Before he could do this he had to replace the bars in the fire-box floor. This was because they were still using the old traditional TR method of lifting out the complete fire, bars and all, and dropping the lot into the ash-pit when putting the engine away at the end of each day's running. The bars were then hooked out of the red-hot mass in the pit and left to cool overnight. It would have been impossible to put them back straight away, as any attempt to quench the cast iron with water to make them cool enough to handle would have been the utmost folly.

2s 6d (or half a crown) seems to have been the going-rate for odd-jobs. The idea of voluntary labour for a commercial concern was something very new, life then being firmly divided between voluntary societies such as the Girl Guides, Boy Scouts, Red Cross and so on and the world of business. In general in the fifties the idea of 'work as play' was totally foreign. The TRPS was one of the pioneers of this social change.

For the first five years the railway was administered from Birmingham. As far as could be managed, Tom and his successors were left with as few financial chores as possible. He just had a petty cash book, with a spending limit of £5 on any one item. The directors appointed by the committee were allowed to authorise expenditure on items up to £10 without its prior approval. The first item in the Cash Book was on 1 June 1951 'To Cash. Ex wages cheque £10.' The first entry on the expenses side was '6 June Stamps 15s (75p), followed by 'Basil Jones 1 dozen sheets of carbon paper?', 'Trunk call to Boyd-Carpenter at Worksop 3s' (must have been from a call box as there was no telephone on the railway at that time), 'Sandwiches for Adams, photographer 2s'.

All other financial matters were dealt with from Pat Garland's office at 36 Waterloo Street, Birmingham. Every fortnight a cheque was sent off to Wharf station for wages. The Talyllyn paid its staff fortnightly on a Thursday, and still does, following what had been normal railway practice. These arrangements, centred on Birmingham, continued almost until the time Bill Faulkner went to live at Tywyn, on becoming unpaid managing director. It was not that the general managers were incapable of paying wages, but they had so many other things to do, and this chore was one that could be taken off them. The Talyllyn Railway owes a great debt of gratitude to the family firms of Pat Whitehouse and Pat Garland. These two Companies' resources of staff time, telephones, stationery and so on were made available to what gradually became a fair-sized commercial undertaking. Using these firm's facilities also gave credibility and standing, and thus extended credit, to a Company that was by no means financially robust. By September 1956, however, the work had grown so much that the committee agreed to pay Messrs B. Whitehouse and Sons Ltd £150 a year for clerical assistance over the past year, and as a token payment for the next twelve months.

Pat Whitehouse gave up as hon secretary in 1965 as he felt it was time 'for new blood'. The railway had by then become much more democratic than it was in the late fifties and early sixties. At that period the committee was rather ineffective, and the Company ran the railway – in fact just the three of them, Pat Garland, accountant, Pat Whitehouse, secretary, and Bill Faulkner, managing director. In the early sixties younger members came to the fore. Neither Pat Whitehouse nor Pat Garland, unlike Bill Faulkner, were the types who 'took their coats off'. Their indispensible work was done behind the scenes. Pat Whitehouse considered that from the sixties onwards it was appropriate that every effort should be made to check any tendency for the Society and the Company to drift apart, to let the latter withdraw into itself. The railway had to be run by its members, or it would die.

Pendre .block post .

CHAPTER 6

'A Workers' Co-operative'

Following the inaugural meeting of the Talyllyn Railway Preservation Society in October 1950 there was a great deal of discussion about how the railway should be acquired, administered, staffed and operated. Bill Trinder told the committee at its second meeting on 11 December 1950, that he, Jim Russell and Tom Rolt had suggested to Mr Arthur, Lady Jones' solicitor, that a limited liability, non-profit making, trust be formed to take over. There should be no unknown liabilities. In particular the trust was to have no obligation to repay the loan of £5000 that, it was then thought, had been made by Sir Haydn to the Railway Company. As a personal loan it would be included as a potential asset in his estate, but as part of any agreement, should be written off. All monies subscribed to the trust should be devoted to the running of the railway, as Lady Jones would be presenting it to the trust free of charge. She would become an ordinary trust member incurring no liabilities beyond this. The trust should receive the line from Wharf to the quarries, but not the quarries themselves, nor anything pertaining to them. The trust would operate the railway for at least three years 'subject to prevailing conditions'. (The outbreak of World War III as an extension of the then raging Korean conflict was envisaged as a distinct possibility.) The trust would undertake not to sell the railway once it was handed over. Mr Arthur was to put all these points to Lady Haydn Jones and recommend she accept them.

Mr Garland suggested Mr Arthur should be asked to draw up articles for the trust, and the committee should appoint a solicitor to examine them. An offer by a well-wisher to vet any legal document had been accepted with thanks. Mr James I.C. Boyd who had also been co-opted on to the committee, in addition to Mr Wilkins, because of his knowledge of narrow-gauge railways, suggested that the new body should be a 'holding company', as the title 'trust' was open to various interpretations and investigations. Mr Whitehouse pointed out the railway could only be operated by a statutory Company authorised by Parliament. Mr Garland suggested it might be better to obtain a majority holding in the shares of the existing Company, the railway be valued, and that on the transference of such shares to the preservation trust death duties on them might be remitted. It was understood (incorrectly, as George Tibbitts later pointed out) that in any case the land belonged to Lady Haydn Jones, not to the railway Company.

Mr Wilkins reported he had examined the line as requested. The track was in very poor condition, the sleepers were rotted, and fifty per cent of the rails were unusable. The main requirement for safe running was now a new sleeper under every joint, and the replacement of unserviceable rails. The ten tons of Corris rail available would only go a small way towards this. The locomotive *Talyllyn* was a complete 'write-off', and *Dolgoch* needed urgent inspection before its boiler could again be insured. The engine was not in good order, being eighty six years old. He estimated the cost of putting the track into good shape at £11,000 (£200,000 in 1989 money). One of the causes of deterioration was that No 2's fixed wheelbase was too large for the track. He agreed to obtain a new insurance report on the two Corris locomotives, so a true value could be placed on them. BR were understood to be asking £85 each which was considered too high. A new approach to BR was authorised. Messrs Boyd, Wilkins and Whitehouse agreed to guarantee the purchase price of one of the Corris engines.

Mr David Curwen, an engineer from Devizes, who was present at the meeting – Tom Rolt must have asked him along – offered to place his experience before the Society, by working on the locomotives at Tywyn and supervising other engineering activities. It was suggested an open 'toast-rack' bogie car be obtained. Names for a suitable president were also discussed.

The third meeting was on 2 February 1951. Various members offered to buy the Corris engines and donate them to the Society now BR were asking only £25 each. The secretary reported he

was still waiting for an estimate from BR for the cost of transporting them from Machynlleth to Tywyn. He had been offered
ten ex-Corris wagons by BR. Mr Boyd offered to meet the cost
of these. Circulars and membership cards designed by Mr Rolt,
the printing being arranged by Mr Cope, were approved. Mr
Garland pointed out that it was unlikely the Society or the
holding Company would be liable to income tax, nor would the
Tal-y-llyn Railway Company have to pay any, due to the losses
sustained and the renewals needed. He would discuss with the
local Inspector of Taxes at Carnarvon the position should it become necessary to wind up the railway Company. It was agreed
Messrs Garland, Trinder, Rolt and Whitehouse should meet Mr
Arthur and Lady Haydn Jones on the lines suggested in Mr
Garland's original letter. This set out the proposals for forming
the holding company and running the railway. A legal discharge
should be sought for the £5000 debt. The generous offer of Mr
Wilkins to send out the new Talyllyn leaflets with those of the
Fairbourne Railway, to supply two gross of fishplate bolts, to
obtain a supply of Corris sleepers and rail, and to store these
items until the Society was in a position to use them, and not
to ask for payment until funds became available, was gratefully
accepted. Messrs Curwen and Wilkins were asked to investigate
the engineering work that needed to be done.

At the fourth meeting on 23 February, the committee approved
the memorandum setting up the railway, agreed at the meeting
with Mr Arthur and Lady Jones at Machynlleth on 8 February.
Mr Garland reported that the total assets of the Railway Company as valued by Mr Edward Thomas were £1350. As soon
as the agreement had been reached a large number of circulars
and membership forms had been sent out, and to date £300 18s
had been received, plus two locomotives. Seven life members
had contributed more than the £15, and there were 88 ordinary
members, some paying more than the £1 minimum. Nominations
were sought for the three posts of director and one of secretary
of Talyllyn Holdings Company Limited. Mr Garland suggested
the same people should hold the same offices in the Talyllyn
Railway Company. The holding company was purely nominal.
It existed merely to hold the shares in the Railway Company.

The guarantee required from each director would be limited to £5, and this would be refunded by the Society should the need arise. The proposers and seconders as well as the nominees are of interest in the light of events yet to unfold. Trinder was proposed as chairman by Jim Russell, seconded by Tom Rolt. John Wilkins and Ken Cope were chosen as directors, the former proposed by Pat Garland and seconded by Tom Rolt, the latter proposed by Pat Whitehouse and seconded by John Wilkins. Mr Fuller suggested Pat Garland as secretary, but he proposed Mr Whitehouse and Mr Fuller agreed to this, Mr Wilkins seconding. Mr Rolt was unanimously voted into the post of general manager, which he accepted on a provisional basis. Three sub-committees were formed: finance and general purposes, engineering, and publicity.

Mr Rolt suggested a public meeting to be held at Tywyn, to inform local people of what was happening and to seek their support. He would also ascertain their views on opening the railway on a Sunday. Mr Whitehouse said he had arranged with the leading railway societies for the TRPS leaflets to be sent out with their monthly magazines. Mr Wilkins reported that *Dolgoch* had been stripped ready for the boiler test, and that he was making arrangements for public liability insurance. He also offered the assistance of his railway manager at Fairbourne for £5 per week, plus his rail fares, an offer gratefully accepted.

The fifth meeting, preceded by meetings of the sub-committees one hour earlier, was on 9 March 1951. Mr Wynne-Thomas of Aberdovey had agreed to chair the meeting at Tywyn on 27 March, and one hundred notices were to be printed and distributed. A rota of private cars to take members from Birmingham to the railway was to be drawn up, as public transport was too expensive. Mr Curwen was to receive £60 for the month he expected to spend on the Corris engines, to cover the cost of renting a caravan, petrol, use of his car, and welding material, as well as his labour and professional expertise. He was authorised to spend up to an additional £20 on any items of equipment, such as tools, he might need. Mr Wilkins was authorised to spend up to £300 on rails, and he would approach Messrs Williams of Harlech about purchasing scrap from the Corris railway. The men employed were to be given a rise of 10s per week and their wages were to be checked 'against the minimum wage obtained by union men'. The engineering committee reported that quarter mile posts were to be set up and the bridges numbered. Mr Oliver was to start preparing the track on the Village Incline ready for lifting, and to use any weekend voluntary labour for this purpose. An electric cable was to be laid to the machine shop, and Mr Walker was to order half a ton of 5in dog spikes. They should look for a petrol driven locomotive. All bridges and abutments should be inspected for ingrowing trees. Time and work sheets should be made out by working parties. The publicity committee was allocated £20. Volunteers were to be paid one penny per week, although this decision does not appear to have been implemented. The publicity committee considered making a film. It appointed a representative to the Tywyn Festival of Britain Committee, and agreed to a request by the Tywyn Advertising Association to supply material for insertion in the town guide. The railway should be kept closed on Saturdays and Sundays, the days most volunteer labour was available. This would give the members' working parties full track possession to carry out urgently needed essential repairs.

At the fifth meeting on 12 April, the idea of camp beds to meet the accommodation needs of volunteers, and Elsan portable loos to meet other needs, was abandoned, as there was no water supply at Wharf. The Crosville and Midland Red bus companies said they might include a trip on the railway as part of their bus tours if a train service could be guaranteed. Name boards and other notice boards, including six glass-fronted ones, had been obtained free of charge by Mr Cope. Five thousand member tickets and twenty seven thousand others, all of the 'Edmundson' card type, had been ordered from Messrs M. Harland & Son, Manor Street, Land of Green Ginger, Hull. All obsolete tickets were being sold as souvenirs.

In July 1951 it was reported that insurance for public liability, workmen's compensation and boiler insurance had been arranged in the name of the Railway Company, and one for personal accident in the name of the Society. Western Region of British Rail would not exchange posters as the TR ones were not the 'Double-Royal' size required, so it was agreed TR posters in future should be 'Double-Royal'. The general manager was asked to prepare a scale of charges for goods traffic. The secretary reported that the Earl of Northesk had kindly agreed to become president and the following to be Vice-Presidents: J.N. Maskeylene, president of the Stephenson Locomotive Society; Hugh Griffiths, a noted Welsh actor; Dr Dickinson, secretary of the Newcomen Society, the American Branch of which had given the Society $500; and Alderman G.F. Hamer, Lord Lieutenant of Montgomeryshire. (If it should be asked why not of Merioneth, the reason is that Mr Garland was Alderman Hamer's accountant.) Griffiths and Dickinson were friends of Tom Rolt. The bank balance at June 1951 was £1011 6s 8d, with liabilities of £717 18s, and further commitments of £309, so about £18 'in deficit'.

In August rules were drafted to be put to the first annual general meeting in September. Committee members, elected at the Society's AGM were to appoint the chairman and two directors of the railway and holding companies, also the general manager, accountant and secretary, and these must be Society members. If they should not already be members of the committee they should be able to attend meetings, but not vote, as also may the two family directors appointed by the executors of Sir Haydn Jones. The three directors appointed by the committee were not allowed to sanction any financial outlay exceeding £10 without its knowledge and approval. (The Society directors, who under Company law serve in a personal capacity, have to lodge the necessary papers with the honorary solicitor to enable their removal should they ever fall out with the elected council.) There was to be no doubt of who was running the railway!

In effect what is now known as a 'worker's co-operative' was created – although nobody thought of it in those terms at the time, and few since. The difference with the Talyllyn railway is that almost all the workers are unpaid volunteers. In theory the Society membership as a whole elects the council (formerly committee), and thus indirectly controls the Company through the three directors. In practice, as there is no postal voting, those present in the AGM constitute the electorate. With the passage of time these have increasingly been drawn from the ranks of the active working volunteers, who now

represent the great majority of those attending and voting.

In September the treasurer said there was no money for a
petrol engine unless absolutely essential. In October Mr Faulkner
became vice-chairman. Mr Rolt was to visit Mr Arthur regarding agreement on items on the railway to be taken over by the
Society (sic). In November Mr Wilkins was thanked for paying
the fourteen guineas cost of paper for the AGM. Mr Garland was
authorised to negotiate a bank loan in the name of the Company.
At a meeting in January 1953, Mr Gray pleaded that there should
be no cutting of hedges in May and June as this was the nesting
season. This was agreed, especially when it was pointed out there
would in any case be other more important jobs to be done at
this time'. The following month there was a complaint that the
TR timetable was not in the January edition of *Bradshaw*. It had
been sent in late, but would appear in the February issue. Mr Rolt
had arranged for the Talyllyn to be mentioned, and be given due
recognition, in the advance publicity and souvenir programme of
a popular film called *The Titfield Thunderbolt* about a branch line,
due to be closed, but kept open by the local people.

In October 1953 the committee ruled that the Society could not
agree to the running of trains on Sundays, as this would be contrary to the wishes of Lady Haydn Jones, in addition to other factors.
The 1953 AGM was attended by Lady Haydn and Mr Edward
Thomas, who thanked members for the very warm welcome they
had received. At a special AGM in Tywyn on 25 September 1954,
tankards were given to local farmer and Society member, and another of Tom Rolt's friends, Mr Morgan Roberts, for cutting the
railway's hedges and letting the Army helpers camp in his field;
to 'Chips' Harrison for building 'the best coach bodies outside
Swindon'; to Geoff Hayes for good service on the locomotives both
on the footplate and in the workshops, and to Charles Uren for
installing the first telephone system, between Wharf and Pendre
and beyond, and for general engineering services. He had been appointed locomotive superintendent at Pendre that year, and it was
remarked that 'his impeturbable manner and cheerful appraisal of
difficulties should help considerably in disposing of our inevitable
emergencies'. The withdrawal of the winter train was bemoaned

by a local, Mr Jones, but it was pointed out the track must be relaid if the line was to remain open. The railway could not afford to lose twenty seven days required for the service. If there was a serious accident the Ministry of Transport would close the line: the inspector had been horrified at the state of some of the track.

In January 1955 the committee learned that the Rev Wilbert Awdry, a keen member of the Society, would base his next book on the Talyllyn. It was to be called *Four Little Engines* and would have the following note appended: 'If you have enjoyed these stories you will certainly enjoy a visit to the Talyllyn Railway in Wales'. On 6 July 1955, a very successful lunch was held at the Whitehall Hotel in Tywyn to honour all those businessmen who had given so much help to the Society in its earliest years. This was followed by a tour of the railway. The Midland Red Bus Company had four coach tours that year which featured a trip on the railway, and they were very successful. After the special general meeting and AGM at the Whitehall Hotel in September, Mr & Mrs Wyatt the proprietors provided a buffet free of charge. The committee agreed to sell the book *Mary Jones and Her Bible* published by the British & Foreign Bible Society. In November 1955 Mr Woodhouse agreed to search Wharf station for the original plans of the line. In January 1956 it was agreed a Sunday special train could be run for a Mr Brown of Manchester, and there could be other non-advertised specials on Sunday afternoons.

In May 1956 the TRPS held cordial talks with the Festiniog Railway Society, and agreed there should be mutual free travel for their respective members. In March 1957 it was agreed the AGM should be held in the Drill Hall, Brook Street – where it has been held ever since – followed by the usual party in the White Hall Hotel. The following year the arrangements at the White Hall were not satisfactory, and a licence was sought for the Drill Hall, with the buffet to be held there too.

MR ROLT AND THE COMMITTEE

Tom Rolt as general manager and as committee member did not always see 'eye-to-eye' with the majority of his colleagues. He was of a very different temperament; relations were not easy, at times acrimonious and even tempestuous. Tom was a visionary, as well as a competent engineer, but he was not a businessman, did not suffer fools gladly, sometimes lacked tact and was not given to a general kind of bonhomie; somewhat of a loner'. He was very much his own man, and in no way a 'committee' person.

Tom's original idea, as expressed at that first public meeting in October 1950, was that a strong working committee should be formed, either to acquire the railway, or to form a society to keep the line running under its then existing ownership. There were two priorities, track improvement, and the provision of additional locomotive power so there could be trains six days a week instead of three. He suggested they acquired more rails from the closed Corris, and should re-lay them with voluntary labour. At the first committee meeting on 23 October 1950 Tom Rolt was made public relations officer and assistant secretary to the new society.

It was at the fourth meeting of the committee held on 23 February 1951, only a fortnight after the signing of the agreement with Lady Haydn Jones handing over the railway to the preservation society, that Tom was unanimously voted into the position of general manager on the proposition of Mr Walker seconded by Pat Garland. Mr Rolt accepted on a provisional basis. He said 'that he would do everything that he could to fulfill the post'. The committee asked him to accept their 'best thanks' for his generosity. As Pat Garland pointed out much later Tom was the only one of their number whose commitments allowed him to spend the summer at Tywyn. Mr Rolt suggested a public meeting should be held to elicit support in Tywyn, and that the views of the locals on Sunday opening of the railway should be ascertained. This perhaps showed that he was slightly out of touch with local feeling, certainly with that of Lady Jones! It was to be several years before the railway operated Sunday services, and decades before the pubs opened on Sundays.

A major row took place even before the first regular public service started on the 4 June 1951. The first advertised train service under Society auspices with tickets sold to the public was on Whit Monday, 14 May 1951, when a successful shuttle service was operated between Wharf and Rhydyronen. There the train

Price 1d.

Tal-y-llyn Railway

(The oldest surviving passenger carrying narrow gauge railway in the world).

No visit to Wales is complete without a journey on this historic railway which traverses seven miles of magnificent mountain scenery from the sea coast to Dolgoch Falls and Abergynolwyn near the slopes of Cader Idris.

TIME TABLE
JUNE 4th. to SEPTEMBER 28th. 1951.

Up Trains (Mondays to Fridays inclusive).

		a.m.	p.m.
ABERDOVEY (B.R.)	*Dep.*	*8.41*	*1.20*
BARMOUTH JUNC. (B.R.)	,,	*9.35*	*2.0*
TOWYN (Wharf)	,,	10.30	2.45
TOWYN (Pendre)	,,	10.35	2.50
RHYDYRONEN	,,	10.45	3.0
BRYNGLAS	,,	10.55	3.10
DOLGOCH	,,	11.10	3.25
ABERGYNOLWYN	*Arr.*	11.30	3.45

Down Trains (Mondays to Fridays inclusive).

		a.m.	p.m.
ABERGYNOLWYN	*Dep.*	11.45	4.0
DOLGOCH	,,	12.5	4.20
BRYNGLAS	,,	12.20	4.35
RHYDYRONEN	,,	12.30	4.45
TOWYN (Pendre)	,,	12.40	4.55
TOWYN (Wharf)	*Arr.*	12.45	5.0
BARMOUTH JUNC. (B.R.)	,,	*1.40*	*6.38*
ABERDOVEY (B.R.)	,,	*1.6*	*6.17*

Towyn Wharf terminus is 3 minutes walk from Towyn B.R. station.   Special trains may be run for organised parties on Saturdays only by prior arrangement.

L. T. C. ROLT,
General Manager,
Tal-y-llyn Railway Co., Towyn, Merioneth

J. BASIL JONES & CO., Cadvan Press, Red Lion Street, Towyn.

could only be turned by carefully manoeuvring *Dolgoch* into the old siding, and then manhandling the coaches further up the line beyond the platform. That evening it was agreed that when the full public service was introduced it should operate over the whole length of the line to Abergynolwyn, the only location besides Pendre where there was a loop to enable the engine to run round its train. A timetable was drawn up, printed, advertised and distributed. Late in the afternoon of Saturday 26 May, ten days before the new service was to start, Tom Rolt received a telegram from Birmingham to tell him the service was only to run to Rhydyronen, and then be extended from station to station up the line as condition of the permanent way permitted. On purely engineering grounds a sensible move, but disastrous from a revenue earning and image point of view. Also how were the trains to be turned, unless a host of volunteers happened to be on hand, or were the able-bodied passengers to do it themselves?

'Maggie' Maguire, then a volunteer, but soon to be a Company employee, wrote on the 30 May 1951, in a letter to his friend Owen Prosser, a member of the committee: 'Master Wilkins submitted a 'Progress Report' behind the GM's back saying the track was unsafe, and everyone in Birmingham panicked, including the insurance company. They had a directors' meeting in Towyn on Monday and eventually decided to open with a 5 mph restriction on 'unrepaired' sections after Rolt threatened to resign on the grounds that 'he was the gaffer or he was not'. Tom Rolt says that at that directors' meeting it was Edward Thomas who swung the decision by saying 'I think you are taking things much too seriously, gentlemen. Let me tell you that if Lady Haydn had asked me to run the railway this year I should have run it without any of your help.' Mind it was this same Edward Thomas when asked, in pre-society days when the railway was in its most decrepit state, by a somewhat nervous prospective passenger, 'Are you insured?' replied, 'No, but we are very careful!'

Another rebuff to the general manager by the committee occurred in September 1951 when Tom offered to give the Society the petrol engine from his canal boat *Cressy*, then being broken up. Mr Curwen, the engineer working at Pendre, had given his opinion that the cost of putting it on a chassis to act as a motor trolley should not be too great. But the chairman whilst thanking Mr Rolt, said a definite decision would only be given when detailed costs had been submitted to the treasurer. At the committee's meeting on 8 February 1952 Mr Rolt offered to serve as general manager for the 1952 running season for £40 a month. He would endeavour to get down to Tywyn rather earlier in the year at no charge to the Society in order 'to keep an eye on things'. This led to further discussion which then became acrimonious. Mr Cope said the ticketing was not being done properly. John Wilkins said, very shortly and patronisingly, in his Black Country brogue: 'Give him another chance'. This was like a red rag to a bull to Tom who felt, as did some other members of the committee, that directors Cope and Wilkins regarded themselves as 'superior' to their general manager; in fact they seemed to look on Tom as just another employee. Tom rose in anger, gathered his papers, banged the table, and walked out, after commenting that he was obviously not giving satisfaction to people who were eager to emphasise his shortcomings but did not appreciate his successes. He said he would not be general manager unless the discontented directors, Cope and Wilkins would give him a vote of confidence. Owen Prosser noted on his personal record of the meeting: 'An evening of criticism and recriminations'.

The meeting was adjourned to 19 February, when Mr Cope recommended that sole responsibility for dealing with the commercial accounts should not rest with the general manager. It was agreed that Mr Rolt should be appointed general manager from June to September inclusive, with expenses of £40 per month on the understanding that a person be appointed to assist him in discharging the commercial duties covered by his office. This was carried with one abstention, that of Mr Wilkins, who asked to be relieved of his position as a director of the railway and holding companies. John Wilkins never got on with Tom Rolt from the first. They were two very different types. There was also personal antagonism between Ken Cope and Tom Rolt.

On 18 August 1952, the committee considered a letter from Mr Rolt about the company's rules. He pointed out that he had drawn up a set of simple operating rules for staff and volunteers. These, should it prove necessary, could easily be amended to satisfy the Ministry of Transport (as subsequently proved to be the case). But his version of the rules, he complained, had not been placed before the committee. Instead a considerable amount of detail had been added by others, and the number or rules increased from thirty to forty two. Rules should be as simple and concise as possible, consonant with public safety. He particularly objected to a section concerned with the receipt and issue of tickets, (a task his wife Sonia was by then undertaking). He considered this a matter to be dealt with as the exigencies of the service and limited staff allowed. It was simply not practical in peak periods to follow the new rules, and they were not a matter of public safety. The people who drew up the new rules did not realise the narrow margin there was between success and failure, and that one was being forced to work on a series of priorities. The top priorities were the locos, stock, track, and punctual running. Therefore paper work should be kept as simple as possible, at least until the practical improvements that were essential had been made. Since the possibility of staff dishonesty could be ruled out, any losses were due to normal errors. The background to this was that Ken Cope had seen a lot of loose change left lying about on the open booking office counter at Wharf, and had spoken to Tom about it. He had replied that safety was paramount, and he would continue to leave cash lying about if necessary. Tom then persuaded Sonia to do more work in the office. (It is relevant to note that at the AGM in September 1952 the treasurer, Pat Garland paid tribute to Mrs Sonia Rolt for her work as booking clerk and business manager. The returns and books were all kept in a most business-like manner.)

Mr Rolt said the operating rules were in order, but he could not obey rule 17 regarding the locking of facing points on running lines unless the committee provided the locks. Nor could he issue detonators as required by rule 28 unless the committee made them available. How could the line be patrolled 'twice a week' with the staff available, and at the same time keep the railway running. (The committee was attempting to institute main-line GWR practices, with which they were familiar, on a decrepit railway with a maximum speed of 10 mph and 5 mph on unreliable stretches of line.) He went on 'Despite all this I would have signed my acceptance of the rules if I felt that I enjoyed the confidence, goodwill and trust of the committee in my efforts down here. Events both last season and this have, however, made it abundantly clear to me that this is not the attitude of certain members. So if anything went wrong at Towyn these members would make use of the rules as a pretext for absolving themselves from any responsibility that occurred and seek to place it on my shoulders. Therefore I am unwilling to sign my acceptance of these rules and after the end of the season I will not accept any further office as long as it continues under the present administration, except for the members Mr William Trinder, Mr William Faulkner and Mr Edward Thomas, whose unfailing confidence, trust and support I most appreciate. If the committee want to put someone else in I shall be happy to tender my resignation now instead of at the end of the season.' Pat Garland's response is reported to have been 'I'm getting fed up with this sort of thing from Tom Rolt'.

The committee decided that as Mr Rolt would not sign the rules there was no point in pursuing the matter further, and agreed to have a discussion with him at the end of the season. At its meeting on 22 October the committee thanked Mr Rolt for his invaluable work in the early days of the Society. Mr Rolt announced he was unable to accept the post of general manager in 1953. The committee wished to record their appreciation of Mr Rolt's excellent work and agreed to advertise the post. The opposing forces came into the open at the next meeting in November. Mr Whitehouse proposed, seconded by Mr Gray, that the existing directors, namely Trinder, Cope and Faulkner be elected en bloc. Mr Rolt proposed Mr Gray as a director. Mr Gray declined to stand. The proposition was carried with only Mr Rolt voting against. He could not agree to Mr Cope continuing as a director. Mr Rolt did however continue as an active member of the committee. In April 1953 he was asked when signing TRPS letters, in the interests of accuracy, to put 'Co-Founder' instead of just 'Founder' under his signature. Also arising out of Rule 23 the committee said it would like to read the manuscript of his forthcoming book *Railway Adventure* so far as it concerned matters connected with the Society. At the next meeting Mr Rolt was reported to have written to say that it would not be possible for the committee to see the manuscript as it was already in type. In May 1954 there was again one vote against the appointment of the directors; presumably Rolt against Cope. Mr Rolt however was appointed a vice-president of the Society, at this same meeting, along with Mr Trinder, his 'co-founder', who had resigned as chairman of the Society and Company. At a special general meeting of the Society in Tywyn on 25 September 1954 it was reported that Tom Rolt's book *Railway Adventure* had brought in many new members. In May 1956 Mr Rolt took over as Press officer 'as not enough coverage' of the railway in the media was, in his view, being achieved. In August 1958 Mr Rolt felt that several matters of policy had been decided by the Company and not by the Society, and whilst this might be understandable it should be avoided if possible. The committee duly took note.

Tom Rolt always continued to work for the railway in spite of his disagreements with some of the polices pursued. Pat Garland wrote of him after his death: 'It is a tribute to his character that those who were most opposed to him in the early days were to become his staunchest friends and supporters in later life.' In 1963 he was elected chairman of the council, and chairman of the Talyllyn Railway Company and Talyllyn Holdings Ltd. Before that he had held the title, 'Superintendent of the Line'. Four years later he retired from these posts, and in 1968 resigned from the council as he was disenchanted with the commercial policy of the management. The last straw was the refusal by council to back his proposal that Dr Geisl from Vienna should design and supervise the construction of a new locomotive. He had wanted to resign in the January but Richard Hope persuaded him to stay on until the AGM in September. But he was back again to launch the Nant Gwernol extension in 1970 and to preside at the 1971 AGM, before increasing ill-health curtailed his activities.

He died in 1974, having seen the railway grow and become well established, to an extent he could hardly have dreamed of when he first set about saving it. It is perhaps symptomatic of his relationships with others, his idiosyncratic place in the scheme of things, his non-conformity, that fourteen years after

Dolgoch the railway's only working locomotive with the company's complete
passenger stock at Wharf in August 1949 (a note on the original photograph,
taken by British Rail, states Talyllyn Railway – runs to Dolgoch
(British Rail)

Bill Trinder, chairman of the Talyllyn Railway Preservation Society, cutting
the tape before the first 'official' passenger train under Society control left for
Rhydyronen on 14 May 1951 (Talyllyn Railway)

A 'dead' No 1 *Talyllyn* pulled out into the undergrowth of Pendre yard by No 2 *Dolgoch* for a photographic session in the summer of 1951 (Talyllyn Railway)

John Snell on *Dolgoch* in June 1951, before number plates had been cast (Trinder Album)

No 2 at Quarry Siding in June 1951 with the young Dai Jones on the footplate (Talyllyn Railway)

No 2 *Dolgoch* cutting its way through the 'jungle' approaching Cynfal with an up train in June 1951 (Talyllyn Railway)

Ex-Corris locomotives Nos 3 and 4 delivered to Wharf Station by British Rail staff in March 1951 (Talyllyn Railway)

Douglas Abselon handing over No 6 in his factory yard to the Society's president the Earl of Northesk. Pat Whitehouse is on the footplate. April 1953 (John Adams)

The team that ran the railway in the Society's early years. David Curwen (engineer), Ken Cope (commercial), Pat Whitehouse (secretary), Tom Rolt (general manager), Pat Garland (treasurer) (Talyllyn Railway)

Wharf station in late 1951 when a make-shift platform has been constructed and some track realignment and re-laying has taken place (Talyllyn Railway)

Wharf station in the mid-fifties with some improvement to the island platform. The locomotives are No 6 *Douglas* on the right facing up the line, with No 3 *Sir Haydn* 'wrong-way round' (John Adams)

Wharf station on 8 August 1956 soon after the completion of an additional
siding to the left and the erection of the narrow-gauge Museum building
beyond the office. Note BR coal wagons in the siding along 'the wharf'
(J. J. Davis)

Wharf station extended with a completely new platform and track layout, a
canopy and extensions to the original office to provide shop and catering
facilities, and considerable development of the museum building. 25 July
1966 (J. J. Davis)

Pendre yard looking east in late 1951. Pendre station is visible on the left
(J. J. Davis)

Pendre yard looking east in the 1980s with volunteer Martin Lester on the
footplate of No 1, with the West carriage shed on the right and the North
carriage shed to the left. Diesels No 9 *Alf* and No 8 *Merseysider* can be seen
parked up the yard (Talyllyn Railway)

Inside Pendre works in October 1952. The carriage 'set', with the TR van No 5 at this end, can be seen on the right projecting from its wooden shed into the workshop (J. B. Snell)

Inside Pendre works in October 1983. The workshop has been extended into the old carriage shed but the doors on the left are much the same. The loco shed is visible through the door on the right including part of the inspection pit. John Slater is cutting a metal plate, and Graham Cox is at one of the lathes (J. B. Snell)

The old hay barn on the north side of Pendre yard about 1951 with No 1 laid up under the sheeting, never to steam again in the view of many at the time. A couple of slate wagons can be seen on the siding which now leads into the North carriage shed (J. J. Davis)

No 6 *Douglas* leaving Pendre, passing through the old crossing gates, with volunteer driver, Graham White, in the early 1980s (John Slater)

Up train at Rhydyronen in June 1964. Engineering trolley in siding (John Adams)

Rhydyronen station in 1951. Note siding off to the left, now replaced by an extended platform. Apart from this, the station remains virtually unchanged (J. J. Davis)

Up train at Brynglas around 1955 with Lord Northesk on the footplate of No 6 *Douglas*

(John Slater)

No 1 *Talyllyn* with vintage coach and 'opens' on an up train passing Brynglas
block post in 1987. Driver: volunteer Roy Smith (John Adams)

Guard and fireman keeping a good lookout at Brynglas road crossing with No
6, c 1985 (Talyllyn Railway)

The Quarry Siding block post 27 July 1971. (J. J. Davis)

No 2 *Dolgoch* crossing Dolgoch Viaduct with an up train in June 1951 (John Adams)

No 127 Construction Unit R.E. (TA) relaying track in Dolgoch station in July 1953 (P. B. Whitehouse)

Loco No 2 *Dolgoch* taking water, unusually on a down train, at Dolgoch in 1951 (J. J. Davis)

No 2 *Dolgoch* taking water at Dolgoch station in 1951, with a worried looking guard, Tom Rolt, and some young passengers on the platform (P. B. White-house)

his death, no permanent memorial had been established on the railway he founded. Only in 1989 was it decided at the Society's AGM, and then by a narrow margin, that the railway's new locomotive, No 7, should be named *Tom Rolt*. It is perhaps also symptomatic that no memorial to his co-founder, Bill Trinder, has even been proposed.

Brynglas · block post ·

CHAPTER 7

The Committee, Hugh, Dai, Herbert and Other Employees

Hugh Jones and his sons Dai and Herbert worked for the Talyllyn Railway Company before and after it was taken-over by the preservation society. The family's connection stretched back for many decades, for Hugh's father and uncle had also been in its employment. Particularly in the middle years of this century, the family were key employees, and the railway's survival owes much to them. They were the ones who did most of the work and grind, day after day, winter as well as summer.

Dai's first job was as a 'postman' (unofficial) based at the Post Office at Bryncrug. He was then only thirteen, and had left school to supplement the family income. The official school leaving age was fourteen but the 'schoolie' knew the motherless family needed the extra money. He delivered the post to the farms and cottages along the railway from Fach Goch to as far as Brynglas, riding his bike along the edge of the track wherever possible. This took him up to about half past one each day except Sunday, and earned the family thirteen shillings (65p) a week. In the afternoons he did gardening or helped out at neighbouring farms.

Hugh suggested to Dai that he join him on the railway. Hugh was trying to keep the near-derelict loco, stock and track working with no money, little assistance and completely inadequate tools and equipment. Dai remembered being dubious about whether the company would survive. But there was at that time virtually no unemployment, even in Tywyn: he could always get another job if this one folded up, and he had always been keen on working on the railway.

His employment with Sir Haydn had started in a way that much recruitment still takes place today, by word of mouth. Hugh had a word with Edward Thomas, and he in turn had a word with Sir Haydn about taking on the young Dai. Peter Williams, the platelayer and driver had gone, and Hugh was finding it almost impossible to keep *Dolgoch* operational on his own. There was only Edward Thomas besides Hugh, and they had to have a fireman if the trains were to run.

Dai was keen, but not that keen. He told Edward Thomas that he would not work on the railway for less than £5 per week. Edward Thomas said Sir Haydn would not agree to that. So Dai answered that in that case he was no longer interested. Edward Thomas returned to say Sir Haydn had agreed to pay Dai what he wanted. (Owen Prosser stated Edward Thomas told him the amount involved was £4 10s). The irony was that his father, with all those years service, was still on £4 per week. It was months before Dai dared to tell his father that he was getting a pound a week more. Dai recalled that his father nearly let go. He thought he was going to hit him. But eventually he simmered down, and after a word with Edward Thomas he too got £5.

Dai first met his wife June in the loco shed at Pendre. She was the daughter of another Edward Thomas also employed on the railway, but as a platelayer – at least it said so on his job description – and hedger. One day she was sent up to Pendre by her father to report that he was sick. The only sign of life she could find at the Pendre works was a series of muttered expletives coming from beneath an engine parked over the inspection pit. Having finally made it clear that she was there, a dirty faced grimy youth appeared – and it was apparently love at first sight. They had not met before, as he had been at school at Bryncrug and she at Tywyn. She and her father were living in a council house at Faenol Avenue, in Tywyn, not far from Pendre. After their marriage Dai moved in too, and there they stayed and brought up their children, Carol and David.

Hugh had returned to work on the Talyllyn in July 1954, after leaving it in 1951 following disagreements with the new management. He began to work closely with a fitter, called Morris Jones, who had been coming over from Portmadoc three days a week since 1952 to work on the engines at Pendre. Morris Jones was the last employee to be made redundant from the old Festiniog railway. That was in March 1947 when he was at its Boston Lodge works. The Festiniog's only surviving resident employee was then Robert Evans at Portmadoc, who collected the rents, and acted as a sort of agent for the residual company. When the Festiniog was reborn in September 1954, Morris resumed work at Boston Lodge, but on condition that he would be free to help out if any sudden emergency should occur on the Talyllyn. By December 1954 Morris was on full time at Boston Lodge, with an apprentice to help him. Hugh learned a great deal from Morris Jones. According to one of the original TR volunteers, Peter Bold, an engineer, and chairman of the Talyllyn Railway Company in the late 1980s, it was largely due to Hugh's unstinting efforts with the locomotives in the mid-fifties that the railway was able to have sufficient motive power to cope with the increasing traffic that brought in the revenue needed for its expansion.

However if Hugh got stuck he would still get in touch with Morris, who would come over, and lend his advice and assistance. After all, Hugh was a local Welshman too, 'one of us'. One big difference between the Talyllyn and the Festiniog Railways was that in the former, except for the years 1951-54, local people still had a large say in the running of the railway: notably the Jones family. In those early years too, Edward Thomas was very much on hand giving good advice as required, as Tom Rolt gratefully acknowledged. Today, apart from the two family directors, and the general manager, both of whose parents were Welsh, there are no Welshmen on the Talyllyn senior staff. But both David Woodhouse, general manager, and John Bate, chief engineer, whose wife is Welsh, have been resident in the area for nearly thirty years; their children have gone through local schools and speak at least some of the local language.

Across the track facing the platform at Pendre Station is a plaque, commemorating Dai's brother Herbert, who died in Tywyn Hospital on 20 January 1983, at the early age of forty-eight. How appropriate that it should be on the outside wall of the cottage where Herbert and his wife, Margaret, went to live after their marriage in 1959.

Herbert used to travel on the engine as fireman to his father during the school holidays. Whilst still at school he also helped out as carrier boy in Sir Haydn Jones' ironmongery shop for five shillings a week delivering paraffin. This was carried in a large box over the front wheel of a specially designed carrier bike, then very common. On leaving school he began to work full time for Sir Haydn. When not on the footplate, Herbert would be working either on the track or on Sir Haydn's farm. Later he worked full-time for another farmer up the valley, but gradually began to feel unwell if he pushed himself too hard. When the time came to do his National Service he signed on for a three-year contract as a regular soldier in the Royal Artillery, probably because the pay was higher. But he was found to have diabetes and was invalided out, aged twenty, in 1955.

Herbert then joined his brother Dai and father Hugh working on the railway. He fired for Dai for a time, and then started driving when he was twenty-one. Herbert, like his father, was dedicated to the locomotives, and gradually took over the role of fitter, becoming locomotive foreman in 1962. He too would work through the night if necessary to have an engine ready for service the following day. His wife would lie in bed listening through the wall to the clanking and banging in the adjacent engine-shed – if she had not already been dragged into the workshop to act as 'fitter's mate'. In 1965 Herbert was appointed locomotive super-intendent, but ill-health and failing eye-sight forced him into early retirement in 1978.

In the mid-fifties before Dai and Herbert got married they still lived with their father at Plas Goch at Rhydyronen. They were in the habit of using a locomotive, preferably No 6 *Douglas*, as a staff train. At the end of the day they would fill the loco with water and coal, drive her up to Rhydyronen, sometimes having attached a coach to take volunteers back to their camp at Tynllwyn-Hen, and park the engine under the road bridge, with just the funnel protruding beyond. They would then bank the fire down, with good coal underneath and slack on the top. They would put a bit of wood over the chimney so there was only a little hole, thus reducing the draught. All this was done very carefully, in the hope, usually fulfilled, that the fire would last till the next morning so as to save lighting up again.

This had the enormous advantage that it kept some steam pressure in the engine, usually about 10lbs per square inch, next day. With no lighting up needed at Pendre, the three of them could stop in bed for another couple of hours. They took it in turns to nip out early to stoke up the fire again to build up pressure. The unlucky one could then go back to bed for another hour or so! With No 4 locomotive which lost water, someone had to get out to her in the middle of the night, so they much preferred No 6. Roy Smith, later a volunteer driver and Society director, recalls that when he was involved as a volunteer fireman in the parking of the engines at Rhydyronen the fire was always taken out: so perhaps the Jones family had a different routine when other folk were about. However it became no longer necessary to take the locos home when there was a change of policy, and more than enthusiastic volunteers became responsible for lighting up in 'the wee small hours'.

Herbert was a practical joker, with a wicked sense of humour, particularly in his younger days. His wife Margaret, a Lancashire lass from Prescot, shared his 'joie de vivre'. The story is told of when they had a volunteer staying with them they would place a wardrobe across the outward opening door of his bedroom. Then when he wished to visit the loo he would have to climb out of the window, and go round outside. Another trick, after the electric light was put in, was to sellotape the light switches, so in the darkness the hapless volunteer would bang his head on the low beams, to the sound of Herbet and Margaret laughing away in their bedroom. Another ploy he used, this time against Margaret, was that when she rang Pendre works and said 'Can I speak to Herbert, please?', he, having picked up the receiver would reply. 'No, you can't, I'm out', leaving his wife fuming!

Dai left the railway in August 1951. Hugh, his father, had left a few months before, after the locomotive of the engine hauling a special had become derailed at the entrance to Six Bends above Brynglas and next day newly arrived enthusiast, Bill Oliver, had leant over the frame giving instructions on what to do. Hugh came back in early 1954, almost immediately after Tom Rolt was replaced by a retired professional railwayman, Ken Marrian, and stayed on until 6 October 1973. It was not easy for the proud

Welshmen to adapt to the English class system, unconsciously taken for granted by Tom and his colleagues, and indeed by others who came to work on the railway, like Bill Oliver. It must have been very galling for men who had kept the railway alive with virtually no input of financial resources, and who knew the engines inside out, to be told what to do by newcomers. In *Railway Adventure* Tom Rolt simply said that Dai let them down, like his father had done, by walking off the job 'without notice or cause'. It was however not so simple as that. The attitude of others, especially Bill Oliver and John Snell, had much to do with it.

Bill Oliver was known to Owen Prosser in the late nineteen-forties through their having met at Light Railway Transport League events. Owen took him along to the inaugural meeting of the TRPS and he became a member of the first committee. An ex-Marine, tall and thin, who never seemed to stop talking, he was one of the first working volunteers of the line. He met a local girl from Llanegryn, moved to Tywyn and married her. She was the daughter of Isaac 'Pop' Davies, Talyllyn employee doing noble work on the track and the locomotives in those first difficult years after the Society took over.

For a time Bill was the local representative of the Kleen-ee-zee Company, travelling round selling brushes and polishes from door to door. He was also a member of a local dance band. But he enjoyed working on the railway and was taken on to the permanent staff to work on the track, while still a member of the committee. From Easter to Whitsun, 1951, he was employed at £2 10s a week working under Mr Vaughton. In July he was employed full time along with another volunteer, A.D. Maguire, known from the first as 'Maggie', at £5 a week.

In February 1952 Bill Oliver asked for a rise to £6 15s on the ground he had been offered a council house. He was given a rise to £6 immediately and to £6 15s when he moved in. This was agreed subject to his services being devoted exclusively to the railway. In August 1952 he was given a £10 bonus for good work on Mr Rolt's recommendation. However by November the committee was expressing dissatisfaction with his work, and refusing his request for a pay increase of 8s per week. He was also told not to authorise sales of scrap metal. In his engineering report

Mr Faulkner said he had seen a local scrap dealer loading scrap without supervision and without weight tickets. By January 1953 Bill Oliver's work had improved and he was paid a bonus of £2.10s. In February however he resigned from the Committee because he could not afford the fares to Birmingham where the meetings were held. In April the Committee warned him about excessive use of the telephone at Wharf. And in November the Committee agreed the monies not paid in by Mr Oliver in respect of the winter's workings be deducted from his bonus for work done the previous summer.

In the spring of 1955, at the magistrates' court Bill Oliver was convicted of stealing rail and scrap from the Talyllyn. He later worked as a BR guard before emigrating to Australia. Many years later he was joined there by his eighty-six year old father-in-law, 'Pop' Davies. The dealer who received the scrap was given a prison sentence. Apparently a member of the Society had seen railway material being loaded on to a lorry and told Hugh Jones. The member then wrote an 'anonymous' letter, and on the police approaching Bill he confessed all. He was just a man who liked to put on a show. TR wages were not sufficient for that, and he succumbed to temptation. There was virtually no supervision during the winter; Tom Rolt and his successor only being at Tywyn from spring to autumn.

In a letter dated 21 August 1951, A.D. Maguire wrote to Owen Prosser: 'Last Tuesday, just a week ago, Dai Jones, the driver, walked out on us as his father did before him. Luckily David Curwen was down at Towyn and he soon trained up John Snell to the point of letting him take No 2 engine out alone. Also we had available the shed foreman and a driver from Norwich B.R. So the Jones' attempt to do us dirt failed ignominiously. The saving of Dai's wages has enabled the Company to offer both Bill (Oliver) and myself permanent employment through the winter when a large programme of re-laying is scheduled. Patching as a long-term proposition has failed – we had two derailments last Friday. Re-laying with proper sleepers and fish-plates on top of the old 'bed' with new ballast is the only hope of survival for the Tal-y-llyn'.

Dai recalled that John Snell, who had just left Bryanston

School prior to going up to Balliol College, Oxford, was staying at Dolgoch where David Curwen and Tom Rolt were also living. John was commuting with them by car so had to rush off at the end of the day when they were ready to leave. Nor did he arrive until 9am in the morning, the time when the general manager and chief engineer were accustomed to start on the day's work. Dai understood that Tom Rolt had told John Snell that it was his job as fireman to cut the wood the night before so it was dry and ready for lighting up the next morning, and also to clear out the fire-box. But he did not do it, rushing off for supper and then not coming back again. Every morning Dai had to clean and oil the coaches, as well as cleaning and oiling the locomotive. One morning it was very cold, and when Dai arrived about 6.45 am, half an hour earlier than usual, he found he had once again to chop up the wood before he could light the fire. Steam locomotives have to stand for about two or three hours after first lighting up in order to build up an operating level of steam pressure. That morning the firewood was particularly wet, and the fire would not draw. At 9 am John rolled up and said 'Oh! No steam'. Tom Rolt was very short indeed with Dai when the train finally arrived at Wharf, half an hour after the scheduled time of departure.

Dai knew Tom Rolt always called in at the Post Office every morning just before 9 am to collect his mail. Tom must have become very familiar with the 'Poste Restante' system from his years of wandering on his canal-boat *Cressy*. So the following morning Dai met him there, told him his engine was in steam and he was off. Tom said he could not leave like that but he did. He went to work for the River Board.

John Snell has since commented that in retrospect Dai and Hugh must have resented all the changes. To a large extent it had been their private railway. At the end of each operating day they had taken the loco home to Rhydyronen, where it stayed parked under the bridge until the next time it was needed. No doubt they were very upset when Tom Rolt stopped this procedure. Dai must also have got fed up with having a succession of young newcomers to train. He agreed it was probably the fireman's job to chop the wood the day before, but pointed out that at that time morale was low. High hopes had been dashed when their new loco No 3 had failed to stay on the track during its trials a couple of weeks earlier. The staff were all getting a little ragged from the pressure of simply keeping the train running on such appalling track with a single, just usable, locomotive. What particularly upset the other staff was that neither Hugh nor Dai ever said anything. They were always friendly and pleasant until the moment they left without warning. All John Snell remembered about the morning of Tuesday 14 August, the day Dai walked out, was a vivid image of arriving about 9 am at Pendre with either David or Tom, and finding *Dolgoch* in steam, alone in an empty shed.

In April 1955, after Bill Oliver's departure under a cloud, a deputation arrived at Plas Goch, where Dai was still living with his father, Hugh, who had retired on 6 October 1973. He died on 18 September 1989 and his body was conveyed by a special funeral train from Rhydyronen to Wharf station on 22 September. The deputation consisted of the railway's three TRPS nominated directors; Lord Northesk, who had succeeded Bill Trinder as chairman, Pat Garland, and Bill Faulkner, together with Ken Marrian, who had by then taken over as general manager from Tom Rolt. When Dai went out he was told they urgently needed another driver and would he come back. He replied he would let them know. Next day he gave in his required fourteen days notice to the River Board, where he had been happy. But as Dai has remarked many times the railway had been in his blood ever since he was a little lad. The pleasant sequel to this unhappy episode is that when Tom later saw him, on a family visit to the railway he said: 'It's nice to have you back'. Thereafter they were on good terms. Dai made his last 'official' trip on the footplate of his favourite *Dolgoch* on the Society's AGM day, 27 September 1986. His fireman was his son, David, and Dai was presented with the special headboard from the locomotive at the following meeting. He was made a vice-president in 1987, an honour extended to his father in 1975 and to his brother Herbert in 1978. Dai's departure from the paid employment meant that for the first time for almost a century there was no member of the Jones' family working for the Company; but son David remained a volunteer fireman.

CHAPTER 8

Volunteers, The Track
and Signalling

Volunteers had started some tidying-up operations on the line even before the February 1951 agreement, but it was only after this was signed that work really got under way. Regular working parties began coming to Tywyn every week-end. The five-day week was becoming general at about this time. It was thus possible to travel down to Tywyn after work on a Friday night and return home again late on Sunday afternoon. It was one of the tasks of the permanent staff, Hugh Jones and Dai, with Mr Vaughton as foreman, to have the tools and materials ready in position for the volunteers to get started on the Saturday morning. Most of these early volunteers came from around Manchester, but the first organised working party, or so Bill Faulkner claimed (see John Slater's newsletter No 16) was in March 1951, and consisted of himself, Owen Prosser, Bill Walker and Bill Oliver. The volunteers were accepted by the permanent staff because they knew the railway needed all the help it could get. Most of the men concentrated on track-laying whilst others, and the ladies, got on with painting everything in sight. While the underlying structure might be more than somewhat suspect, the outward appearance could be quickly and cheaply improved. Packaging was regarded as important right from the start, and certainly served to give the volunteers and the passengers the impression of a growing, successful enterprise.

Some of the first new rails put in after the Society's take-over were between Pendre and Rhydyronen. This was a most urgent task. The track, except for one short section, remained in the position in which it had first been laid eighty years earlier, probably in a four to five month period in 1865. With the sixty-hour week prevalent at that time a track gang could probably have completed 100 to 150 yards a day.

Delivery of the rails commenced in early 1865, the order having been placed the previous year, probably in South Wales. The rails would have come to Aberdovey by sea, and then up the newly opened coast railway to Tywyn. About 500 tons of rail was bought at a cost of £3000–£3500. Until 1964 it was generally thought that all the rails were made of wrought-iron, as steel rails were then only at an early stage of their development. However in the *Talyllyn News* in December that year Mr W.K.V. Gale, an iron trade historian, reported that he had sent away for analysis a piece of original rail given him by Rolt. To his considerable surprise the British Iron & Steel Research Association reported that the metal was steel. All that can be said is that at least one of the rails in the original TR track was made of Bessemer steel 'at a time when steel was still viewed with disfavour, and some distrust by the main-line companies'. The metal 'is a very mild steel and would behave in many ways like wrought iron . . . and sold as wrought iron scrap . . . would get by'.

The rails, whatever the metal they were made of, were flat bottomed, and although the weight was supposed to be 44 lbs. per yard, and indeed was recorded as such by Captain Tyler, the government inspector, it was barely 40 lbs in practice. Largely because the wrought-iron rails were hand-made they varied greatly in quality, and some rails failed many years before others. They had a tendency to split longitudinally. The rails were mainly in seven yard lengths, although a small proportion of shorter length six yard rails were included to avoid waste, a practice followed by rolling mills to this day.

The rails were abutted on a common chair made of cast iron. There were originally no fish-plates. Without these, the lines tended to come apart, and so rather rudimentary fish-plates were fitted over much of the line at a later date. Each seven yard length had seven sleepers to support it one of which was under the joint with the next rail. Only the joint sleeper and two others had cast-iron chairs to support the rail. On the other four sleepers, two in the middle and one at each end, the flat-bottomed rail was spiked directly into the softwood with brobs – nails with a half-inch head to hold the rail. Some of these brobs were later replaced with dog-spikes – a five-inch spike with a turned over head to clip the bottom of the rail to the sleeper. The rails were secured in the chairs by hardwood keys. By the 1930s the Talyllyn was almost certainly the only railway in the world still laid entirely in wrought iron (with a few early steel?) rails.

By the 1930s the track condition had become very poor. In 1935 Sir Haydn had purchased twelve tons of steel rail made available by the closure of the Glyn Valley Tramway, nine miles south of Wrexham. The simple expedient was adopted of lifting the old iron rails out of their chairs and putting in the already well-worn steel rails on the existing sleepers. However as the rails were 28 feet long with properly fish-plated joints, they gave a much smoother ride. When the Society took over in 1951 this was the only stretch of rail in reasonable order, and even this was largely covered in turf. The remains of ballast had long since disappeared beneath a thick covering of grass: only the tops of the rails were visible, so the train wheels acted as a kind of automatic mowing machine. In *Country Life* on 28 September 1951 Graham Dukes wrote: 'The Tal-y-llyn is more than ever a part of the country, for the hedges have grown high, and in places the line runs through a tunnel of over-hanging trees while the locomotive brushes aside the gorse and tall grass lining the track.' Even in October 1952 a writer in *The Link* (the Journal of the Manchester Model Railway Society) describing a trip on the railway by fifty four members could write: 'By this time the younger members of the party, and a few older ones, had discovered that the TR runs between seven miles of almost solid blackberries, and were acting accordingly'. (He added: 'The Society's thanks are due to Lady Jones for permission to run this special train on a Sunday, to Mr LTC Rolt for his assistance in securing this permission, and to John Snell and Gareth Jones, the loco crew'. It was the first Sunday train on the TR for many years.)

Both the steel and the wrought iron rails corroded greatly in the base and web because of the railway's habit of ballasting up to rail level. Many of the wrought iron rails just collapsed into the ground, having simply rotted away. However one advantage of having the rails buried was that it helped to keep the line in gauge.

No other rails were replaced until the Society took over. Sir Haydn had however started to do something more. When the Corris Railway was dismantled in 1948, he bought about eight tons of rail intending to continue the relaying down from Cynfal. The rails were actually laid out alongside the line. But there was no labour available to fix them until 1951, when John Wilkins sent over a gang of men from the Fairbourne Railway. Until then Dai and Hugh had been merely trying to keep pace with the increasing deterioration by replacing collapsed rail with odd bits and pieces.

The Society was able to purchase another thirty tons of Corris rail and a quantity of Corris sleepers from the scrap-merchant W.O. Williams of Harlech. This was used to complete the re-laying of Cynfal Bank. This section later became known as the 'Corris Straight' an odd title, as the 'new' rails were slightly curved, and being laid without being straightened, the track became a curious succession of 'dog-legs'. The rest of the Corris rail was used to relay the Wharf-Pendre section. This carried the heaviest traffic, especially as there was no water-tower at Wharf until 1966, and locos had to go back to Pendre to refill.

The usable iron rails released were used for patching collapsed individual lengths of rail. The rails removed from the Alltwyllt and Abergynolwyn inclines, not so worn as the others as they had not to carry locomotives or passenger stock, were used to relay a continuous stretch west of Brynglas, starting in 1951 and continued in the winters of 1952-3 and 1953-4. The work was carried out partly by permanent staff, but also by the first volunteer working parties. Ex-BR sleepers were bought by the thousand from dealers in the West Midlands. Generally they were of the cheapest grade, as money was tight. They were cut in half for use on the narrow gauge. Many of these sleepers were used by a Territorial Army unit relaying the track between Brynglas and Dolgoch in the summer of 1953, using old rails on new sleepers with new fishplates. But these old rails, together with others removed from the mineral extension between Nant Gwernol and the Abergynolwyn Winding House, proved completely unsuitable when placed on new sleepers. Thus there arose an urgent need for a fresh supply or rails, especially with the prospect of further Army help in 1954.

In June 1954 about fifteen tons of assorted rails arrived from a quarry near Clitheroe, in Lancashire. These were 'industrial' rails as opposed to the 'railway' rails previously used. The 'industrial' rails were very much of a job lot. The rail sections ranged from 40 to 80 lbs a yard, the latter rolled for the Midland Great Western Railway of Ireland in the 1880s but never delivered. There was also some rail from a lot destined originally for New Zealand Railways. Some rail was bought from the well-known scrap merchant, George Cohen, later the 600 Group, and some of this may have come from the dismantling of the Welsh Highland Railway, and also the Dinas branch of the Festiniog Railway. The Talyllyn also bought much other material from the Festiniog, whose managing director, Allan Garraway, a TRPS member and former volunteer worker, was most helpful.

But all this was not sufficient, as only one mile of track had been relaid with steel rail, and barely half the line re-sleepered. The sharp rise in traffic with an increasing frequency of ever more heavily-loaded trains was causing the old track to deteriorate rapidly. Then a large amount of rail became available from Hartshill Quarry near Nuneaton, where the owners were going over to road vehicles. It was arranged that the TR would buy the track as it lay, all three miles of it, and provide the labour to lift it and remove it to Tywyn. In retrospect this was not a wise decision. Getting enough volunteer labour, as and when needed, proved very difficult. As the work of removal did not proceed as quickly as the quarry company required, they had to use some of their own men to do the lifting, and this put up the cost. What however put the cost up even more to the TR, was that the rails were of very uneven quality, and quite a lot were useless and had to be sold for scrap.

The rails had to be stored up the line as there was insufficient storage space at Wharf, and piles of unsorted rails lay alongside the track for years to come. To cater for this heavy traffic, six 3-ton slate wagons were purchased from the Festiniog in 1956, regauged and converted into bolster and flat wagons. The only ex-Hartshill rails remaining in the track in the late eighties were some British Standard (BS) 45 lbs a yard rails, rolled for the War Department in World War I. Of the 242 tons that arrived at Wharf, usually in ten-ton lots by road, only sixty per cent or 143 tons could be used, and the other 99 tons had to be cut up and sent back to the Midlands as scrap. It seemed a poor reward for the hard work put in by Midland Area members. In 1954 the Area fielded twenty six working parties moving 88 tons in 192 shifts, and a further twenty one parties in 1955, moving 106 tons in 88 shifts. They moved a further 47 tons in 53 shifts in the following two years, 19 tons being rejected on site. This enormous and not very rewarding job was superintended by a volunteer member, Don Gardner, a technical engineer from Coventry, introduced to the railway in 1951 by Owen Prosser. In the end the total cost of the rails to the railway was not far short of that of buying new ones! But it is easy to be wise after the event, and those rails saved the day for the railway at the time. Many useful lessons were learned for the future.

By 1957 there still remained three miles of track needing re-newal. The next lot of rail came from another closed quarry, at Crich, near Matlock in Derbyshire. This project was managed by volunteer, Mr J.M. Davis, from Sheffield. Some of the early work was done by TR permanent staff travelling up in the original TR lorry (a 1930 Morris Commercial) with a load of tools, but volunteers, mainly from the North West and Yorkshire Areas, soon took over. Profiting by the Nuneaton experience every piece of rail was carefully examined before despatch. The good stuff was sent to Tywyn by rail; the unusable was taken away by a Gloucester scrap merchant. Some of the Crich rail originally came from the USA and some from Belgium. On arrival at Wharf the rails were slid off the BR wagons on to stacks at the Wharf edge. They were then graded. Code letters were painted on, and using the small TR wagons and the Wharf-edge turntables, they were then re-stacked in Wharf yard in graded lots. When sufficient rails of any particular type had accumulated, a batch was taken up the line. Because of the care taken in sorting and stacking, and getting the right fish-plates, most of the Crich rails are still in the track and likely to be so for some time to come. Crich rail amounted to about 100 tons and provided 2500 yards of track, roughly twenty per cent of the total rail length, chiefly in Hendy cutting, Brynglas cutting, a section to the east of Abnergynolwyn and in the station there. Some of the lighter rail was used for sidings in the north carriage shed at Pendre. Mr Davis was also a member of the Tramway Museum Society and when he heard that it was looking for a place to run its trams, was able – thanks to the TR link – to suggest Crich quarry, which subsequently became the major national centre for preserved trams.

That was the last occasion on which TRPS members were involved in lifting rail on site. It was expensive in man-hours and diverted volunteer effort from Tywyn. Since then rail has been lifted and delivered by the suppliers. But by 1958 the crisis was over. The line had been completely re-sleepered. The trains no longer fell off the lines. The last of the original 'main-line' rails was taken out in 1961 near Quarry Siding, and the last of the wrought-iron rail, which had come from the incline, was taken out of the running line west of Brynglas on 27 January 1968. There is however still some iron rail on the line: on the locomotive siding at Pendre, and more historically, over one hundred and twenty years old, genuine, original and untouched, on the north end of the Wharf edge siding.

In mid-November 1957, fifty feet of embankment between Brynglas and Dolgoch disappeared into the valley below, leaving the track standing at the edge of a near vertical slope. Apparently a culvert through an earth embankment, carrying the railway across a small gully, had become blocked. This resulted in water collecting between the embankment and the hillside. The water, seeping through the bank, caused a softening of the material, and the embankment gave way after a period of heavy rain. The failure was probably enhanced because of the weight of a low slate wall which had been constructed two years earlier at the top of a previous limited slip, in an effort to retain the bank. There had apparently been trouble at that particular spot for decades, as there was evidence of rough slate slabs, laid against trees, being used as the base for crude supporting buttresses. The site had also been used for dumping domestic refuse, thereby choking the culvert.

It was obviously necessary to make a proper job of any repairs if trouble was to be avoided in the future. A series of trial holes were dug, and as these showed no solid rock within easy reach of the surface it was decided to build a concrete retaining wall, to be carried on piles made of old rail driven in at an angle of one in three to the vertical. Whilst searching the country for a small pile-driver with which to drive in the 'piles', which were actually old rails no longer suitable for track purposes, the vegetation was cleared, and a trench dug for the wall. At the same time preparations were made to slew the track, by moving it into the hillside. Eighty wagon loads of fill, waste stone from the ballast quarry, were tipped into the space between the embankment and the hillside. The track was then relaid another two and a half feet into the hillside, away from the edge, and a 5 mph speed limit imposed. It took from February to May to do the piling, and work commenced on the concreting in June. By the end of the year about three-quarters of this had been completed, and the chief engineer reckoned the job was only half done. Another one-thousand man-hours of work, mostly by volunteers, would be required to see it through, chiefly on earth back-filling behind the retaining wall. In the winter of 1958-9, for work had to cease during the running season, the old culvert was dug out and replaced with a new 15in diameter pipe; with a catchpit upstream to intercept any rubbish that might block the new drain. The work was finally completed in the autumn of 1960. This was a major undertaking and the railway was very fortunate in having a chief engineer of Mr Bate's calibre, able to take such tasks in his stride.

SIGNALLING

In the days of Sir Haydn, with only one engine in steam, there was no need for any control or signalling system, and there was none from 1866 until 1952. The need arose when the railway, having acquired additional locomotives and thus being in a position to cope with more traffic, needed to run light engines between Pendre and Wharf. At first there was just the one train staff marked on one side 'Wharf to Abergynolwyn' and on the other 'One engine in steam'. Possession of this was necessary before a loco could venture out of the sidings on to the main running line. Then it became desirable to be able to run an engine with a works train, and later with passenger stock, down from Pendre to Wharf whilst another train was still up the line. So the single staff was abandoned and two others made, marked 'Pendre/Wharf' and 'Pendre/Abergynolwyn'. Unless the driver had the appropriate staff he could not take his engine on to that section of the main line. The staffs would be changed at Pendre so if one engine was up the line beyond Pendre in possession of the 'Pendre/Abergynolwyn' staff, this meant another loco could have the other staff and thus operate between Pendre and Wharf. After a loop was added at Brynglas in 1953, a metal staff with tickets – the Train Staff and Ticket system – was introduced instead of the wooden staff, the Pendre-Abergynolwyn section being split into two. The new train staffs incorporated a metal ticket for each direction of running; a square metal ticket for the up direction, and a round one for the down. The metal ticket could be removed, to allow a train into the section, and given to the driver as his authority to proceed. He had to check personally however that the round metal ticket was still in place on the staff, thus ensuring there was no train coming the other way. Then a second train could follow into the section taking the staff with it.

By 1966 the staff and ticket system was too limiting, and was replaced between Pendre and Wharf by a miniature-electric train staff system. This consisted of two instruments of Webb-Thompson design manufactured by the Railway Signal Company of Liverpool. One machine was located in the running shed by the telephones at Pendre and the other in the booking office at Wharf. They were powered by accumulators charged continuously from the mains. Each machine contained ten miniature train staffs, set of course so that only one staff could be out at a time. They could be operated by the driver from either end: only one end needing to be 'manned'.

In 1973 this system was replaced by the electric key token (EKT) system over the whole line. This consisted of a series of machines, two for each section, one at each end, interlocked so only one token staff can be withdrawn at a time. In emergencies, for example a breakdown, there are special procedures so that a rescue train can be sent up into the section, with strict instructions to proceed with the utmost caution. The train staff and ticket system is still used from Abergynolwyn to the terminus at Nant Gwernol, as normally only one train is on that section at the same time.

These signalling changes were introduced to accommodate more trains. The loop at Brynglas was constructed in 1953 as trains were terminating there while the Army had possession to relay track further up the line. Thus it became possible for two trains to be run from Wharf in the afternoon – a non-stop between Wharf and Dolgoch in addition to the 3.0 pm, and for relief trains to pass on busy days. The three trains a day service, with the traditional 10.25 morning departure remaining unaltered, remained much the same until 1959 when an additional morning service was introduced, making four trains a day Monday to Friday. In addition two services were introduced on Saturday afternoons, and for the first time in the railway's history a regular advertised train was run on a Sunday.

There had been Sunday afternoon services since 1957 on an 'ad hoc' basis. If there were enough volunteers and plenty of visitors around, Bill Faulkner, then a volunteer deputy general manager, or someone else 'in authority' who happened to be around, would decide a train should be run. The locomotive would be lit up. A chalk notice on a blackboard would be stood up outside Wharf Station, bearing at its foot the initials H.J.P. - being those of Harold James Parker, the general manager. Not that he would travel to Wharf from his home at Llanbedr, some miles to the north, for such 'last minute specials'. So the unfortunate booking clerk had to open up without change, as Harold had the key to the safe. This was all before the days of the commercial department, and the poor booking clerk was also expected to sell pencils, postcards and so on as well as the tickets. Each sale was supposed to be recorded in its correct column, one of a considerable number ruled on large sheets of paper. Needless to say the figures rarely balanced.

In those days there was a cheaper evening fare. Passenger to booking clerk: 'By how much are the evening train tickets reduced?' Booking Clerk: 'Actually they're much the same as regards size as our other tickets.'

Passenger to volunteer guard, who thinks he is a fellow volunteer, while the train is stopped at Abergynolwyn: 'How long are you here for?' Guard: 'Till next Tuesday.' Exit confused passenger.

In 1960 the number of scheduled trains a day in the peak season was increased to five, and in 1963 to seven. This was the limit that could be achieved with two train sets. With the introduction of the miniature-electric train system in 1966, and construction of a further loop at Quarry Siding in 1969, it became possible to introduce the three train service. The adoption of the electric key token system in 1973 meant that the railway's signalling system was more than adequate.

Tom Rolt was always anxious to retain as much local traffic as possible, and was also sensitive to local feeling. So a winter train service was run in 1952. It was on Fridays only, with a morning and afternoon train to enable passengers to shop in Tywyn. It was suspended in 1953 to enable essential track work to proceed, but re-introduced in 1963 at the request of a few young wives of army personnel living in cottages at Rhydyronen. Improvements in the track, and the use of a much more economic diesel engine had made it a practical proposition. But it was withdrawn in 1965 through lack of patronage: often there was only one passenger. A Christmas service for the week from Christmas Eve till January 2nd was begun in 1977 manned solely by volunteers. They tended to be particularly well patronised on Boxing Day as it gave the hotels with Christmas packages something to offer their guests. 'Santa specials' were first tried in 1985 and after a poor start began to gain in popularity.

In 1950 the railway carried 5,235 passengers; in 1951, 15,628; in 1956, 36,928; and in 1957, after the BBC television programme in May with Huw Weldon and Wynford Vaughan Thomas, 57,632. By 1973 the figure had risen to a peak of 103,787 bookings. In 1987 it had shrunk to 58,000, although revenues had risen in every year, except 1986 when there was no rise in fares.

The Talyllyn has never had an accident involving a collision between trains. The only accident involving injury to fare-paying

passengers occurred on 31 July 1953, as a result of a breach of
the company's rules. At 6.20 pm a special train with a party of
Scouts, left Abergynolwyn for Tywyn. It had four empty slate
wagons attached behind the passenger coaches. A number of
the Scouts were travelling in the empty wagons, contrary to rule
40. At approximately 6.50 pm the rear wagons jumped the rails
between Dolgoch and Brynglas and the passengers were thrown
out. Four had to go to Tywyn hospital with cuts and bruises and
one was detained. The train was travelling at 8 mph at the time
and pulled up in 44 yards.

The passengers did have to walk back to Towyn earlier that
month, when on the 17th at 5.15 pm, a down passenger train,
headed by No 3, derailed itself, in the process damaging over
forty yards of a stretch of track recently re-laid by the Army.
The locomotive finished up periously close to toppling over the
bank. The driver was John Snell, the fireman Hugh Jones and
the guard Phil Glazebrook, who was still an active volunteer
thirty five years later. The speed was 12 mph. The loco, after
much effort by volunteer permanent way workers who happened
to be on board, was re-railed late that evening, and the rest of
the train the following morning. There were no injuries and no
serious damage.

There was an accident to a member of staff on 14 July 1958
when Hugh Jones, leaning a long way out of his cab to locate
an unusual noise, was knocked off the footplate when his head
came into collision with a telephone pole near Fach Goch. He
broke his collar bone and a leg injury meant plaster from thigh
to ankle. For the next week Gareth Jones got time off from being
a BR fireman at Machynlleth depot in order to replace Hugh as
driver at Pendre.

The only occasion on which the Talyllyn Railway appeared
in the Railway Inspectorate's annual report was in 1986, when
(paragraph 85, 'Accidents at Level Crossings', under the side-
heading 'Gated Crossings(MG)', it states: 'A motorised trolley
skidded into the gates of Pendre (Tal-y-llyn Railway) in the
rain.' One of the more elderly, sober and responsible volunteers,
driving the small motor trolley, fitted out to carry tools, failed
to realise how wet the rails were, and thus the limited braking

power of his lightweight vehicle. As a result the trolley slid gently into the gates.

The electrical and signalling department, headed since 1963 by Don Southgate, is under the general direction of the chief engineer. The Talyllyn ceased having an independent S & T (signalling and telegraph) division in 1960, after one of its relatively few traumatic 'bust-ups'. At the Society's AGM in September 1959, Major Robinson, who had set it up, said that the S & T, disgusted with a general lack of co-operation from the operators, was standing down. References were made to 'Big Brother', British Rail, where (in those days) this sort of thing was always happening. The committee were disturbed at the suggestion that a dossier of alleged irregularities was being built up, and pointed out that the correct procedure was for these to be notified to the secretary, who would bring them to the Company's Board. The committee received a very critical memorandum from a meeting of the telecommunications section (as it had renamed itself) in Manchester on 19 December 1959. A sub-committee consisting of the Earl of Northesk, and Messrs Cope, Faulkner, Gardiner, Robinson and Rolt was appointed to meet Major Robinson and the S & T members, provided they withdrew their threats. No one was quite sure what Major Robinson had actually said at the AGM, so it was agreed to employ a shorthand writer in future. This did not happen, but John Slater, editor of *Talyllyn News*, began to take very comprehensive minutes, published in full in the December issue.

The full committee eventually decided that in future signalling and telegraph work should be done under the direction of the engineering department. 'Experience has shown that it is not possible to ensure effective co-ordination of activities if a separate section has sole responsibility for planning and organising S & T work.'

Major Robinson had made the first telephone call between Abergynolwyn station and Wharf at 7.03 pm on 30 May 1954. He and twelve of his men from 96 AG, Royal Artillery (Anti-Aircraft Command) Signal Squadron, TA, had arrived from Atherton, near Manchester, at Wharf at 8.30 am the day before. In filthy weather using a special train they started laying a new telephone wire from Hendy Bridge. Communication was established with Brynglas by Saturday lunchtime, and Sunday being a fine day, the wire laying was completed. The wire was at first laid in the hedge, but over week-ends later in June the job was completed, by putting the wire, complete with insulators, on three hundred donated wooden telegraph poles, which had also to be prepared and planted: no mean task. (The wires were placed underground in 1987 under Don Southgate's direction using a mechanical trenching machine, and permanent staff labour). In March the following year Major Robinson reported that due to the reorganisation of the Territorial Army his unit could only do two more week-ends. He would spend his annual holiday on the railway 'and if the work has not been finished by then I intend to press on with it myself. I shall be grateful for the help of any stalwarts and can promise interesting work with tea every hour on the hour in true Signals style!'

In the days of general manager Ken Marrian, a professional railway man, whose knowledge and judgement was respected, and therefore whose orders were accepted, relations were pretty smooth. But when he was succeeded by Harold Parker, his assistant, a much more cautious and commercially-minded man, relations deteriorated. However perhaps the crucial factor was that for years Major Robinson suffered from symptoms of an illness which led to him going blind, and from which he eventually died of a brain tumour in 1964. After the onset of his blindness his enthusiasm for the TR continued undiminished; his last wish was that all the telephone equipment he had gathered for use on the railway should come to Pendre – as indeed it did.

As has already been hinted, in the early years, when it was most needed, the TR received a great deal of help from the Army. Assistance was originally offered by army units based locally in 1951; but such was Tom Rolt's character that relations with the officers in charge were none too good. As Tom admits in his *Landscape With Machines* he was not a good mixer - and he was by nature and conviction an anti-militarist. His usual dress of open-necked shirt and sockless sandals complete with bee-keeper hat was hardly in keeping with what was expected at the time. However some help was received from locally-based service personnel in

1952 particularly in lifting rail on the Alltwyllt incline. Early in 1953 a TA unit at Smethwick, looking for something worthwhile to do at their annual camp, rang Bill Faulkner to say they would like to do a training exercise. Mr Roberts lent his field for their tents, and Mr & Mrs Wyatt,, of the White Hall Hotel provided a barrel of beer. The 160 men from No 127 Construction Unit (TA) Royal Engineers, re-sleepered some of the track between Brynglas and Quarry Siding in 1953. In July 1954 185 Squadron (TA) Royal Engineers relaid the quarter mile approach to Abergynolwyn station.

But this Army help was nearly torpedoed by fears of union objections. Bill Faulkner received a phone call from the unit's adjutant telling him that the training exercise was 'off'. He found out that the local union office had received a message from Mr Victor Feather, assistant secretary of the Trade Union Congress, to say they did not approve of the Army doing this kind of work. The committee appealed to its president, Lord Northesk, for urgent assistance. He got in touch with Vic Feather and invited him to lunch. Vic Feather, like many trade union officials and most of their fellow men and women, liked lunches and Lords. Mr Feather pointed out that Merioneth was an area of high unemployment, even then, and it was wrong for trade unionists, when doing military training, to work for a commercial company, thus depriving their comrades of jobs. Lord Northesk pointed out the Company did not have any money so could not employ any more people, that it was not a commercial organisation, and the re-laying work would have to be done by volunteers or not at all. When Vic Feather understood the situation the TUC objections were withdrawn.

Former Army officers were also of great help to the Society in matters concerned with the Ministry of Transport Railways Inspectorate. In 1951 an early member of the Society, Lt Col Woodhouse, himself a former HM Inspector of Railways, warned that it was likely that his former colleagues would soon be taking a closer interest in the Talyllyn, as a result of all the publicity it was receiving and with the considerable growth in passenger traffic.

In March 1952 the chief inspecting officer of railways requested an interview. The Committee decided it would be prudent not to open the railway for public services that Easter, and asked Bill Trinder, its chairman, Pat Whitehouse, its secretary, and Tom Rolt, the general manager, to represent the railway at a meeting at the Ministry. This took place on 18 April, and was described as 'pleasant but thorough'. It resulted in a visit to the line by Lt Col McMullen on 12 June. This, as subsequent visits, was a traumatic occasion. Tom Rolt and the Committee were well aware they were treading a tight rope. They needed to be able to keep the trains running to earn the revenue to make the railway safe: without an inflow of cash their venture would fail. But Rolt and McMullen got on well, and later had much to do with one another when Tom came to write *Red For Danger*. It has been suggested McMullen recognised there was a good man on site, and therefore quietly accepted things that clearly would have to be tightened and improved later.

On that first visit the inspector emphasised the priority of making the track safe. An overall speed limit of 12 mph was recommended, with 5 mph where the track was exceptionally bad. He indicated that if the line had not been open and running, he would have not allowed it to re-start. The implication was clear: if there was an accident, the line would be closed. But while a statutory railway is still operating, safety is the responsibility of the Company. The Minister only has powers to close an operation after the report on an accident. By the time of his next visit in July 1954, Col McMullen was able to report 'I was very glad indeed to see the improvement in the track and I appreciate how much work you must have put into it. It is, of course, still far from being good throughout, and in fact there are sections which are still distinctly bad. I know that you are well aware of this and that you are, quite rightly, making it your first priority.'

CHAPTER 9

Aspects of Society Life Since 1953

Talyllyn News, the quarterly journal of the TRPS, has long been considered one of the best railway society magazines. It first appeared in September 1953 under the editorship of R.W. Inkster, who was responsible for the first thirty nine issues. The first ten issues, entitled *Tal-Y-Llyn News* [sic], were duplicated on a machine belonging to the Manchester Model Railway Society. The TRPS' president, Lord Northesk, wrote an introduction in the first number in which he stated the objects were to serve 'as a means of keeping in touch with what is going on those (members) who, for one reason or another, cannot visit Towyn', and to 'be an introduction to the fascination of our line to any non-members . . . and lead their becoming active members of the Society'. He continued: 'The objects of the Society – the preservation of this unique old railway for posterity – are regarded with sympathy by all who become aware of its existence, as is exemplified by the many spontaneous and practical gifts, and offers of help, received from all over the wold.'

In August 1954 the Committee agreed that the magazine could be produced three times a year instead of quarterly as planned, due to the 'vast amount of work involved in its production'. Within a year however it had reverted to being quarterly and so it has remained. In May 1956 the joint editors Mr and Mrs Inkester were formally congratulated by the committee and Society on their marriage.

Issue No 11 in May 1956 was the first to be printed, and had a black-and-white photograph of No 6 *Douglas* at Wharf station on its front cover. The first two-colour printing was on the cover of issue No 27 in September 1960, and the magazine was given a colour top-strip front in December 1961, which also carried a splendid reproduction of Terence Cuneo's magnificent painting of No 1 *Talyllyn* with train at Dolgoch. Mr Cuneo generously contributed this picture to the Talyllyn so that prints could bolster Society funds, and to use on a poster. The first colour photograph was on the cover of the June 1986 issue, No 130, and subsequently the policy was to confine colour photos to the June issue as this was the one that sold most to non-members through impulse buying at the railway's shops.

John Slater, was the second, and so far only other editor, taking over in December 1963. A volunteer since 1952, he has spent most of his week-ends over the last thirty years in the railway workshops where he feels at ease having once been an apprentice with the engineering firm, Mather & Platt of Oldham. He later became editor of *Railway Magazine*. He was first elected to the Council in 1963, when he became editor of the *Talyllyn News*. He has also written over 1100 weekly newsletters on his visits to Tywyn since 1952, and these, together with *Talyllyn News*, are prime sources for information on events of the time.

The magazine has changed little since its earliest years. It soon acquired a correspondence column and in each issue the chief engineer reports on the progress, or occasionally lack of it, on permanent way, locomotives, carriages and wagons, workshops and building and civil engineering. The general manager supplies a traffic and operating report, and other members contribute regular reports or occasional articles on their sphere of activities, or their views on the activities of others. There is a personal column for births, marriages, and, as Society members get older and the years pass, inevitably more deaths. Well illustrated, the magazine is produced to a high standard,. There seems no shortage of material, and the editor's 'spike' is by no means unused. Nor is the editor afraid to be controversial, and would probably have incurred the declared displeasure of Council on more than one occasion, were it not that he usually topped the poll at election time!

The Coronation of Her Majesty Queen Elizabeth II preceded the magazine's birth, but events on the Talyllyn Railway were extensively covered in an early edition of John's weekly bulletin.

He reported that this notice was displayed at Tywyn (Wharf):

TAL-Y-LLYN RAILWAY
Special arrangements for
Coronation Day,
2nd. June 1953.
The Company is glad to announce that on
Coronation Day, June 2nd.,
Both the regular morning and afternoon trains will
be specially decorated in honour of
Her Majesty Queen Elizabeth II,
and that subject to the rules and regulations of the
Company, all children under the age of 14 will
be carried FREE OF CHARGE on these two
trains to the limit of their capacity.
By Order of
The Directors

No 4 *Edward Thomas* carried a headboard, devised and ex-
ecuted by Jim Lloyd and Bob Inkster, surrounded by a scroll
which read: 'Rheilfford Talyllyn. Tren Arbenig Dydd y Coroni.
Mehefin 2 1953'. Roughly translated that is: 'Talyllyn Railway.
Special Train. Coronation Day. June 2 1953.' EIIR plaques and
flags were fixed to the loco and the carriages. John wrote:

The kids were waiting at Wharf for their free rides from
9.0 am – a whole platform full of them . . . The train ran down
to Wharf at approximately 9.45 am and a brave little sight it
made with little triangular pennants fluttering in the breeze,
and the brass all polished up. The BBC Welsh Home Service
were there to see the train out . . . Bill Oliver surreptitiously
placed two detonators under the wheels of the loco and a
further six under the Aberdovey road bridge. The children
were all aboard, and began singing, their taste ranging from
Welsh songs through 'God Save the Queen' to·'How much
is that Doggie in the Window?' Sharp at 10.25 am the train
whistled and moved off – immediately two detonators roared
and, a few seconds later the six beneath the bridge went off

... Altogether sixty seven children boarded at Wharf and another twenty seven got on at intermediate stations, making a total of ninety four, so the train was loaded 'to the limit of its capacity' as several adults were travelling as well . . . The afternoon train was no so crowded as the Towyn 'junketings' were on at that time. Altogether during the day, £4-1-8½d was taken by selling refreshments, so our 'free rides for children' were not a complete loss.'

At the Centenary, on 1 June 1965, John Betjeman CBE, the Poet Laureate, opened the re-built Wharf booking office. First came the formal luncheon in the Corbett Arms hotel, customary on such occasions. He then inaugurated a specially 'named' train, *The Centenarian*. This consisted of No 1 *Talyllyn*, complete with special headboard, the original Talyllyn coaches and van, the latest new carriage, No 18, just completed in the Pendre works, and for good measure, one of the Glyn Valley coaches. For the rest of the season the 13.10 up-train from Wharf, and the return service, the 14.10 from Abergynolwyn, ran as *The Centenarian*.

A special service was held in the ancient parish church of St. Cadvan's, Tywyn, on Sunday, 4 July: the day before the actual centenary of the Royal assent being given to the Talyllyn Railway Act on 5 July 1865. The first lesson, taken from Ecclesiasticus XXXVIII verses 25-34, was read, and indubitably chosen, by Tom Rolt. The sermon was preached by a '1951' TRPS member, the Rev W. Awdry MA, the famous children's author. On the chancel steps, standing on a few lengths of rail, was placed a permanent way push-trolley, carrying a slab of slate, a quarry hammer, a shovel and *The Centenarian* headboard.

On 30 June there was a Victorian Cavalcade, to celebrate not only the Talyllyn's century, but also the half-century of the Women's Institute. The procession was led by Society members including Council vice-chairman Eric Gibbons in a governess's gig, followed by the Towyn Silver Band. Then came about a hundred WI members, most in victorian dress. After parading through the streets they arrived at Wharf station to join a special train, consisting of *The Centenarian* set, headed by No 2 *Dolgoch*, plus the Corris van to carry the band and their instruments. The driver, Herbert Jones, and the guard, David Woodhouse, rose to the occasion; the former being resplendent in york straps and buff waistcoat, and the latter even more so, in high button tunic and red-striped trousers.

There was also a historical exhibition in the Grammar School opened by Wynford Vaughan Thomas, supported by TR director, Edward Thomas. There were sections on the Cambrian and Talyllyn railways and on each of the surrounding villages and quarries, as well as on Towyn and Aberdovey. The Talyllyn exhibit consisted of a large 7 mm model of a section of the line, brass buttons from guard Jacob Rowland's uniform of fifty years before, a one-ton iron wagon, sections of rail and point-work, a 1903 account book, and numerous plans, tickets and photographs from the past.

A book, *Talyllyn Century* with contributions from J.B. Snell, J.I.C. Boyd, J.L.H. Bate, L.T.C. Rolt (who also edited it), D. Woodhouse and H. Dalston, was published by David & Charles. A special supplement was published in *The Cambrian News*. 8500 first-day covers, carrying a special two-colour centenary railway letter stamp, were prepared and sold – a very sticky job co-ordinated by member, films officer, and later Society chairman, John Adams, a professional photographer, from Birmingham. Twelve years after it was made, *Railway with a Heart of Gold* was received from the USA: a magnificent film, by far the best on the TR so far; directed, shot and produced by Carson Davison, it showed the railway as it was in 1953.

In 1971 the Society celebrated its twenty-first birthday, commemorating the inaugural meeting on 11 October 1950 at the Imperial Hotel, Birmingham. It did so by running a three-hour canal trip from the Gas Street basin, in the centre of Birmingham, out to Tyseley, then the home of Standard Gauge Steam. At Tyseley, GWR No 7029 and an ex-GWR, ex-London Transport pannier-tank were in steam. Some members had foregone the canal trip to make their own way to Tyseley for an excellent lunch in one of the Pullman cars. After this they combined with the canal party, which had by then arrived, to make a close inspection of the depot, before rejoining the narrow-boat *David* for the return journey. This was via the Birmingham Navigation, and its numerous locks, 'giving a view of Birmingham and its industrial archeology vouchsafed to few'. In the evening an informal social evening was held in the Imperial Hotel, Tom Rolt and the Society's then president, Viscount Garnock, being among the company. At the speeches after lunch it was announced that Prince William of Gloucester had agreed to become the Society's patron. Next morning two bus loads of members left the Birmingham Bull Ring to spend the day on the Severn Valley Railway at Bridgnorth, including a train ride in reserved accommodation on the 15.00 to Hampton Loade and back, hauled by another ex-London Transport pannier tank.

Unfortunately Prince William was not destined to be patron for long, as he was tragically killed in a flying accident on 2 August 1972. He had first visited the railway whilst staying with a vice-president, Colonel J.F. Williams-Wynne, the Lord Lieutenant of Merioneth, at his home at Peniarth. He rode on the footplate of No 2 *Dolgoch*. He had only time to make one more visit to the railway before he died. Lord Garnock in his letter to the Prince's equerry wrote 'Prince William will be everywhere mourned . . . and sadly missed amongst groups such as our own in which he was playing an increasingly prominent part.'

On Monday 15 May 1972 a special train was run to commemorate the twenty first anniversary of the Society's inaugural. After a cold collation in the museum, there were some brief speeches before the 'inaugural' train made up of the original TR stock, headed, as on the original occasion, by No 2 *Dolgoch* left for Abergynolwyn. However it only proceeded as far as Pendre, where it waited in the loop, whilst a following train containing the Press and headed by No 1 *Talyllyn* overtook it, and preceded it to Rhydyronen. There the Press were able to see the arrival of the 'inaugural' train and witness the hand-shunt of the coaches around *Dolgoch* as had been done in 1951. The two trains combined into one and then went on to Abergynolwyn to witness progress on the Nant Gwernol extension before returning to Wharf.

But on that occasion, unless necessary for safety, none of the engines sounded their whistles, for only three days before had come the sad news that Mr Edward Thomas, to whom the railway owed so much, had died at the age of 92. By the time he resigned as a director in 1967, owing to ill-health, he had served the railway for over seventy years. To mark a record of continuous service that must be unique he was presented with a silver salver, now in the Museum at Wharf. Mr Thomas' funeral was fixed for 15 May and the TR ceremony only went ahead after consulting the family directors, Mr Hugh Mathias, Sir Haydn's grandson, and Mr B.J.P. Williams. Together with Hugh's mother and Sir Haydn's daughter, Mrs Mathias, they made a brief appearance at the buffet before going on to the funeral, as did also former Society chairman Eric Gibbons, and locomotive superintendent Herbert Jones, respectively representing the Society and the Company. The locomotive No 4 *Edward Thomas* carried a wreath all that day, which was later placed on the grave.

During the spring bank holiday in 1977 the railway mounted an exhibition in the north carriage shed in honour of the Queen's Silver Jubilee. This included various models, some working, of the Talyllyn, together with old photographs and drawing of the railway and quarry.

On 25 November 1982, the Prince and Princess of Wales visited Towyn, in the course of a tour of north and mid-Wales. After leaving the Royal train at Aberdovey, they arrived at the Neuadd Pendre social centre by car, to meet local dignitaries. They then walked up Brook Street to Pendre station where they were to join the Talyllyn's Royal train for the journey to Rhydyronen.

In the best traditions of railway practice a pilot engine was run up the line twenty minutes ahead. This was No 6 *Douglas* carrying a 'royal train pilot' headboard. The driver was Maurice (Tug) Wilson, a volunteer fireman, later to become Society chairman and a Company director. The fireman was another volunteer, Dr John Burton. Volunteer Peter Twigg acted as traffic inspector as befitted a senior manager in British Rail. And there were also two security men on the footplate. It was just as well No 6 has a large cab.

The royal train was headed by No 2 *Dolgoch* with Dai Jones driving, with another member of the permanent staff, a former volunteer, Mike Green, firing. The guard was 'Chief Bodger,' John Smallwood, a manager with British Rail. His title as Chief

Bodger was given him because he looked after the repainting of locomotives and carriages, and general maintenance of the latter: task mainly carried out by volunteers. The Royal saloon for the day was the Corris coach, No 17, which was coupled next to the engine. The rest of the train was formed by two bogie-coaches, No 19 for invited guests and No 18, for the Press; four-wheel open-sided coach No 12, requested specifically for the television camera crews; and four-wheel brake van No 5 of 1866, specially fitted with an extra bracket so it could carry two tail lamps.

A headboard of the Prince of Wales 'feathers' was carried by *Dolgoch* with six flags: the Prince's Standard, the Union flag, two Welsh dragon flags, one Scottish lion and the three legs of the Isle of Man. Arriving on Pendre platform by the wicket gate, the royal couple were welcomed by general manager David Woodhouse, and introduced to the Company's chairman and Society president Patrick Garland, and Mrs Garland; director Hugh Mathias, Sir Henry Haydn Jones' grandson; Sir Haydn's daughter, Mrs Mathias; Society vice-president Hugh Jones; chief engineer John Bate and his wife Olwen; and John Macdougall, representing the permanent staff.

Patrick Garland, on behalf of the Society, gave the Prince a specially bound volume of Tom Rolt's *Railway Adventure*; Sara Woodhouse, the general manager's daughter presented the Princess with a bouquet, and Judith Bate, the chief engineer's daughter, gave her the three Rev W. Awdry children's books, based on the TR, for Prince William.

The Prince was then offered a ride on the locomotive footplate as 'third man'. The sleeves of the overall to protect his clothes were too long, and he is reported to have said this was nothing unusual. All the overalls with which he was provided on such occasions appeared to have been made for 'anthropoid man'! The chief engineer had already been asked to travel in the front saloon of the Corris coach with the royal party, but the Princess gave Sara and Judith the thrill of their lives by asking them too to join her on the journey.

At 11.36 the train left Pendre, the royal 'third man' relaxing on the footplate and reportedly expressing considerable interest in the veteran locomotive, its controls, and the coal burned.

Prince Charles was fascinated to learn that Dai's brother, father, uncle and grandfather had all worked on the railway. The TV news reporter who claimed that the Prince was sternly told by the driver not to touch anything must have made it up, as Dai certainly said no such thing. At one point, the Prince tapped on the back window of the cab and waved to the Princess, remarking as he saw the chief engineer opening a window that it must be rather stuffy in the coach.

In the front compartment of the Corris coach were the Princess, Anne Beckwith-Smith, her lady-in-waiting; John Bate and daughter Judith; and Sara Woodhouse. The Princess is reported to have asked Judith if she found learning Welsh difficult, and was told it was harder than French, but easier to practice as there were plenty of people around who spoke it.

During the journey, the engine crew made their own presentation to the Prince, giving him on behalf of the volunteers a painted wooden plaque. This carried a transfer of the railway's heraldic device, the Prince's own 'feather's bade'. He was obviously delighted with the plaque, which, like the headboards, had been made by Dale Coton, a volunteer guard and blockman, and former Society publicity officer, a teacher from Nuneaton.

The journey ended at Rhydyronen where the royal party rejoined their cars to go off for a private lunch with Col William-Wynne. The royal train proceeded, with the Press still on board, to Brynglas, where *Douglas* had been waiting. *Dolgoch* ran round the loop, and the now double-headed train returned in triumph to Pendre. This was not quite the end, for at the Prince's specific request, *Dolgoch* was at Wharf to see the 'big' BR royal train off. As Their Royal Highnesses waved from a window, *Dolgoch* whistled, and this was acknowledged by the horns of the two British Rail engines, Nos 25,259 and 25,278, heading the BR royal train – a royal salute returned!

AREA GROUPS

For members who live away from Tywyn the Society has Area Groups or local branches. These arrange for social occasions, working parties to go to Tywyn, publicity through exhibitions

The Talyllyn News
Southern Edition

Being news from the London Area Committee, Talyllyn Railway Preservation Society

THE SPRING REUNION
OF THE LONDON AREA WILL BE HELD AT
THE KINGSLEY HOTEL
Bloomsbury Way, W.C.I.
[Near commencement of New Oxford St.]

on Saturday, April 18th, 1953
from 4 to 9 p.m.

COME and hear about YOUR Railway, YOUR Society, and YOUR Area
See Programme overleaf
Licensed Bar - Soft Drinks and Tea - Postcards, etc. on sale. - Raffles.

TRIP TO TOWYN. It is hoped to arrange a trip to Towyn by railcar during the season. The cost is expected to be about £3 10s. but before arrangements can be completed the Committee must know they have the support of at least the smallest coach load. So even if you are not coming to the Reunion please complete question 5 on the form below.

Model Railway Club Exhibition. We would remind members that the Area is running a stand at this Exhibition during Easter week, 7 - 11th April and look forward to seeing you there.

P.T.O.

CUT HERE

To: T. W. Robertson, Area Sec. 23, Portway, Ewell, Sy.

1. I shall be attending the Reunion. ....

2. I shall require .... tea(s) *at* 2/- per head.

3. „ „ „ .... dinner(s) *at* 8 6 per head.

4. I enclose .... prints for showing on the epidiascope.
S.A.E. enclosed for return.*

5. I am interested in and will support the proposed rail-trip to Towyn....

6. To save double postage I enclose £ .... as subscription for 1953 and or donation.* Alternatively I will pay at the Reunion.*

7. Some suggestions are overleaf.

Signed.................................. Address...............................

*Delete inapplicable words.

The prompt return of this form will assist the smooth running of the Reunion,

and illustrated talks. They also take money-raising stalls at model railway events and traction engine rallies.

The first of the groups, originally known simply as 'Areas', was set up in the North West in 1951, largely at the instigation of James Boyd. It was the first area to send working parties to the railway; they were responsible for some of the very early track work. The establishment of a London group soon followed in 1952, the Midlands coming later, after the East Midlands and Yorkshire. Later groups were set up in the South West centred on Bristol; in 'Wessex' centred on Southampton; in East Anglia; at Milton Keynes; in Tywyn and Mid-Wales; and there is even an overseas group for members scattered round the world, which keeps together by correspondence. After that first year in 1951, when Pat Whitehouse had a publicity stall at the International Model Railway Exhibition, the London group have organised and manned it. In its early up-market days, the group held spring reunions at the Kingsley Hotel in Bloomsbury (tea at 2s) and places for dinner through the secretary; in 1960 meetings were moved to the more prosaic premises of the Model Railway Club.

A poignant note from James Boyd in the September 1954 edition of *Talyllyn News* regretted the death of member Donald Mackreth, who had been a prisoner-of-war in South-east Asia, and had returned home a sick man with only a few years to live. 'His interest in the Festiniog and Talyllyn railways did much to cheer him in his illness. It is good to know we helped to give him some little pleasure before his recent death.' It is this comradeship in promoting something without personal financial gain that appeals to the men and women who make up the area groups.

THE SPECIAL TRAINS FOR AGMs

An early feature of the activities of the TRPS was the organisation of a special train from London to its AGM. The first of these was on 26 September 1953 by diesel rail car. The departure time from Paddington was 6.50 am, due in Towyn at 2.15 pm. The return trip was to leave at 6 pm arriving at Paddington at

7 am on the Sunday. The cost of the return trip was just under £3. This first charter was of a somewhat informal nature. The car was not equipped with toilets, so 'lavatory stops' had to be made with the guard tearing his hair out at some remote station to get the train re-started. Passengers were even asked 'where-they-wanted-to-get-out' on the return trip which proved somewhat eventful. The diesel's engine seized at Lapworth, between Birmingham and Warwick, due to a loss of cooling water. The passengers descended at dead of night on to the track in an unsuccessful attempt to push it into a loop. An ex-GWR 2–8–0 steam engine was detached from a goods train passing on the down line, to haul the failed diesel car to Leamington. The BR staff however were puzzled on how to connect up the rail car as it had apparently no coupling gear. Some of the passengers, Society members, came to the rescue by pointing out that the towing bar was stored in a small compartment at one end of the vehicle and that the budget lock could be opened with a carriage key. On reaching Leamington Spa a smaller 48-seater diesel car was substituted, and twenty unfortunates had to stand all the way to Paddington, where, one and a half hours late, the epic journey ended at 8.30 am.

In 1954 eighty members travelled in a diesel triplet set, the outward journey being via the long-since closed Ruabon and Dolgellau line, thus approaching Tywyn from the north. In 1955 the Society had expanded so much that a steam-hauled special train, complete with cafeteria car, was organised. It left Paddington at 7am with calls at Birmingham and Shrewsbury. The tickets cost 50s return from London, and 25s 6d from Birmingham. A specially cleaned 'Star' took the train to Shrewsbury, where it was replaced by a Southern T9, reinforced by a GWR 'Duke-Dog' from Welshpool. The last steam-hauled train was in 1966. The specials came to an end in 1981, when reserved space was provided on a BR 'Merrymaker' excursion, and thereafter support was insufficient to make group travel arrangements. The decline was due to many members wishing to spend the whole of the AGM week-end at Tywyn, the omnipresent motorcar, and the demise of many elderly arm-chair members. And with the introduction of much faster through trains Euston - Tywyn both ways, it had become quite feasible to travel to the AGM and get back home the same day, comfortably and relatively cheaply on a 'Blue Saver' ticket, using scheduled services.

OTHER GENERAL MANAGERS

Ken Marrian, who succeeded Tom Rolt in 1953, had worked as a civil engineer, first for the Cheshire Lines, and then for the LMS. In World War I he had been a captain in the Royal Engineers in charge of a railway construction company. But when the railways were nationalised he took early retirement. With a reasonable pension, he was willing to work on the Talyllyn during the summer for a relatively low salary. He commanded authority and respect as a professional railwayman. But he was a friendly, open relaxed kind of chap, not touchy like Tom could be, and very good at public relations; 'good with people'. He was noted for his remarkable penchant for 'Double Diamond' beer. He always had a bottle in his desk drawer. He even arranged, when he was travelling on the up-train on British Rail, to have supplies of his favourite beverage transferred to it, either at Moat Lane Junction or Newtown, from the buffet car of the down-train. It is also rumoured that contrary to regulations, TR trains at that time also carried emergency supplies of Double-Diamond.

At the end of the 1954 season, Ken decided he would only be able to work part-time in 1955. It was agreed to appoint an assistant to look after the 'paper-work' side of the growing business. Harold Parker was appointed in 1955 as assistant general manager. He was another amiable character, and a first class book-keeper. In January 1958 Ken Marrian died, and Harold was appointed full-time general manager from 1 February at a salary of £550, together with a 'vehicle at the Company's expense'. Provision was also made for the appointment of an assistant for the 17-18 weeks of the season at a wage of £5 per week. After Harold Parker resigned at the end of the 1965, a volunteer, David Woodhouse became full-time traffic manager, and Bill Faulkner, who had been deputy general manager since 1964, became managing director, still in a voluntary capacity. Another volunteer, Eric Gibbons, became unpaid commercial manager. Bill Faulkner gave up the post of managing director in 1967 on becoming general manager of the Dart Valley Railway. In 1970 he resigned from this post, settled in Aberdovey, and was re-appointed managing director of the Talyllyn in 1973. David Woodhouse became general manager after Bill's death in 1982.

MUSEUMS

The Talyllyn is a railway preservation society, and proud of it. It is its *raison d'être*. As an editorial in the *Talyllyn News* pointed out when a senior member of the staff was reported to have said, no doubt in a moment of exasperation, that he was trying to run a railway, not a museum, he was in fact running the latter. Whilst the most difficult thing about running a preserved railway is reconciling preservation with operation, the TR has managed to do it successfully for over thirty-five years. Those who did not like it that way soon left. Alan Garraway left the Talyllyn to take up with the Festiniog railway, whose manager and engineer he became in 1955, the first full-time employee after its restoration. He first visited that railway with Bill Harvey in July 1951, when they were no doubt having a day off from wrestling with the locomotives at Pendre. He is recorded as saying that the Talyllyn was in such a decrepit state it was a wonder it still worked. The permanent way was just two bars of metal embedded in the turf. But the Festiniog was different. That was the railway they ought to be restoring. That was a proper railway. After taking over as manager, Alan is reported to have said 'I'm here to run a tourist attraction, not to preserve a railway.' On the Festiniog and most other private railways, the Society members do not control the railway as they do on the Talyllyn. While the Festiniog has restored its original locomotives, and other historic stock, partly no doubt (and why not?) as an additional tourist attraction, and possibly because it is cheaper than having new locomotives built, it is essentially a tourist and not a preservation business. The Talyllyn is a living museum, which only has to pay its way. The Society members, who include almost all the permanent staff, derive great satisfaction from preserving something of our national heritage, for the enjoyment of others as well as themselves.

The idea of a museum, a static display of artefacts as opposed to the 'living' museum of the Talyllyn itself, was there from the very beginning. In 1951, when member Harold Dalston was visiting the Festival of Britain in London, he saw on display there a new narrow-gauge diesel locomotive destined for the Guiness Brewery in Dublin. That meant the old steam locomotives were about to be displaced. So he wrote and asked for one, and somewhat to his surprise was not only promised a locomotive but given it carriage paid. The Society could hardly do otherwise than give it house-room. It was thus forced into actively considering the question of a museum, and in time-honoured fashion set up a committee, the museum sub-committee. From 1954 it started collecting suitable relics, and looking for somewhere to put them. In 1955 the ex-North Wales Narrow Gauge Railway's locomotive *Russell* arrived in somewhat dilapidated condition soon to be followed by the de Winton locomotive, *George Henry*, with its vertical boiler, on loan from the Penrhyn Quarries. James Boyd lent a number of items from his private collection, and he and Patrick Whitehouse secured other artefacts. These were placed in the old gunpowder store at the far corner of Wharf yard, which by 1955 was no longer required by Lady Haydn Jones for storing her car and mowing machine. It was converted into a temporary museum building during the winter of 1955-6. In August 1956 the Guinness locomotive arrived. The sub-committee had to be very selective in its acquisitions because of the lack of space. It tended to go for narrow-gauge passenger items rather than the more plentiful industrial relics, and then for only one of each make or type. 'Narrow-gauge' was interpreted as anything less than the standard 4ft 8½in.

In 1957 the museum sub-committee secured possession of the old lock-up goods yard beyond the office, on which the Midland area undertook to construct a museum building. They were as good as their word. The new building, successfully designed by Society member and architect, Robin Butterell, to fit into the existing fabric of Wharf station, was opened by John Scholes, curator of relics at the then British Transport Commission, in September 1959. The exhibits filled the new building from its inception, and an extension was started in 1963. A deed of trust, giving the museum charitable status, was signed on 26 September 1964. There were seven trustees, four from the Society and one each from the Newcomen Society, the Railway Correspondence & Travel Society, and the Stephenson Locomotive Society. The new Trust was given a lease of seven years on the premises at Wharf. The extension to the museum, much of which was built by volunteers from the North West area group, was opened by Lord Kilmaine, secretary of the Pilgrim Trust, on 15 June 1967. On 1 June 1970, the trustees, were granted a lease of twenty years at a cost of £20 pa with the usual wayleaves and covenants, for a Narrow Gauge Railway Museum at Wharf. In the summer of 1987 one of the exhibits, an 18-inch gauge 0–4–0 tank locomotive, *Pet*, built at Crewe in 1865 to the design of John Ramsbottom, was taken back there for the Crewe Heritage Festival. The loco is on loan from the National Railway Museum for exhibition in the Narrow Gauge Museum. Transport between Tywyn and Crewe and back again was arranged by P.E.T., Tool Hire Ltd of Crewe.

THE SHOP AND REFRESHMENTS

The railway derives a considerable net revenue from its retail shop and catering services. The shop grew out of the side-line, originated by Ken Cope, publicity director of the railway from 1951 to 1965, of selling postcards, calendars, Christmas cards, guide books and souvenir items from his home, and from the ticket counter at Wharf. Since then the range of goods sold has expanded enormously: especially since the shop became separated from the booking office when Wharf station was rebuilt in 1964, and even more so when extended in 1979. The shop really began to play a major part in the Company's activities, and as a source of revenue, after the appointment in 1965 of Eric Gibbons as unpaid commercial manager, and Tristram England, formerly an active volunteer from London, as his paid assistant. Eric was a leading Black Country businessman, a fuel engineer, who had been chairman and managing director of his family engineering company. Founder and secretary of the Midland area group he arranged for his firm to rebuild locomotives Nos 1 and 2, as well as leading working parties which installed a hopper and conveyor at Quarry siding, built the first part of the museum, rebuilt the south carriage shed, extended the north carriage shed and fitted smoke vents into the engine shed and extended it into the old cottage. He was chairman of Council 1967-9 and of the Company 1968-9, and was made a vice-president in 1973, a year before his death. Eric was not married, and was not universally popular. One member described him as 'just a boy in many ways, who could be petulant if he did not get his own way'. But there is no doubt he gave much of his life in dedicated service to the TR.

The shop carries a large range of souvenirs of the railway and the locality, along with railway books and model railway equipment, and conducts a vigorous mail-order business. There is also a quite substantial catering facility. Tristram England succeeded Eric as commercial manager in 1971. The Company then made the classic mistake, after easing Tris England out of the job in 1979 as Eric Gibbons had been eased out in 1971, of engaging a 'professional' as its commercial manager. He was apparently a 'go-getting' entrepreneur, with almost no interest in railways or railway preservation as such, and little sympathy for the volunteers. He did not want them in the shop, except as customers! In any organisation where volunteers are an integral part of the set-up it is essential, with rare exceptions, that the paid staff have had experience of being volunteers themselves. In the early eighties the shop made a thumping loss. The post of commercial manager was then abolished, and replaced by that of commercial assistant, under the direct control of the general manager. Mary Davies was appointed as the first commercial assistant. She was followed by Liz Green, a former teacher, and wife of Mike Green, one of the permanent engineering staff. This job enabled Liz to live at home in Tywyn. She was also a volunteer fireman, Mike being a keen volunteer, and occasionally paid, driver. If the Duchess of York could become a helicopter pilot like her husband, Liz could become an engine driver like hers!

Refreshments were first served at Abergynolwyn station from the ticket office. By 1964 with increased traffic these facilities became hopelessly congested. so from 1964 until a new station building was opened in 1968, No 7 van, converted into a mobile tea bar or 'take-away', was brought up each day on the end of the first train, and parked in a specially built short siding, at the east end of the station. With the onset of the age of the car, more and more passengers began to use Abergynolwyn as a terminus. Many fathers and the children now travelled by train in one direction while mum drove.

The refreshments were organised and served by a Miss Zelah Thomas, a redoubtable lady, a niece of Mr Edward Thomas. Woe betide any guard who left her, or her van, behind at Wharf. The van was inadequate and cramped. There was not enough covered accommodation for both waiting and eating. The new station, opened for the 1969 season, included a new refreshment room. This, and a small non-food sales counter, is run as a branch of the railway shop at Wharf station.

THE RAILWAY LETTER SERVICE

After the nationalisation of the railways in 1948, only British Rail, the Northern Ireland railways and the Talyllyn Railway, as a statutory railway, were permitted to run a public mail service by carrying 'railway letters'. They were authorised to accept and convey letters by the first available train and ship. Such letters must either be passed on by the railway's officials to the Post Office carrying an ordinary first class stamp in addition to the railway's stamps for delivery to any address in the normal way, or they may simply be addressed 'to be called for' care of any TR railway station. Until 1978 railway letters could also be sent to any manned BR or Northern Ireland Railways' station. In 1969, authorisation to run a 'railway letter service' was extended by the Post Office to the Festiniog and the Ravenglass & Eskdale and since then to other private railways. The Talyllyn Railway issues its own stamps and the first specially printed railway letter stamp issued by the Society was on 23 May 1957. Since then first day covers have been issued to celebrate special TR events or anniversaries, or in connection with new Post Office issues, mainly as collectors items. The 'railway letter service' provides a useful income, and a source of pleasure and interest to many specialist philatelists. In 1989 a volunteer, Sara Eade, was appointed postmaster.

CHAPTER 10

On To Nant Gwernol

Extending the line beyond Abergynolwyn, since 1865 the upper terminus for all passenger trains, proved a major task. It was the largest single new project undertaken by the Company under preservation society control.

From the earliest days there was a feeling amongst members that the railway ought to be extended. A Christmas card issued by the Society in 1951 bore a stylised diagram of the railway ending at 'Bryn Eglwys: site for future passenger terminus!' In 1957, when the railway had achieved some degree of normality, and members were looking for new fields to conquer, various ideas were put forward: most notably that of pressing on to the Talyllyn Lake. The damper was cast on this by an estimate of John Bate's that the cost, without land, would be of the order of £83,000, and would take 10-20 years to complete at the then current rate of volunteer effort. But Nant Gwernol was regarded as not beyond the bounds of possibility, once the main line was in reasonable order. After all, some members on No 2 *Dolgoch* had reached Nant Gwernol and the foot of the Alltwyllt incline in the earliest days of the Society, and the line was in use when Bill Trinder first saw it on 14 March 1947!

Nothing much happened until 1959 when member George Tibbits offered his services as solicitor free of charge. At that time it was assumed the extension, at least as far as the foot of the incline, formed part of the Talyllyn Railway. George's immediate concern was therefore over what to do with the hundreds of passengers dumped on a platform with no exit other than back down the line. The incline was too steep to serve as an exit. He therefore suggested a bridge should be built to link the station to the footpath on the other side of the ravine. This footpath, known mysteriously as 'Shanghai', linked Abergynolwyn with the quarries via a footbridge much further up stream. But soon a major impediment arose, perhaps best described by George himself in *Talyllyn News*.

In the summer of 1959 I was asked whether I could apply for a Light Railway Order to enable the Railway Company to carry passengers from Abergynolwyn to Nant Gwernol . . . The number of Light Railway Orders obtained during the last fifty years is probably very small, and few solicitors now in practice have ever seen one. However, having obtained a copy of the Statutory Rules and Orders relative to Light Railways I suggested to Patrick Garland that I ought to walk the track of the proposed extension with him. A trip was arranged on 2 July 1959 and we travelled to Towyn with Bill Faulkner in his car. I was thrilled with the proposed extension to Nant Gwernol and determined to spend some time in Abergynolwyn later that summer, so that I should be acquainted with the neighbourhood, and this I did in August 1959.

I inspected the deposited plans and book of reference in the office of the Clerk of the Peace which confirmed that the Statutory Railway ended at the gate east of Abergynolwyn station. I made a fairly lengthy report to the Council of the Society in October 1959 and asked if I could see the Deeds of the Railway. It will be appreciated that every piece of land taken for the construction of the railway has to be conveyed to the Railway Company. To my dismay I was told there were no deeds. At this time everyone believed that the railway eastwards beyond the gate of Abergynolwyn was, and always had been, an integral part of the railway, though by that time I was beginning to suspect the snag which subsequently appeared. There were notices in various places along the route as far as the foot of the second incline to Bryn Eglwys proclaiming that the land belonged to the Talyllyn Railway Company. It seemed to me if a Light Railway Order was to be sought, we should soon be in difficulties unless we could prove our title to the land. Even a nodding acquaintance with such matters must indicate to the railway enthusiast that if the land over which a railway is to be run does not belong to the Company wishing to operate the railway, or cannot be purchased by agreement, powers of compulsory purchase must be included in the Order and acquisition under those circumstances is costly. It became evident therefore that somehow I must find the deed, and establish beyond question the Company's title to the land. Quite apart from this I was anxious to find, if I could, the lost records of the railway and in this I was helped by another of my hobbies, namely writing local history.

In 1960 I was ill and could not do very much but after several excursions into Wales as far north as Caernarvon I was partly successful in my quest, which ended at Dolgellau. I discovered that when the McConnel family sold its interests in Abergynolwyn and Bryn Eglwys to Mr (afterwards Sir) Henry Haydn Jones in March 1911, the track from the end of the Statutory Railway eastwards to a point about three-quarters of the way up the Alltwylly incline was included in the conveyance to Sir Haydn, he being, on the face of it, the owner of the fee simple in the land. Subsequent researches revealed that although this was so, the Talyllyn Railway Company had exercised absolute control of this land for over ninety years without, as far as is known, ever having paid any rent or giving any acknowledgement to the owner of the freehold, and therefore had a possessory title. Such title, which depends upon adverse possession, is not the best of titles and is usually looked upon with suspicion in the face of deeds showing someone else is the freeholder. In the case of dispute, proof is of course the main difficulty.

That such a position should have arisen is not difficult to understand. The McConnels and subsequently Sir Haydn Jones has possessed certain leases of land at Bryn Eglwys which enabled them to work the quarry and they had also owned all the shares (sic) in the Railway Company and much land in the vicinity of Abergynolwyn. In those days the railway and the quarry depended upon one another. Neither could exist without the other but the fact that the shares were owned by the McConnels and later Sir Haydn Jones did not mean that the Railway Company was not a separate entity, being a legal person quite distinct from those who owned the shares. This is so today and cannot be too clearly understood. That it was not understood in pre-Society days is evident for reasons which may be known to some but upon which I do not intend to be drawn. It will be understood from what I have written above that from the time of this discovery I was dealing with the solicitor for the personal representative of the late Sir Henry Haydn Jones. I would like to say that, consistent with his duty to his client, this gentleman showed me the greatest possible courtesy and patience on the many occasions I met him. He was most helpful in allowing me to look through a box of old deeds in his office in June 1961, as a result of which I have recovered a deed of conveyance of the greater part of the land upon which the railway was subsequently built. This conveyance has attached to it a most interesting strip map of the whole railway as far as Dolgoch.

I must draw a veil over the protracted negotiations which followed, my hopes of success were raised during the summer only to be dashed again early in August this year [1964]. However, towards the end of that month I received an unexpected letter from the solicitors for the party from whom I had been trying to obtain a confirmatory conveyance saying that their client had signed the document which I had submitted in the hope some time previously. In jest, our chairman (Tom Rolt) had said that if I succeeded in this matter a bust of me ought to be erected on Nant Gwernol station when built. On the 1 September this year I went to collect the long desired conveyance and at once sent a telegram to Tom Rolt saying: 'Funds permitting bust may now be ordered.' The girl in the Post Office at Towyn who accepted the telegram looked a little surprised, as well as she might, but she did not, nor did I intend her to, know what it meant.

It is disappointing the extension cannot be opened in 1965 (Centenary Year) as was intended but the delay has its compensations. There is still much to be done and it would be foolish to extend, with all that is involved, before the line from Towyn to Abergynolwyn is as good as it can be made.

Before a Light Railway Order can be made there remains a considerable amount of paperwork to be done but at least the land is now firmly within our grasp.

Whilst tracking down the ownership of the various plots of land, George Tibbets located the previously unknown owners of the half mile horse tramway which had linked the Alltwyllt and Cantrybedd inclines. Acting for the Company, having bought the land he re-sold it to the Forestry Commission, which had been after it for years, and negotiated a public right of way along it as far as the point where the 'Shanghai' path crosses the stream. Talyllyn Holdings Ltd actually purchased the land from the gate east of Abergynolwyn station to half way up the Alltwyllt Incline in September 1964.

A considerable amount of time was spent in trying to get hold of the land on both sides of the ravine. The plan, originally floated by Tom Rolt in 1963, was to persuade the National Trust to purchase the Nant Gwernol ravine as a whole, lease the forestry rights to the Forestry Commission, and then let the TR run its railway under some sort of tenancy agreement. There were still hopes of a grand terminus at Nant Gwernol with a two level station, and a self-service restaurant on the upper deck. The whole scheme foundered in May 1969 when the owners of the east bank refused to sell on any terms.

In May 1964, Colonel Robertson, a railway inspector from the Ministry of Transport, visited the extension, and outlined what would be needed to obtain a Light Railway Order. The principal initial requirement would be detailed plans and sections for each 100 feet of line. Considerable improvements to the existing track formation would be needed, and he also stressed the importance of adequate public egress from, and access to, the terminal station. By 1965 George had prepared a draft Order, but it was another three years before the drawings were ready. These were sent to George a few days before his untimely death on 31 October 1968.

Without the efforts of George Tibbits it is quite likely that the Talyllyn Railway would still end just beyond Abergynolwyn station. Tom Rolt wrote:

No one knew better than I did how hard he worked to bring the extension scheme about. That bust became a private joke between us as he plogged doggedly on in the face of a seemingly endless succession of frustrating legal difficulties that would have discouraged many a lesser man. All this work, representing an astronomical sum in legal fees, he did in his capacity as honorary solicitor to the railway Company, moved solely by two things: his love for the railway and his unbounded faith in, and enthusiasm for, the project to which he had set his hand. His sole reward would have been to see a train steam into Nant Gwernol station, but, alas, it was not to be.

For the last nine months his health was so bad that he knew his time was running out. Yet, ignoring the advice of his friends, he persisted in carrying on and paid his last visit to Tywyn in September, 1968, when he spoke at the annual general meeting. He died almost exactly one month later, on the last day of October, in Warwick Hospital, at the age of 64.

So passed a very gallant gentleman. I use the last word advisedly for he was to me much more than a valued colleague; he had become a very dear friend on whose sterling quality I knew I could utterly rely. In George Tibbits the railway lost one of its most devoted and selfless supporters, a man of great and loveable character.

George Tibbits exemplified the selfless service given to the Talyllyn. Jeremy Wilkinson, his successor as honorary solicitor, continued the good work. In July 1969 the Council decided against seeking compulsory powers in its Light Railway Order. Instead it negotiated with the Forestry Commission the provision of a whole series of public footpaths. These were largely built, and are maintained, by TR and other volunteer effort. The railway constructed a footbridge over the ravine, high above the rushing torrent below, only a few yards from the platform end, thus giving easy access to the 'Shanghai' path. These forest paths, somewhat similar to nature trails, for which an illustrated leaflet is available have proved a very popular attraction, and many a day's, or even longer, walk, now begins or ends at Nant Gwernol station.

In 1980 the Talyllyn received the Prince of Wales' award for the footpaths project. The citation read:

The Project comprises the development and opening up of a network of footpaths and a new footbridge in an area of natural ravine and forest at Nant Gwernol, Abergynolwyn, where the narrow gauge Talyllyn Railway now terminates after its extension in 1976.

Apart from the temporary employment of two men for the footbridge and a certain amount of stone walling, the entire scheme has been undertaken by volunteer workers from the Talyllyn Railway Preservation Society. The Forestry Commission carried out the work on the footpaths which traverse its forests. The Countryside Commission gave a grant towards the costs of the footbridge and a local landowner was very helpful.

The work carried out on the footpaths, steps, stone walls and fences has been done with great care taking into consideration the high amenity value of the area. The footbridge has been constructed to a high standard, the design and use of natural materials adding to its setting in the ravine.

The completion of the project has opened to the public an area of natural beauty and forest allowing them to explore where there is no access for vehicles. The footpaths now provide a major open-air attraction within the Snowdonia National Park which can be used by local inhabitants and the passengers of the historic Talyllyn railway.

The footbridge was formally opened by Lord Parry, chairman of the Wales Tourist Board on 3 May 1980. But it was ten years earlier, back in July 1970, that the main scheme really started to get off the ground when the Society's council set up a Nant Gwernol Extension Project Group. It retained the part-time services of Bob Gunn, a mining engineer from Tywyn, as consultant in charge of the project, under the general direction of the railway's chief engineer, John Bate. The group's chairman was Richard Hope, and its secretary, Jeremy Wilkinson. The official inauguration of work on the extension took place on AGM day, 3 October 1970. There had however been some preliminary work, notably the demolition of the winding house, and later, causing much less anguish, some site preparation, such as the provision of a hut as store and workshop, the widening of the first two cuttings, and clearing of undergrowth, and the laying out of a siding for materials.

At 10.30 am on 3 October, a fine day, No 2 *Dolgoch* steamed out of Wharf station with a 'vintage special', comprising the ex-Corris coach, and the five original TR passenger stock. On arrival at Abergynolwyn the crowd and invited guests gathered round the water tank, on which stood Tom Rolt ready to perform the opening ceremony, accompanied by Eric Gibbons, chairman of the railway Company. After some appropriate remarks, and assuring the crowd 'we are not, as it might appear, up to our knees in the water tank', Tom duly pressed the button and the work literally started with a bang! A couple of minutes later, the Abergynolwyn policeman was observed striding up the drive from the main road clutching a large lump of rock. The company of invited guests, the Press and railway officials and others, including presumably the policeman, then retired into Abergynolwyn station for buffet refreshments. In the afternoon there was a second 'big bang'. This was for the benefit of members attending the AGM, who had come on the special train from London and Birmingham. Tom again pressed the button, and this time there was an even bigger explosion from up the line. Although he had no silver spade to keep, he did have a certificate issued under the Explosives Act.

There followed a successful call for extra volunteers. There is a particular breed of volunteer that likes hard physical work, building something new, but is less keen on actually 'playing trains'. The work proceeded steadily towards the winding house, clearing and widening the cuttings, erecting a retaining wall at Forestry Crossing in conjunction with the Commission, and renewing the bridge by the boundary gate; this last job being carried out by a unit of army cadets. The 'public notice' relating to the Light Railway Order was published in English and Welsh in *The Cambrian News* early in 1971, and no objections were received. The Order itself was issued by the Department of the Environment on 21 February 1972.

The work proceeded in fits and starts, much more being done in the summer months when more volunteers were available. These were of all sorts: Birmingham University students toughening up as part of their rugby training; Venture Scouts, the 'Hammers' from the 24th Hammersmith; another scout troop, larger in numbers but smaller in stature; a school party from Bridgnorth; a group from the Leighton Buzzard Narrow Gauge railway; and another from the Rhowniar Outward Bounds girl's school at Tywyn. The machines occasionally gave trouble. No 5 *Midlander* had to be 'pull started' on occasions by engines Nos 3 and 4 penetrating up the new line. An air shovel from Portmadoc was overhauled and regauged, and proved very useful for loading the 'arisings' (broken rock from the blasting) into wagons. Besides blasting and levelling the track bed, there was a considerable amount of other work, including concreting, often in very difficult conditions. Much of this was required to provide proper drainage,as being a very wet area with innumerable mountain streams, there would have been a grave risk of the track formation being washed away in flash floods, if culverts and other works had not been constructed. Temporary track, using old TR wrought-iron rails, was put down initially. These old rails had the advantage of being easily bent into shape, but the disadvantage that nearly half of them proved unusable on site. The laying of the permanent track was one of the final operations.

The method of operation was to lay the temporary track near the outside edge of the formation, blow up the rock, clear away the arisings, and slew the track closer into the cliff face. This sometimes had to be done as many as four times. The excavated material was dumped at the west end of Abergynolwyn station, providing 'fill' for the extension of the platform and the provision of additional track. The last stretch of original wrought-iron track, including chaired joints, was removed on 22 January 1972, from the embankment at Ty Dwr. By the end of the year the temporary track had reached the site of the old winding house.

Trouble occurred with the blasting in the autumn of 1972. Complaints were received that stones were being thrown as far as the southern edge of Abergynolwyn village. The reason for the debris being thrown so far was an indirect result of the coal strike on at that time. The powder previously used was apparently made for colliery use. This not being available, as there was no demand as the pits were closed, the quarry supplying the TR with powder sent a stronger variety, with twice the original range of scatter of about 500 feet. So blasting was suspended until the usual powder could be used; and from then on observer/sentries were posted in the village and on 'Shanghai' path. Happily there was no injury to people or property. The railway continued to benefit from gifts. An ageing wire rope broke, and a watching bystander offered to explore the possibility of a replacement. In due course a splendid new length arrived, supplied by John Shaw Ltd of Worksop.

The '10-RB' mechanical excavator, known as 'Mr Rusty,' was released from work at Pendre, and arrived on the extension on 1 July 1973, after some refurbishment in the workshops. It was brought by road to Forestry Crossing – the loading gauge (clearances) were far too narrow on the railway generally to allow the wide 'Mr Rusty' to pass – and there loaded on to a purpose-built trolley called a 'whitebait'. The mechanical excavator saved an awful lot of volunteer sweat. It was equipped on one side with a special 'waistcoat' of planks of wood to protect it from blasting scatter.

In the autumn of 1973 the compressor gave up the ghost, and whilst another one was being got ready for use, the volunteers were put to work making footpaths beyond the station site. They found the body of an old wagon still in good condition way down the slope, and salvaged it with block and tackle. The project engineer ('Head Gwern') acquired an assistant, thus reducing the number of untoward incidents: supervision of volunteer labour was much improved, and track and other repairs could be undertaken in time, thus reducing derailments to a negligible level.

In 1974 the project group put back the target for opening until spring 1976. Fifty tons of BS 50lb rail arrived at Wharf, enough to complete the extension. Because of the deteriorating security situation nationally, the police required tighter arrangements for the transport, storage and use of explosives. This somewhat delayed operations until new and acceptable procedures could be introduced. An unusual accident occurred at this time. The project engineer was making the tea and emptied the old tea leaves out of the mess van - No 7 – window. The honorary secretary's dog, 'Boston', came up to investigate. The project engineer then warmed the pot with boiling water and threw that out of the same window, scalding the unfortunate creature's rump. There was then a considerable commotion, but fortunately the dog quickly recovered, although it is said the honorary secretary lost his usual 'cool'!

The temporary track reached Nant Gwernol at Easter 1974, twenty two years after it last saw a train. At the end of the year the project group had to consider three unexpected developments. Bob Gunn felt he had to get a full time job, and this took him to Tavistock in Devon. The grant application to cover 49 per cent of the cost had to be re-submitted to the Wales Tourist Board, because the project had taken longer than expected. Thirdly, due to errors on the Ordnance Survey and TR plans, another fifteen hundred cubic yards of rock had to come out of what was known as 'Big Bend' in order to maintain the 300 feet minimum radius required. This meant that over half as much again of rock still remained to be removed as had already been excavated in the previous four and a half years since the start of the project (2400 cubic yards). As it turned out, in the final weeks, the chief engineer was persuaded by the secretary to open with a 'temporary' radius of 270 feet which has become permanent. The job had to be ready for an opening in May 1976 at the start of the season, otherwise it would slip a whole year. The police then insisted that only the supplier could deliver explosives, and ICI would not be bothered with very small loads to such a remote location. Advance notice had to be given, and the blasting take place on the day the explosives were delivered. The bangs would thus be big ones! Council therefore agreed in December to hire a contractor to finish the blasting, and urgently appealed for volunteers to get the job finished in time.

Contractors were also employed to do the stone walling necessary to support the track formation in sections where infilling was needed to ease some very erratic gradients: raising the line by up to two feet in places. Fortunately the Forestry Commission gave the railway permission to take slate from the old cutting sheds on the Cantrybedd level at Bryn Eglwys. This was brought down by lorry to Forestry Crossing, where it was loaded on to rail wagons. A large tree had to be removed from the massive stone retaining wall supporting the terminal station site at Nant Gwernol, and a buttress was also required to prevent further movement. James Wilkins was able to act as foreman during the summer months. The stone walling contractor, Alan Forster from Durham, and his gang also built a retaining wall at the eastern end of Abergynolwyn station, together with a massive base, fourteen feet high at the rear, for the new signal box. Two hundred pieces of slate suitable for platform edgings were recovered, by arrangement with the Forestry Commission, from old buildings at Bryn Eglwys.

On 5 October, the day after the 1975 AGM, the track through Abergynolwyn station was lifted prior to the realignment of the platform. The platform was extended outwards and lengthened, the signal box was erected, and the new track layout was in position by the start of the 1976 season: albeit with points clipped due to the absence of rodding. During the winter a further one hundred yards of permanent track was laid in order that the Festiniog could have the old temporary track for use in the construction of its new Moelwyn Tunnel. An inspection of the new track layout and signalling at Abergynolwyn was carried out by Major P.M. Olver of the Railways Inspectorate on 11 May 1976. These were approved as were the arrangements for the opening on 22 and 23 May. However he considered the track on the extension needed additional 'fettling', that is tidying up and doing minor adjustments, and therefore the line beyond Abergynolwyn should be closed to passenger traffic from 24-28 May to allow this to be done, re-opening on 29 May.

On 22 May the inaugural train left Wharf station promptly at 10.30, behind No 2 *Dolgoch*. Dai Jones was the driver, volunteer Philip Guest, the fireman, and the guard was member Michael Howard, the Society's archivist, arrayed in a silk top hat. The locomotive carried a large headboard with the Prince of Wales' feathers in white arising out of a gilt coronet on a blue background, the gilt lettering being in both Welsh and English. *Dolgoch* was also decorated with evergreen boughs along the sides. As the train came to a halt in Abergynolwyn station the Aberystwyth town band played the tune 'See the Conquering Hero Comes', without which no similar Victorian occasion would have been complete.

The guest of honour, Wynford Vaughan Thomas of Harlech Television, took the stand, flanked by the directors of the Company and officials of the Society. After the speeches he drove the symbolic gold-plated spike, kindly supplied by a North American member, into a specially prepared sleeper with a 'special' soft hammer. The party rejoined the train, the band struck up again, and to the plaudits of the crowd, *Dolgoch*, with whistle blowing frantically, broke through the white tape and proceeded a few yards into the extension. She stopped to pick up the photographers and then became the first public passenger train ever to reach Nant Gwernol.

The official party inspected the station and its environs, whilst the locomotive ran round. Fourteen minutes after its arrival the train departed for Abergynolwyn where Mrs Elen Thomas, the wife of the local MP, Dafydd Elis Thomas, Plaid Cymru, unveiled a commemorative plaque in English and Welsh, which is now securely fixed to the signalbox. The official train set off for Pendre, where the guests and their hosts descended for a short walk to the Neuadd Pendre social centre in Brook Street, for the 'cold collation' traditional on such occasion. Toasts were drunk, and speeches were made. Wynford Vaughan Thomas was reminded of the occasion when on the first live television broadcast from the Talyllyn - a 'Now' programme with Mr Huw Weldon exactly nineteen years earlier, 22 May 1957 – his buttons gave way. He was presented with a set of Talyllyn Railway buttons in case such a disaster should occur again.

During the rest of that day, and the next, special trains galore were run. It was very pleasing that over one hundred of the Abergynolwyn villagers took advantage of a free travel offer, in some recompense of the one or two extra lively bangs that had scattered stones amongst them. That evening 110 gallons of real ale were consumed by about 280 people. Railway building is thirsty work.

CHAPTER 11

Engines and Stock

The railway's first locomotive, *Talyllyn*, arrived in Tywyn in September 1864, having been brought by sea from Fletcher Jennings' works at Whitehaven in Cumbria. She was a small engine without a tender, with only four driving wheels and with large overhangs, particularly at the back. *Talyllyn* arrived soon after work on building the railway had started. In order to provide the motive power for the transport of materials as construction of the line advanced up the valley, and to take away the waste. But the ride, with the large overhangs, must have been somewhat like that on a bucking bronco in a Wild West Rodeo. The inspector from the Board of Trade, Captain H.W. Tyler, described it in his report in 1866, – for even in those days government permission was needed before a passenger railway could be opened – as having 'excessive vertical oscillation'. So the designers tried something entirely new with the next narrow-gauge steam locomotive they built for the TR. They attempted with No 2 *Dolgoch*, rather like those who designed the 'Mini' auto nearly a century later, to put the four wheels one in each corner. But this meant that the rear driving wheels were a long way from the drive cylinders, and indeed from the front pair of wheels. So rather complex linkages were needed, causing problems which took another 120 years to resolve. After *Dolgoch's* arrival at Tywyn in 1866, it was possible to send *Talyllyn* all the way back to Whitehaven to be fitted with a pair of wheels under the rear overhang. She thus became a 0–4–2 locomotive; no supporting wheels in front of the driving wheels, and two behind. *Dolgoch* of course remained a 0–4–0 engine.

Most of the drivers preferred to work with *Talyllyn* as they considered her to have a more comfortable ride than *Dolgoch*. For after the lengthening of her mainframe to accommodate a pair of trailing wheels, *Talyllyn* was the more rigid of the two locomotives. The permanent way gang however would have much preferred to see *Dolgoch* out on the line as she apparently did less damage to the track. Because her rigid wheelbase had been increased from 4 feet to 8 feet 4 inches, *Talyllyn* tended to push the track out of gauge, particularly on curves. But the track gang had no say; they were at the bottom of the railway's pecking order. But they too were able to make life easier for themselves. They simply re-gauged the line a little wider than the original 2ft 3in and built up the outside of the sharper curves rather more than before.

Records of the original two locomotives are scarce, and according to the TR's chief engineer, John Bate, it is uncertain exactly what repairs or overhauls were undertaken or when. However it would appear that before 1951 *Talyllyn* had undergone only one major overhaul since she had been sent back to the Lowca works at Whitehaven in 1866 to have her trailing wheels fitted. This was probably sometime in the 1890s when she was returned to Whitehaven for a new firebox and boiler repairs. Shortly after her return she was rebuilt with new steel frames in the Pendre works.

In 1952 *Talyllyn* was moved out of the works, where she had languished unused since 1944, and was deposited in the hay barn on the north side of Pendre yard. Most members at that time considered *Talyllyn* was a complete write-off and likely to remain so, with a completely worn-out boiler, a cracked cylinder casting – the final blow which had led to her being finally laid up – and the rest of her in a very poor state.

But some other TRPS members regarded it as a duty to put the railway's original locomotive back into working order, if at all possible. By 1957, with sufficient locomotive power available to run the required services, and a track that could carry the trains without them falling off, members had enough energy to look again at what to do with No 1. Besides, they wanted the space occupied by the barn and No 1 for the new north carriage shed! The Midland Area of the Society, notably in the person of its chairman, Eric Gibbons, chairman and managing director of Gibbons Bros Ltd, engineers of Brierley Hill, offered to put the locomotive back into service. *Talyllyn* left Pendre on 24 March 1957, as the return load for the lorry that had brought a four-wheel Ruston diesel locomotive, No 5 *Midlander*, from Jee's quarry at Nuneaton.

After loading up No 1 the vehicle was parked outside the cinema at Tywyn, whilst the working party members and lorry crew took lunch in the upstairs dining room of the White Hall hotel opposite. One of the party had produced a pair of notice boards which were fixed to the loco. They proclaimed, in Welsh, 'I shall return home again'. This was an attempt to reassure the local populace that the engine was not being taken away for scrapping. After lunch it was discovered the notices had been removed. It was explained that the Welsh used was not the local variety but that used in South Wales. On Jane, the hotel waitress certifying she understood what was written, the boards were re-instated, and the lorry and *Talyllyn* departed for Brierley Hill, where the loco underwent a complete re-build.

Another story told of No 1 is that whilst laid up in the barn she was used as an egg repository by William Jones, the old hedger. He used to keep chickens at Pendre in the early and mid-fifties, and was in the habit of leaving new laid eggs in the sandbox of *Talyllyn*. A volunteer discovering this practice one day added two very hard-boiled eggs to those already stored in the sandbox. It was never discovered whether the owner of the eggs intended to boil or fry them!

Unfortunately Gibbons Ltd, not being locomotive engineers, did not realise that the apparently minor changes they made to the original design of *Talyllyn* would have quite serious effects. Immediately on her return to Tywyn on 14 June 1958 modifications were required. She was three inches higher than before, so the couplings did not match. The track was now in gauge at 2ft 3in, but the locomotive wheels were not, so flanges had to be removed. Nor did she steam well. This was partly due to trouble with the valves, and according to Roy Smith, an early volunteer and driver, formerly an engineer with ICI, no bottom on the smokebox. It was quite some time before it was realised that in fitting a new welded boiler Gibbons had not appreciated that the original design was what gave the engine its stability, the boiler being part of the rigid frame. The engine had to be withdrawn again in 1968 for another overhaul, this time at Pendre. She did not reappear again until 1972. Whilst better, she was still a rather shy steamer. Her pulling power was such that she was limited to a five-coach train. Generally she was satisfactory, but with occasional somewhat irritating mechanical failures. In 1982 the engine again underwent a major rebuild at Pendre. The valve gear was re-designed and an entirely new rear frame section fitted. The engine was now longer than it had ever been, with a nine-foot total wheelbase. Again it was four years before No 1 re-appeared in time for the 1986 AGM, at first without cab. She re-entered passenger service on 31 October. In over thirty years John Bate had learned almost all there was to know about *Talyllyn*, and incorporating his knowledge into the last re-build, the engine was probably running better and more efficiently than at any time previously in her 120-plus years of existence.

In 1972 No 1 went to London to take part in the Lord Mayor's show. She was put on a low-loader road vehicle at Wharf on 7 November, decorated by the London Welsh Society with the help of the Wales Tourist Board, and became their float in the procession on November 12, with locomotive superintendent Herbert Jones as 'driver' and Roy Smith as 'fireman': and there was a photograph in *The Times* to prove it.

But there was another locomotive called *Talyllyn*, named in honour of the original, and of the Talyllyn Preservation Society. This was a British Rail class 86/2 electric locomotive, No 86,258 (later re-numbered 86501), first used for heading West Coast main line expresses out of Euston. On platform 20 at Euston on 30 April 1984, the then Parliamentary Under Secretary of State for Transport, David Mitchell, named her *Talyllyn*. The words 'First Preserved Railway' also appear on the nameplate. The plate is surmounted with the Talyllyn Railway Company's crest, the 'Prince of Wales' feathers' surrounded by a garter carrying the company name, copied from the common seal of the TR, found by Tom Rolt, hidden away in the old Wharf office. Up against the buffers on adjacent platform 19 at the same time was a BR 'flatrol' wagon with TR loco No 3 *Sir Haydn*, resplendent as part of the *Mid-Wales Express*, then touring the country as a Development Board of Rural Wales promotion. Pat Garland the Society president presented the then Mr (later Sir David) Mitchell with a scale model of *Talyllyn* made by Wessex member Tony Gilmour. Also present were over one hundred members of the Society, including the Rev. W. Awdry and Tom Rolt's widow, Sonia; and David Rayner, once BR area manager at Machynlleth, and by then a senior BR general manager. In October the same year Pat Garland was presented at Euston by Malcolm Southgate, general manager of British Rail, London Midland Region, with a framed coloured photograph of 86,258 *Talyllyn*, prior to being entertained to lunch.

No 2 *Dolgoch* remained largely unaltered. She appears to have had some sort of overhaul during the Boer War. She was being repainted when news was received that the British Army had entered the enemy's capital. So the event was commemorated by re-naming her *Pretoria*, but at the next repaint she reverted to *Dolgoch*.

As already stressed *Dolgoch* was the only motive power available in the Society's first season. The engine was virtually as she had been for the previous eighty five years. The only known major repairs undertaken in that time were boiler repairs at the Britannia Foundry in Portmadoc in 1938, and again at the Atlas Foundry, Shrewsbury in 1945. In 1951 she was in a sorry state and was only kept going with great difficulty. In the following year she could share duties, as other locomotive power became available, and in 1953 was used only as a spare engine.

At this point, with two other working steam engines in the shed, three Midland area members offered to have her overhauled at Hunt Bros at Oldbury in the Black Country. There was a shortage of susitable spare labour and the work dragged on. The old boiler was sent away to Hunslet's at Leeds in 1957 and they sent back a new boiler, virtually replicating the original one, in 1958. Work started again in 1961, but in 1962 the locomotive was transferred to the nearby works of Gibbons Bros for work to be completed. In that year the loco took part in the Coventry Carnival. It was still not realised that the boiler barrel formed part of the locomotive's frame stiffness, and although the boiler as received from Hunslet's had the brackets needed to fix the boiler to the engine's framework, these were removed as 'superfluous'. *Dolgoch* was finally returned to Tywyn, after having been away ten years, in 1963. Preservation can be a slow process.

Various steaming problems were overcome, but still the engine did not steam as well as it should. A great deal of effort went into trying to unravel difficulties with the valve gear. She began to show problems of excessive movement in the frame, just like *Talyllyn*. However she ran quite well for the next ten years until a tube failure in 1973 revealed the need for complete re-tubing. In 1977 she was taken into Pendre for a complete overhaul. The frame was strengthened, and the springing changed. She was put back into service in 1980, and apart from being re-tubed in 1984 and having a different kind of spring fitted in 1985, has since run smoothly. The 1865 patented Fletcher-Allan valve gear had always been a problem. John Bate made a full-size model of it in 1985 to analyse its performance and try out improvements, and some of these have been incorporated into the valve settings with good results. In 1982 *Dolgoch* was taken around England on an exhibition train, and for a time was displayed in the National Railway Museum in York, having to be rushed back to Tywyn because a national rail strike threatened, and she was needed for the summer season.

A somewhat unusual feature of the two locomotives, and therefore copied subsequently on all the other TR vehicles, is the provision of two side buffers, at each end of the engine. Nearly all narrow gauge railways, including the earlier Festiniog, have a single buffer in the centre, incorporating the coupling mechanism. The buffers on the TR stock are rather on the large side in relation to the small size of the vehicles, somewhat out of scale. This is because the makers, Fletcher Jennings, had the habit of using the same components, wherever possible, on all sizes of locomotives.

In 1951 the Talyllyn bought its first new stock for eighty five years: two second-hand locomotives for £25 each! According to Bill Trinder, as he and Tom Rolt travelled to and from the meetings in Birmingham, things came up for discussion in the car. One night he remembered saying that although he was brought up on the

Ten Commandments, one of which states 'Thou shalt not covet thy neighbour's goods', he was tempted by the two locomotives standing under their tarpaulins at Machynlleth. (He was referring to two locomotives belonging to the Corris railway, closed in 1947, after flooding of the River Dovey after the severe winter had undermined the bridge. Before the bridge was dismantled, the two locos, with the brake goods van, and a few open goods wagons were withdrawn to Machynlleth. The story goes that Mr Campbell Thomas, then stationmaster at Machynlleth was anxious that they should go to the TR knowing that Edward Thomas was interested in buying them, but had no funds available at the time. Mr Campbell Thomas therefore made sure that they were swathed in tarpaulins and stabled behind a rake of standard gauge wagons at the back of the yard, well hidden from prying eyes.

'We ought to have them', Trinder said. 'We'll have to do something about it.' He knew two or three of the Banbury drivers well, including one called Hambridge who had driven the Royal train several times, and always asked after the Talyllyn when he met Trinder in the street. One day Trinder asked George Hambridge if he would introduce him to the shed master at Banbury, and as George was going on duty he took him straight along. Trinder explained that he was interested in getting hold of the two narrow-gauge locomotives for the Talyllyn. As the engines had by then passed into the ownership of British Rail, Western Region, Trinder asked whom he should see at Swindon who might be able to help them. He and his colleagues felt it was a pity the engines should be standing there rusting away when they could do with them. It turned out that the shedmaster had, years before, been an apprentice at Wolverhampton with the chief mechanical engineer (CME) at Swindon. So Trinder was given the CME's telephone number, and advised to ring for an appointment, mentioning the shed master as his contact. This he did the next morning, and somewhat to his surprise was put straight through to that exalted personage, the CME. Bill Trinder explained that he was the chairman of the Talyllyn Railway Preservation Society – 'rather a mouthful' was the response – and they were interested in the two locomotives. He was informed they were to be brought back to Swindon for scrapping. Trinder asked for a

Abergynolwyn station around 1960 with No 6 *Douglas* heading a short train, prior to running round at the then terminus (John Adams)

The first refreshment room at Abergynolwyn station. 31 May 1953 (J. J. Davis)

The refreshment van en route to Abergynolwyn behind No 6 *Douglas* in 1967, followed by the Corris coach No 17, a vintage coach, and TR-built standard coach No 18 (Talyllyn Railway)

Refreshment van in use on its purpose-built siding at Abergynolwyn in August 1966. No 2 *Dolgoch* with up train in the main platform (John Adams)

No 4 *Edward Thomas* taking water at the old water point by Ty Mawr on the then mineral extension whilst on a rail-lifting train in 1951 or 1952 (John Slater)

No 2 *Dolgoch* approaching Nant Gwerol station in mid-1976 (Talyllyn Railway)

No 3 *Sir Haydn* beginning to run round its train at Nant Gwernol in mid 1976 (Talyllyn Railway)

No 4 *Edward Thomas* arriving at Nant Gwernol in the mid-eighties. Volunteer driver, dentist Viv Thorpe (Talyllyn Railway)

Top Winding House at Bryn Eglwys and derelict cottage July 1953 (John Adams)

David Curwen on footplate of No 2, probably in 1951 (Talyllyn Railway)

No 5 diesel *Midlander* with works train, when there was a quarry worked by volunteers, loading ballast at Quarry siding April 1961 (John Adams)

North West Area working party digging out and loading ballast at Quarry Siding in April 1961 (John Adams)

Guiness locomotive No 13 at Wharf before being placed in the Narrow Gauge
Railway Museum. 5 August 1958 (J. J. Davis)

No 2 (with barn door to keep out the weather), four wagons and the Corris
van No 6, at Quarry Siding on Sunday 11 May 1952 (John Slater)

Getting No 4 'Edward Thomas' back on the rails after a derailment at
Rhydyronen in June 1958 (John Adams)

No *Dolgoch* being pulled on to a low-loader at Wharf in September 1954,
having been pushed up the ramp by No 3 *Sir Haydn*. Note that No 3 still has its
Corris centre linkage not having yet been fitted with TR buffers. No 6 *Douglas*
in attendance (J. C. Flemons)

The semaphore signal in Wharf cutting on 19 June 1954. A 'lower quadrant home', the arm was painted red with a white stripe. Erected by Charles Uren, Superintendent of the Line, this and a similar signal at Brynglas were soon removed by order of the Railway Inspectorate! (John Slater)

Volunteers at Brynglas ground frame in August 1965 (John Adams)

No 3 *Sir Haydn* ex-Corris, still without TR buffers, on a works train including original TR wagons in 1953; Bill Oliver driving (John Slater)

Rev W. Awdry with *Sir Handel* (TR No 3) from his fictitious Skarloey Railway. 6 June 1982 (Talyllyn Railway)

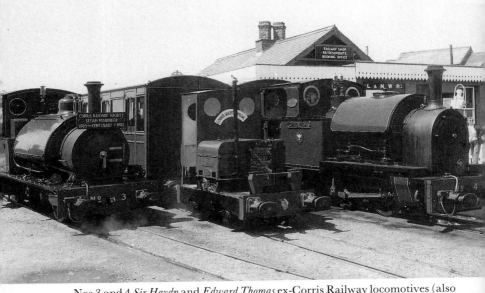

Nos 3 and 4 *Sir Haydn* and *Edward Thomas* ex-Corris Railway locomotives (also Nos 3 and 4), with visiting current Corris Railway diesel engine No 5 *Alan Meaden* 4 July 1983 (Patrick Smith)

Herbert Jones and Lord Northesk with No 4 on 21 September 1956 (J. J. Davis)

The original TR loco No 5, built by David Curwen in his works at Devizes, using the Model 'T' Ford engine from Tom Rolt's canalboat *Cressy*, about to leave Wharf for the first time on 17 October 1952 (John Slater)

The original TR loco No 7 *Charlie's Ant*. 31 July 1954 (J. J. Davis)

The pressure of passenger numbers led to the use of unorthodox means of accommodation! Pendre 29 August 1953. (Note the National Servicemen from local camps) (John Bate)

Ex-Penrhyn quarry coach No 8 at Wharf 12 August 1954 (J. J. Davis)

Ex-Corris large wagon (TR No 1) – one of two large wagons known as *Queen Marys* outside Wharf station office on 11 May 1952 (John Slater)

TR slate wagon July 1958 (John Adams)

Tom Rolt preparing to set off the first charge of the rock blasting at the official start of work on the Nant Gwernol Extension on 3 October 1970. Eric Gibbons, Chairman of the Company is also on the 'platform' on top of the water tower (John Adams)

Tom Rolt as guard selling tickets from TR Van No 5 in June 1951 (Talyllyn Railway)

meeting rather than discuss the matter on the telephone, and was invited over. Bill Trinder was delighted. He had always wanted to go to Swindon. He remarked to Tom Rolt, as they were led through the maze of corridors and got near the 'big door,' that to be in the same office where Gooch, Churchward and Collett and the other great GWR engineers had reigned felt 'like Moses standing on holy ground'.

There had actually been a considerable amount of investigation and heart-searching before Bill Trinder was asked to try and make a contact at Swindon. As Tom Rolt recorded in *Railway Adventure* he, with David Curwen and Jim Russell, had already taken a good look at the engines. Corris No 3 had been built by Hughes of Loughborough in 1878, and No 4 by Kerr, Stuart of Stoke-on-Trent in 1921. This was the firm to which Tom Rolt had been apprenticed, and he described his chagrin when a colleague was sent down to Wales in 1929 to undertake repairs instead of himself. He understood the asking price was £65 for each engine, and with the cost of carriage, and the cost of putting the permanent way in order the Committee felt they could not afford to buy both. No 3 was the more complex engine, but was in reasonable order, and apparently could be put into service fairly quickly. No 4 was a more straightforward, simple type of engine, with its works accessible, built for industrial use, and more suited to the Talyllyn's requirements. But it had seen much heavier service and would require an extended and expensive overhaul. The problem seemed insoluble. Finally Tom, Bill and Jim Russell volunteered to go to Swindon to see if they could get the two for the price of one.

Trinder recalled that he spoke quite briefly for about fifteen minutes and concluded by asking to be given the locomotives. Tom Rolt commented that Bill Trinder put their case so eloquently and with such feeling, that if it had still been the days of the GWR, pre-nationalisation, they would have got the engines for nothing. Trinder in fact states that the CME told them that he would have done just that in the days when his word alone went at Swindon. But now no one there, nor indeed anywhere on BR, was apparently empowered to give anything away. However he said while Swindon had the authority to dispose of the two engines, they had gone out of his jurisdiction, and were now under that of the chief stores superintendent. (Tom Rolt states in *Railway Adventure* that this was the official they saw. Bill Trinder however stated that it was the CME whom they met.) The CME asked them to wait a few minutes while he went off and consulted his colleague. He was away three quarters of an hour. Tom and Bill waited in suspense, but filled in the time by having a good old browse round that historic impressive office.

It was decided that the engines could be written off the books at a much lower figure than previously envisaged, and they could have them for £25 each. Bill Trinder remembered expressing his thanks for this generosity, leaning across the table and shaking hands to clinch the deal, promising the cheque would be in the post next morning. He felt sure that the treasurer, Pat Garland, would raise no objection. He rang up on his return home, 'and the cheque was put in the post immediately, so they couldn't go back on the deal'. Bill Trinder was a very keen Rotarian and used to claim he had addressed fifty five clubs on the merits of the Talyllyn and its preservation. On the Monday following the visit to Swindon he was telling the Talyllyn story to the Rotary Club at Tamworth, 'and old Jimmy Black who had been in a wheelchair for sixty years at that time was so impressed that he wrote out a cheque for £25 on the spot'. The delivery in March 1951 to Wharf cost another £68, still pretty cheap when it is considered a steam crane had to be brought all the way from Oswestry to do the lifting. A member in Leeds had already bought the Corris van for £2 10s, but generously donated it to the TR. It was moved to Tywyn together with the engine. Also included in the move were nearly all the Corris goods wagons, which the Talyllyn had taken the opportunity of purchasing at the same time, for 10s (50p) each. The additional transport cost in respect of the eleven wagons and the van was £7.

No 3 on the Corris became No 3 on the Talyllyn: similarly No 4. They were named *Sir Haydn* and *Edward Thomas* respectively. The naming of No 3 was agreed unanimously in committee, but for No 4 there was a good deal of support for the name 'James Swinton Spooner', to commemorate the engineer who designed and built the railway. The voting was 7 to 4 in favour of *Edward Thomas*. However the names were even more appropriate than those responsible for their selection realised. It has recently come to light (in an article by Richard S. Greenhough in *Railway Magazine*, March 1988) that if it had not been for the actions of Sir Haydn and Edward Thomas in the mid-thirties the GWR would have closed the Corris, and sold off its track and locomotives for scrap. Henry Haydn Jones had taken over the running of Aberllefenni quarry in 1935. Edward Thomas became company secretary there, as he was of the Abergynolwyn Slate & Quarry Co. The amount of slate passing along the Corris railway and through Machynlleth was continuing to decline, in spite of a large tarrif reduction made by the GWR two years earlier in an effort to meet road competition. At a meeting called by an increasingly restive GWR, Edward Thomas pointed out that if customers specified delivery by road, especially if they bought ex-quarry, the quarry management had no option but to comply. Sir Haydn at a later meeting indicated that he had turned down the offer of a local road haulage company to carry all the slate at a lower cost per ton than that charged by the railway. He had turned it down because he wanted the railway to keep running. Indeed he was somewhat miffed because his own workers and their families seemed to prefer to travel by bus rather than using his train services.

Deliveries from Aberllefenni quarry to North Wales took one day by road and three by rail. This was partly due to the fact that one loading and unloading was needed by road and three by rail, the additional two being at Machynlleth and at the ultimate rail head, if the customer did not have his own rail siding. Aberllefenni quarry was accessible by road, unlike Bryneglwys quarry served by the Talyllyn Railway. The quarrymen transshipped the slate at Machynlleth from Corris to GWR wagons. The Corris train arrived at 15.30. Their reaction to a demand that they should then carry out the work so as to catch the 0.15 freight north next morning, so ensuring next day delivery, was that 'it was impossible'. There is nothing new in inflexibility in working arrangements bringing about local unemployment.

In 1900 No 3 was apparently returned to its makers in Loughborough, by then the Falcon Engine & Car Works, now the Brush Company, part of the Hawker-Siddley Group, for rebuilding with a larger boiler. She was also lengthened to incorporate a pony-truck with very small wheels beneath the cab. In 1920 she was rebuilt at Corris using bits from condemned sister engine No 1. John Snell writing about No 3 in 1954 said he had only one grave complaint against her: 'I am six feet plus, and her cab was designed with no one taller than 4ft 6in in mind. In 1878 this didn't matter, since all Welsh narrow-gauge locomotives were driven by this specially-bred race of pigmies. If you don't believe this look at any old photograph of a Corris or Festiniog engine and observe that the relative sizes of it and its driver are exactly the same as those of a main line locomotive and its driver. These pigmies are now unfortunately extinct.

With some very hard work, David Curwen had managed to get *Sir Haydn* steaming by June 1951, but almost catastrophically, in view of the railway's complete dependence on the ailing *Dolgoch*, she proved unusable. A vital point had, quite understandably, been overlooked at the preliminary inspection. No 3 had wheels half an inch narrower in the tyre tread than the other engines and stock. (Locomotive wheels consist of a metal centre on to which are 'heat-shrunk' metal tyres.) Consequently when she ran on the then out-of-gauge unstable Talyllyn track, she simply subsided between the rails. So she had to be stored for another couple of years until 1953 when the track was more or less at last firmly in gauge. On returning to service it was found there was a considerable amount of corrosion, and she had to work at reduced pressure. At this time, because her vacuum brake reservoir was placed on the nearside of the cab closing off the footplate on that side, she had to be run 'wrong way round', with the cab pointing up the line, to give access to the platforms. In 1958, No 3 was withdrawn from service to await the purchase of a new boiler. This came from J. & W. Gower of Bedford in 1964, and the engine resumed service in 1968, after a ten-year lay-up: this time 'the right way round'. New tyres were fitted in 1976. To celebrate her centenary in 1978, the Corris Railway Study Group ran a special train on 6 May comprising the Corris coach and van. No 3 had a special headboard; and for the rest of the season she ran with another headboard 'the Falcon Centenarian'. She was taken on a low-loader belonging to the Brush Group by road to their works at Loughborough, where she was originally built, for exhibition on 1 and 2 September.

In 1982 she was overhauled and re-appeared as *Sir Handel* in a red livery, on loan from the Skarloey railway on the island of Sodor, as recorded in the *Thomas the Tank Engine* series of children's books by TRPS member (since 1951) the Rev Wilbert Awdry. This marketing ploy, launched by Mr Awdry in May 1982, lasted for two years, and resulted in many more passengers. The series included five books about the 'Little Engines' of the Skarloey railway, one of them written by his son and TRPS member Christopher, for whom the original series was created. The Skarloey engines are the exact counterparts of the Talyllyn steam locomotives, and are acknowledged as such in the books which contain an exhortation to visit the Talyllyn. Thousands of children, and their parents, have followed this advice.

Incidentally, when the Rev W. Awdry was asked why so many churchmen are interested in railways, he replied that British railways and the Church had several things in common. They were both large organisations, subject to much criticism, and each one thought it had the best means of getting customers to their destinations.

No 4 had a new boiler, with more tubes, fitted by Kerr, Stuart in 1928, as the original one evidently proved inadequate. The locomotive was worked hard until 1947 when it was taken out of service to await boiler repairs. So it was unusable when it arrived at Pendre. Very little work had been done on it when John Alcock, chairman of the Hunslet Engine Co Ltd (successors to Kerr, Stuart) of Leeds, offered a complete overhaul, provided the TR paid for the carriage and cranage. As this amounted to £56 16s 8d, far cheaper than employing a fitter, the committee accepted with alacrity. The work involved the repair and overhaul of the boiler, a new saddle-tank, the installation of a mechanical lubricator, removal of the vacuum brake-equipment, thus giving access from the platform side, plus the fitting of a second injector, and other renewals and repairs. It was done very satisfactorily, by people who knew what they were doing, on what was a comparatively modern, standard type locomotive, compared with Nos 1, 2 and 3. She was back in service in June 1952 in time for the second running season. *Edward Thomas* provided much needed relief for *Dolgoch*, and has ever since worked reliably and economically. In 1958 she acquired a long narrow fishtail chimney. This was the Giesl Ejector blastpipe and chimney, intended to reduce fuel consumption and increase efficiency. British Rail has proved reluctant to accept an offer of a free trial by its inventor, Dr Giesl-Gieslingen of Vienna. But when he made the same offer to the Talyllyn it was taken up with great enthusiasm, although a few members had their doubts. It brought a considerable amount of publicity, including questions in Parliament, as to why a private railway was making technical fuel-saving innovations, whilst the great nationalised industry even shunned a free trial. (BR eventually did buy two Giesl ejectors, but found they could achieve equally good results by other means, and thus avoid paying royalties to Dr Giesl.) Tom Rolt claimed it was an outstanding success, and it was taken up by standard-gauge railways all over the world. The Talyllyn *Handbook* states that 'on the Talyllyn it did not achieve its intended aim and in 1969 when the Giesl Ejector was in need of major repair, the original chimney and blastpipe [still in store as is the TR custom] were replaced'. No 4 was fitted with a new Hunslet-supplied boiler in 1964. A major overhaul was carried out at Pendre from 1976-8 when the engine resumed service. In 1983 a new inner firebox was fitted into the boiler by Israel Newton & Sons at Bradford.

On 14 May 1988 No 4 re-entered service after a brief overhaul and repaint. But this time in red livery as No 4 *Peter Sam* of the Skarloey railway, whose owner Sir Handel Brown had kindly agreed to loan him to the Talyllyn. Sir Handel also kindly once again arranged for the Rev. W. Awdry, his son Christopher and grandson Richard, 'to visit Tywyn, conduct the handing over ceremony, and convey his greetings to the Talyllyn management with whom his relationship has always been most cordial'.

In 1983 a unique event on the TR occurred when a visiting locomotive ran on its rails for the first time. Serious attempts were being made by the Corris Railway Society to reopen part of the old Corris line. On 2 and 3 July 1983, they organised a 'Corris

Railway Week-end' on the Talyllyn, featuring their diesel loco-motive No 5 (Motor Rail 22258 of 1965), named *Alan Meaden* in honour of their founder, a member of the TRPS, and a working volunteer in the late fifties. This diminutive-sized engine, much smaller than any of the Talyllyn's, hauled a rake consisting of TR coach No 18, designed by Alan Meaden, and built at Pendre for the TR Centenary in 1965, together with TR van No 5. The other Corris special was headed by No 3 *Sir Haydn*, most appro-priately still in its red livery, for that had been its colour when it ran on the Corris. The rake consisted of ex-Corris Coach No 17 – the 'royal' carriage – three ex-Corris wagons, Nos 1, 2 and 4, and the ex-Corris van No 6. A happy occasion, with several Corris pensioners present, including Humphrey Humphreys of the village of Corris. Humphrey, aged 77, had started work on the Corris as a teenager and drove the last train in 1948. Other pensioners who attended were Tom Jones aged over 90, who had been a horse man; Evan Williams, a clerk; Gwilym Jones, a guard and stationmaster; Ieuan Roberts, a shedman; and Mr and Mrs David Owen, who had worked on the Corris buses.

In 1952 Lord Northesk, the president of the Talyllyn Railway Preservation Society, had written to several hundred heads of firms seeking assistance. Pat Whitehouse recalled that he had a phone call one day in February 1953 from a firm called Abelsons offering the railway a narrow-gauge locomotive in their possession. Built in 1918 by Andrew Barclay of Kilmarnock for the Admiralty, it had spent most of its life at RAF Calshot on Southampton Water. Although it was of two foot gauge, Mr Wilkins and Mr Hunt, who inspected it on 28 February 1953 agreed it could easily be converted to the TR gauge of two feet three inches. Mr Hunt agreed to do this at his works, with the aid of Mr Wilkins. Mr Whitehouse arranged free transport to Oldbury, and then, when the job was done, on to Tywyn. The committee accepted the offer with thanks, and agreed that the engine should be called *Douglas* after the donor, Mr Douglas Abelson, and that a suitable presentation plate would be placed on her. Mr Wilkins arranged for this to be done, and Mr Whitehouse organised the public handing-over ceremony. She entered service in 1954. While reliable and economical on normal duties, she was a bit light for trains of more than five coaches. She had a new inner firebox in 1961, and new tubes and smokebox in 1974, while still retaining her original boiler. But in 1988 a boiler inspection revealed parts of the boiler plate had worn thin and working pressure had to be reduced to 120 lbs per square inch.

The Company has another steam locomotive, No 7, first named, after much controversy, at a Society AGM in 1970, *Irish Pete*. The name arose because the engine was bought, very cheaply, from the Irish Turf Board in 1969, when increasing traffic levels suggested there might one day be a need for another powerful reliable locomotive. Built in 1948 by Andrew Barclay, and designed to burn peat – but it wouldn't – she had seen little use. She was dismantled to be rebuilt, and work progressed steadily until 1973. However a decline in traffic meant the urgency became less, and in the allocation of priorities for capital expenditure, work on No 7 slipped further and further down the list, almost out of sight. However when it began to look cheaper to complete No 7 than incur heavy expenditure on the boiler of No 6, council decided in 1988 work should be resumed, and it is hoped the engine will be in service by the Company's 125th anniversary celebrations in 1990. At the Society's 1989 AGM it was decided by a narrow majority of four votes to rename No 7 *Tom Rolt* in preference to *Cader Idris*.

All the locos now have 'foreign' whistles, extracted from 'main line' locomotives long since broken up. Engine No 4 *Edward Thomas* has the large whistle from GWR Castle class No 7007 *Great Western*, on permanent loan from its owner Roy Smith. He acquired it by approaching Harry Cureton, the shed foreman at Worcester BR in 1963. He was told he could not have it because the engine had been sold to Cashmore's of Tipton, and John Cashmore was complaining bitterly of locomotives arriving with many moveable items missing. So Roy, nothing daunted, set off for Tipton. On arrival he asked to buy a loco whistle and was offered dozens. But he wanted the one still on 7007 at Worcester. After parting with £2 10s, he was given a letter of authorisation, with which, on presentation to Harry Cureton, he got his whistle. The whistle on No 1 *Talyllyn* is the small whistle from GWR 7007, also supplied by Roy Smith. No 3 carries the spare whistle formerly kept at

Stratford shed on the Eastern Region for the 'Britannia' class. How it got to Pendre is somewhat of a mystery. No 6 *Douglas* has the whistle from an LNER engine *Sparrow Hawk*, an AF Pacific No 4463(60018). This was presented by TR volunteer David Ratcliffe of Wembley Park, who also provided a whistle from the former Kittybrewster shed for No 2. Engine No 2 previously had the only pre-1923 vintage 'hooter'; reputedly to have come from the Caledonian railway, and now in store at Pendre. It is said to have arrived at Tywyn still fitted to No 6, a relic from its days with the RAF at Calshot.

The railway has three diesel locomotives used for works trains. No 5 *Midlander* came from Jee's quarries at Hartshill near Nuneaton in 1957. The quarry manager is reported to have asked £900 for her. Pat Garland burst out laughing and offered £2, and they closed at £150. From 1963 to 1965 No 5 hauled the short-lived 'Fridays only' winter service for local residents. From 1971-6 it was based at Abergynolwyn for work on the Nant Gwernol extension. Because of difficulties with parts, an identical second Ruston & Hornsby diesel was acquired and cannibalised.

There had been an earlier No 5 intended to run the winter train service and haul works trains. Delivered in September 1952, it had been built by David Curwen in his works at Devizes, using the Model 'T' Ford 20 bph (with luck!) petrol engine taken out of Tom Rolt's canal boat *Cressy*. The engine could just manage one TR coach, plus the Corris van. The TR van was too heavy. The committee's initial reluctance to spend money on this project proved justified, for the gearbox which worked on the boat was unsatisfactory for rail use. The loco lacked adhesion. The wheels spun round on the rail without gripping. It also tended to overheat when the radiator was not facing forward. Its greatest moment, which brought about its last, was on 26 October 1952, when it rescued No 4 *Edward Thomas* after a derailment. This had taken place the previous day half a mile west of Dolgoch. The first No 5 just about managed to bring the 'dead' engine and its load of ballast wagons back to Pendre. In doing so it overstrained its gearbox, and although this was patched up, it was never the same again. The original No 5's last trip was hauling the Friday train on 17 April 1953. Repair was intended, but other diesel traction became available, and after standing around in the yard for several years gathering rust, it was dismantled and its frame became the basis of a flat wagon.

There was also an earlier No 7, irreverently called 'Charley's Ant' after Charles Uren, chief engineer at the time. This was a Mercury Tractor presented to the Society by a member, Major C.S.N. Walker of Gloucester. It was promptly converted to burn paraffin in place of petrol. The idea of this new motorised vehicle was to provide motive power for works trains when it was uneconomic to use a steam locomotive. Introduced into service in mid-1954 it then seemed to have spent a fair proportion of its time being overhauled, adjusted or repaired. It could be turned anywhere on the track by being pivoted on a jack fitted to the underside of the vehicle. It suffered considerable structural damage when some bright spark attempted to drive it off with the jack still down. It began to be used less frequently after the arrival of No 5 *Midlander* in 1957, and after gradually rusting away in Pendre yard was disposed of for scrap.

No 8 *Merseysider* is another Ruston diesel, originally working on the three feet gauge line at Park Gate Steel works at Rotherham. This plant closed down in 1967, and in 1969 three of its locomotives were acquired by the TR and cannibalised into one. It is used for shunting and works trains, and in emergency, with a reputed, but disputed, top speed of 13 mph, can be used for passenger trains. It ran the Abergynolwyn-Nant Gwernol push-and-pull shuttle service, with specially equipped ex-Corris coach No 17, on AGM Day 1987. No 8 can also be driven very slowly, having hydraulic drive, which makes it useful for hedge-cutting. The cab gives full weather protection and it can be driven from either side.

No 9 *Alf* is a standard underground loco built by the Hunslet Company for the National Coal Board and used at Huncoat Colliery, Lancashire. The TR bought two, overhauled one, and dismantled the other for spares. Powerful, but slow and without a cab, the machine is used mainly for ballast and engineering trains. The railway still uses volunteer man and womanpower to shunt carriages and wagons, one at a time, and is reputed to have used a horse in pre-Society days, to bring back home a broken-down No 2: but that's another story.

Over the years the railway has had various platelayers' trolleys. North West Area built a small hand trolley in 1953 and this stimulated London Area, in particular John Bate, into designing and building a powered trolley, for which he still has the original drawings. It was specifically designed from first principles, purpose-built to be powered by an internal combustion engine, and to have space for the track gang and the necessary tools to be carried. The frames and wheels were bought in and delivered to John Bate then living at Capenhurst. The Austin 7 engine was provided by Society member John Wilkes, who at that time was involved in preserving 'Baby Austins.' The completed trolley was sent up by freight train, but without its magneto, retained for security reasons by John Bate. It could only be run-in between Wharf and Ty Mawr Bridge, then under repair, but entered service on 31 December 1954. The Austin radiator proved to be too small for railway use, and combined with unsuitable gearing led to over-heating. So the original radiator was replaced with a larger one from a Morris 10, and the chain sprockets were changed. The trolley, now called *Toby*, for it is still in use, has two gear boxes, one used for reverse. The simple steel chassis on four wheels carries a flat platform on which are mounted the engine, a driving seat and tool box. Three people can sit on the tool box, two on the engine cover, so with the driver, the seating capacity is six. The machine can also haul an additional trolley or wagon.

Carriage No 1 – numbers were only introduced after the Society take-over – is an open carriage with three compartments of facing wooden seats. Each compartment has its own door, opened by turning a magnificent brass handle, and each door is fitted with a drop-slide window with a genuine leather strap. (In more recent years a spectator watching the windows being closed is reported to have remarked 'See, they wear safety belts on that railway.') All the doors on the south side of this and all other passenger vehicles are permanently fastened. This was done soon after delivery, at the command of Captain H.W. Tyler, who in his report to the Committee of the Privy Council for Trade dated 25 September 1866, pointed out that the bridges already built on the line were only 9ft 1in wide, whilst the carriage the Company had bought was over five feet wide, and thus there was but 1ft 11in between the outside of the carriage and the abutments, instead of the 2ft 6in which there ought to be.

> Mr McConnel, the Chairman of the Company, proposes to obviate this difficulty by permanently fastening the door and barring the windows on one side of the carriages, and slewing the rails so as to allow sufficient space between the one side and the abutment. The objection to this course is that if a carriage was turned over on the unbarred side, with the barred side uppermost, the passengers would be unable to escape from it. But it must be admitted that this objection has not the same force in the case of a line of this description, on which only one engine will be employed for passengers and minerals at a speed intended to be not greater than ten miles an hour and on which the passenger traffic will be so limited that it would not be worth while for the Company to carry passengers at all if much extra expense was to be incurred in the works as on lines of higher speed and greater traffic.

The doors were then permanently fastened and barred and have never been opened since. The Talyllyn only has platforms to the north of its lines. However the track to this day remains unslewed, still in the centre of the bridge openings.

No 2 coach is identical to No 1, but while in outward appearance No 3 seems the same, at some time in the past it has been sub-divided with a partition to give a single compartment at one end. Coach No 4 was built by the Lancaster Coach Company and is straight-sided, unlike the three Brown Marshalls which have the curved sides of the old stage coaches. Of the original five vehicles No 4 had always needed the most attention. It was known as 'Limping Lulu' in the early days of the Society due to its peculiar motion. This, it eventually transpired, was because its frame was in such a poor state. Even the axles, it is said, were not exactly parallel. In 1958 the original timber frames were replaced by a welded steel frame, and in 1972 major repairs were undertaken to the bodywork. It was still not quite right due to short buffers making it impossible to screw the couplings tightly. The wheels needed re-profiling, and the draw-gear springs were weak and inadequate. In 1988 these matters were rectified, and the coach then rode better, probably since it was built. In 1980 'Limping Lulu' had her moment of glory. She was sent to Liverpool Road station, Manchester to take part in the 'Rocket 150' exhibition, commemorating the historic 'Rainhill Trials' of 1830.

Metro-Cammell, the railway coach and bus manufacturers, the successors to Brown Marshalls, still hold the original drawings, dated 18 July 1866, for carriage No 5, the brake van. The van has double-sliding doors on the platform side. At the far end of the van is a hatch, which when opened gives access to a handle. This could be turned to apply oak brake blocks to all four wheels. There are also small projecting lookouts in each wall of the brake-van enabling the guard to look up the side of the train without leaning out. The one on the platform side has been altered to include a small ticket window, and just inside it a ticket cupboard and a date press have been provided.

The body of the ex-Corris brake van, No 6, was replaced in 1958. In the early years from 1952 to 1957, it was usually coupled at the front of the train to provide much needed additional passenger capacity. The original body, much decayed, and with fire damage in one corner was then used as a lineside hut at Quarry Siding for another twenty years before being finally scrapped. The underframe required major repairs in 1974, and ballast boxes were added beneath the floor to improve braking power by providing additional weight. By then its use was confined to goods trains.

The seating capacity of the four original coaches was seventy two, and yet it is known that 138 people travelled on one of the early trains: the guards' vans were also packed with passengers. It was vital to increase capacity, if only to increase revenue. The first new carriage stock arrived in the winter of 1952-3, a gift of six open quarrymen's coaches, C,D,E,G,H,P, from the 1ft 11½in gauge Penrhyn quarry railway near Bangor. Two of these, H and P had already been regauged to the TR gauge of 2ft 3in by Penrhyn quarry using TR wagon wheels. These became carriages nos 7 and 8, respectively. E and G were sent unaltered, followed by C and D somewhat later. All four came without wheels or bearings.

Carriage No 7 was given a light roof carried on eight pillars, but on being put into service kept coming off the track. So it was put into storage until 1955, when, after removing the roof and strengthening the frames, it ran satisfactorily as an open carriage until finally taken out of service in poor condition in 1961. In 1963 it was dismantled, and rebuilt at Pendre as a tea van, in less than two weeks 'by half a dozen bods' and the chief engineer. As already mentioned, until 1968 this tea van was attached to the first train of the day to Abergynolwyn where it was man-handled into a specially constructed siding. It returned to Wharf on the last train of the day. After 1971 it was used as a mess and tool van for the Nant Gwernol extension, and finally it was scrapped in 1980 when its body was found to be beyond repair. The original running gear was then attached to a new steel frame, and a new carriage body suitable for accommodating handicapped passengers built on it. No 8 ran as an open carriage until withdrawn from service in 1964, when it was broken up due to its poor condition.

In April 1954 two bogie chassis were brought from W.G. Allen Ltd of Tipton. These were originally built to meet an order for man-riding bogie cars placed by the National Coal Board in 1952, the design being modified for use on the Talyllyn. One of the chassis had a handbrake fitted. Of the four ex-Penrhyn carriage bodies two, C and D, were used, with one of the Allen bogies, to make carriage No 9 at Pendre, where the workshops had been sufficiently improved to allow volunteers to do this kind of work. The other two bodies, E and G, were completely cannibalised, and used with the other chassis to build coach No 10, a semi-open body with a small enclosed brake compartment at one end. No 9 only operated in its original form for the 1954 season, and was then rebuilt into a fully enclosed six-compartment body for 1955. Built of softwood and cheap materials the bodywork deteriorated rapidly. In 1965 No 10 was dismantled, and rebuilt with reinforced underframes and modified bogies to give a better ride. A new hardwood body to a TR design was supplied built by Raymond Tisdale & Co Ltd of Kenilworth. No 10 returned to service in July 1967. No 9 was similarly dismantled and rebuilt after the 1967 season.

Coaches Nos 11 and 12 were built at Pendre utilising the two ex-Penrhyn quarry coach bodies taken off No 9. These were put on new steel frames, using running gear from quarrymen's coaches scrapped by the Festiniog. No 11 entered service in 1955, and No 12 in 1956. The bodies did not last long, and the two carriages were converted into open stock to the same design as No 13, which had been built separately at Pendre and had entered service in 1957. No 12 re-entered service in 1958, and No 11 in 1959.

Carriages Nos 14 and 15 were built by the Midland Railway Carriage & Wagon Company Ltd of Shrewsbury for the Glyn Valley Tramway, which closed in 1935. No 14 was a first-class coach, built in 1892, and purchased from Chirk Vicarage garden in 1956. It took a lot of restoring to its present luxurious condition, and new running gear had to be fitted. Coach No 15 originally a second-class coach and equipped with a brake, was built in 1901, acquired from a farm in 1958, and rebuilt at Oldbury. Both vehicles entered service in 1958 in full Glyn Valley livery, restored as near as possible to that railway's first-class standard. Run as first-class vehicles with a supplementary fare, they formed a worthy addition to the Talylln's vintage stock. In 1985 No 15 returned to its original home at Glyn Cereig, to be put on display in the centre of the village in commemoration of the fiftieth anniversary of the closure of the Glyn Valley Tramway.

The original No 16 was known as the 'Stanton' coach, being obtained for £25 in 1957 from Boden's Stone Ltd of Stanton-in-the-Peak, Derbyshire. It was originally built by Kerr, Stuart to a gauge of three feet. It was in poor condition and required considerable rebuilding. A five-compartment semi-open body was constructed on similar lines to No 13, itself based on the Ravenglas & Eskdale Railways open coach design. A guard's compartment was added later, and additional luggage space in 1969. In 1978 No 16 was withdrawn and the bodywork dismantled. A new body was built to the now standard TR design, on the lines of No 10, and the new No 16 entered service in 1981.

No 17 the 'royal' ex-Corris coach, so called because the Princess of Wales rode it when she and her husband visited the railway in November 1982, is the last of the vintage coaches. It was built by the Metropolitan Carriage & Wagon Co Ltd in 1898 for the

Corris railway, on which it ran until passenger services on the line were withdrawn in 1930. It was brought back to Pendre in May 1959, having been discovered at Gobowen, near Oswestry, where it was being used as a garden shed. The restoration proved a very formidable task. Much of the carriage had to be completely rebuilt, and a new underframe and bogies provided. The carriage work was almost entirely the work of volunteers B.J. and J.W. Green, a father and son team of expert craftsmen. No 17 entered service in May 1961. (About this time the Company was thinking of selling debenture stock to the public in an effort to raise much needed capital. It would have paid a very low rate of interest, but could have proved attractive to richer members and others wanting a financial stake in the railway. However the idea was killed 'stone-dead' when the railway's only carpenters, the Greens, said they would cease work immediately if their freely given labour was to be used to generate distributable profits.)

Because of the increasing scarcity of vintage carriages, and also because their restoration took so long and cost so much, it was decided in 1959 that the railway should build its own carriages to a standard, yet traditional-looking design, in keeping with the railway's vintage character. No 18 was assembled by volunteers at Pendre. The body of No 18 was prepared in Coventry by the Greens to the highest standards. They then re-erected it at Pendre on an underframe. This, together with the roller-bearing bogies, had been constructed in the TR's own workshops. Coach No 18 entered service in 1965, and has proved to be the most durable of the TRs 'modern' coaches. The need for new vehicles became urgent with the rapid increase in traffic. The remaining five carriages, Nos 19 to 23, were constructed by Raymond Tisdale Ltd on underframes fabricated at the Midland Furnace Co Ltd. The bogies were built at Pendre to a new design which followed main-line practice by incorporating coil springs. The wheels for all these last six standard coaches came either from the Welshpool & Llanfair or from Bowaters Industrial railway in Kent.

Following main-line practice, the passenger stock is divided into sets, one for each of the three train services. With twenty one coaches, three of them composite types incorporating a guards van, and two brake vans, this is quite feasible. Using sets, vehicles can more easily, and in a more systematic way, be taken out of service for repair or maintenance in the paint and workshops. But some members are not very happy with the practice of putting at least one vintage carriage in each set. They consider the original and very historic stock should be used more sparingly and they are not sure of the wisdom of mixing the 'old' with the 'new.'

The Talyllyn originally had about 120 wagons, of which about 100 were open-sided slate wagons. One can be seen outside the Narrow Gauge Museum at Wharf. The other twenty wagons consisted of some iron-bodied coal wagons, a few covered vans and one special gunpowder van. Originally they had iron wheels, but later these were replaced with steel ones. They had no springs, and a timber frame. When the Society took over in 1951 there were still about sixteen wagons left on the railway, and a few more in the quarry.

Those in the quarry were cut up by the contractor who bought the scrap. The surviving TR vehicles consisted of ten slate wagons, five iron open-body wagons, and one bolster. Eleven ex-Corris wagons were bought from BR for 10s each: four timber bodies with 1-ton capacity, five 1-ton iron bodies, and two 2-ton iron bodies, all with steel wheels and unsprung axle boxes.

None of the original TR wagons remains in use. Of the fifty-five wagons available for use in 1988, numbers 1 and 2 were former Corris locomotive coal wagons, and were still being used for this purpose in 1988. By then only three other Corris wagons remained in their original condition. The rest, with the TR wagons, had all been cannibalised and put together with new parts to provide twelve 'new' wagons. Three of these had side-tipping bodies, three were flat wagons and six were open box wagons. Two large flat bogie wagons were obtained from Bowaters railway at Sittingbourne in Kent in 1971 and 1975, and a dozen side tipping wagons, or 'Skips', from Bowen's Cefn Coch Quarry in 1969. Six 2-ton iron frame slate wagons were acquired from the Festiniog in 1956; three of them were used as 'flats', and three converted into single swivelling bolsters useful for handling rails. Four hopper wagons were acquired from the Winchburg Shale Oil works in Scotland in 1961, and the TR designed and built its own model in 1983. All the bought-in wagons, with the

exception of those from the Corris, of course, had to be re-gauged.
The wagons are used purely for maintenance of the line, or for
carrying locomotive coal from Wharf to Pendre.

In August 1956 the Talyllyn was presented by the Alton
Motor Company with a 15/30cwt Morris Commercial, of about
1930-1 vintage. The Company had recently bought the vehicle
from the Southern Gas Board, which had acquired it when it
took over the Portsmouth Gas Works on nationalisation. In 1980
it was replaced by a 1969 Ford V 200 lorry. The Hilton Valley
Miniature Railway had acquired it to carry out a short-distance
move in the Birmingham area. After this was completed a Society
member borrowed it to bring some materials down to Tywyn.
The chief engineer saw it and on remarking that the TR could
do with such a lorry, was told it was available for the asking.
The TR acquired it for a modest sum in 1980.

Pendre Station .

CHAPTER 12

Up The Line To Brynglas

Pendre is the railway's supply base, but its operations are controlled from Wharf. The trains are assembled at Pendre and start and finish the day there. So in describing the line and how it was operated in the late nineteen eighties it is appropriate to start from Pendre yard.

The Pendre station platform and hut remained virtually unchanged. Having been used for years for storing engineering materials, the station was cleaned up in 1981 and dedicated to the memory of John Tonkyn from Oxted, Surrey, one of the first people to join the TRPS in 1951. He served as a volunteer guard, booking clerk and chairman of the London area group, and was 'unrivalled as an extractor of cash'. He raised thousands of pounds for the railway by collecting 'anything going for nothing, old magazines and coins' and finding a buyer. The dedication is commemorated by a plaque on the wall of the hut.

Looking directly across the single rail track from the platform at Pendre there appeared at first sight to have been little change over the years. The blank wall of the old loco shed, merging imperceptibly into that of the engine driver's cottage, was exactly as it had been since first built in 1867. The building was constructed of slate-blocks, for the railway was by then in a position to bring the slate down cheaply from the Company's quarry. But appearances can be deceptive. In 1968 the cottage part of the building had 'disappeared' to provide room for an extension of the loco shed. In 1979 the rest of what had been a dwelling-house became a mess-room with showers and toilet, and office space. The adjacent workshop is equipped with heavy lifting tackle – up to five tons, milling and drilling machines,

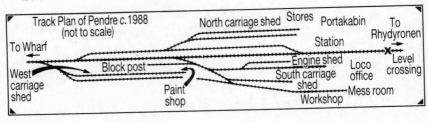

lathes and welding equipment, and even a blacksmith's forge. It was able to carry out almost all the repairs, building and maintenance needed to keep the locomotives, rolling stock and other equipment in good order. It also carried out quite major work for outside customers, and provided a much needed facility for the mining, manufacturing, agricultural, marine, tourist and other industries in the locality. It also did work for other private railways, even of standard gauge.

The main difference from the past was a flower bed beneath the wall instead of a lot of old weeds. In fact this symbolised the major change in the yard generally since the 1950s. It looked like a proper railway, instead of just a field with a few rusty lengths of rail projecting from the gradually all-enveloping vegetation. The grass was now confined to the banks round the edge of the yard.

Jutting out beyond the engine shed and the workshop behind it, the first carriage shed with its timber walls and slate roof looked much the same as it had for the last century or so. But in 1962 it had been rebuilt with a steel frame and timber cladding. Another change since the Society took over, was a large steel water tank on top of a solid stone column, just outside the loco shed doors, replacing the original tank, which had been somewhat precariously perched in the rafters of the shed itself.

North of the line the old hay-barn was replaced between 1959 and 1963 by a second carriage shed, built mainly of asbestos sheets. It had bays to house engineering and electrical stores, the automatic telephone exchange, the carpenter's shop, and, in 1988-9 was extended to house an enormous wheel lathe. Once it had also contained the chief engineer's office but, as pressures on space increase, he was pushed out into a cabin sited next to a toilet block erected in 1961.

The most recently completed building was the west carriage shed at the end of the yard nearest Wharf Station. Started in 1972 it was finally completed in 1987, accommodating ten bogie coaches. One end of the shed had been divided off by large double doors to provide an insulated, well-lit paint shop. At the other, western end was a long inspection pit. When first dug out this had rapidly turned into a duck-pond, as all the water from the banks of the cutting at the foot of the hill-slope drained into it. So a permanent self-starting electric pump had to be fitted.

On the north side of this shed was a block cabin, called a signal box on most railways: something undreamed of in 1951. It houses a fifteen-lever ground frame controlling all the running points in the Pendre yard: those points controlling sidings away from the 'main line' were still mostly hand-operated. Pendre box also controls the main line down to Wharf end up to Brynglas, where the next block posts are located.

In one respect at least things had gone a complete circle since pre-Society days when the Talyllyn Railway was able to keep all its locomotives and coaching stock under cover. From about 1953 when new loco and carriage stock was acquired until 1987 this had not been the case. The stock needing sheltering in 1987 had grown to five working steam locomotives, three diesels, twenty one coaches, and two brake vans, including all the originals. Few other major private railways are in a position to keep all their stock securely locked up indoors.

Let us go back to a typical day in say 1987. The rostered driver is Dai Jones, the only paid regular driver, although other employees could drive when necessary. His fireman is John Robinson, a volunteer, a computer analyst from Hertfordshire. As a senior fireman with long experience, John is able to take over if something happens to Dai while the train is in service. The engine is all sparkling and bright, lovingly cleaned polished and oiled by a bevy of young volunteer cleaners. These are boys and girls mostly in their teens, anxious to graduate eventually to working on the footplate. The carriage stock has been thoroughly swept out and the brass door handles polished by the guard and

Wharf Station.

her assistant. The guard today is Sarah Thomas, a physiothera-
pist, daughter of John Newman, also a volunteer guard; wife of
Graham, an accountant with British Telecom and a volunteer
driver; and mother of a baby daughter herself. With a surplus
of eligible young men it has not always been certain just how
single-minded was the interest in railway preservation of all the
young lady volunteers! Weddings of volunteers have been by no
means infrequent and the Talyllyn has active volunteers even
unto the third generation!

The loco has been prepared and backed on to its rake
of carriages much as in the days of Dai's father, except that
the set has most likely been stabled in the west carriage shed.
As the train drifts easily down the cutting towards Wharf, Dai
looks out from the right hand side of the cab, the driver's side,
keeping a close watch on the track ahead. There is always the
chance that a volunteer or member of staff will be working on
the line or using it as a pathway between Wharf and Pendre.
Towards the end of the cutting he keeps a special look-out for
the coloured-light signal guarding the entrance to Wharf station
and yard. The Talyllyn had apparently abandoned signalling a
few months after the railway first opened in 1866. It was only
when it introduced a two-train operation in 1954 that a signalling system became necessary. For with more than one engine
in steam at a time, and an increase in the shunting of coaches
in the yard at Wharf together with the new practice of coaling

the engines there, it was felt additional protection was required. This is particularly so as the approach is in a deep cutting round a sharp curve cutting off any view of the station and points until the last moment. So early in 1954 a rather primitive semaphore signal was erected a short distance up the cutting. The signal, without spectacles or lamp, for it would not be used after dark, was mounted on a short tubular post. This once formed part of a 'Belisha Beacon'. The signal was worked by a wire linked to a lever alongside the point levers by the bridge. The inspecting officer did not like the system as it could not be locked, could be interfered with by unauthorised persons, and the signal could easily be left at 'Clear' by mistake. So the semaphore signal was replaced in time for the 1955 season by a colour light-signal, mounted on a wooden signal post complete with spiked finial obtained second-hand from BR, and worked from inside the station office.

The gradient into Wharf is quite steep, and if a stop at the signal is required it is as well to apply the brakes as soon as

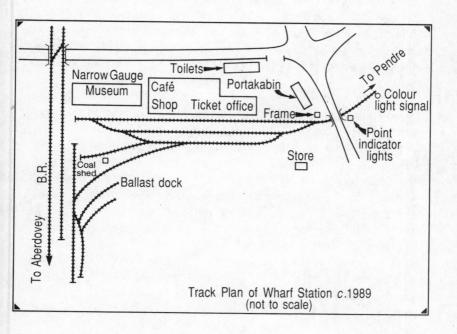

Track Plan of Wharf Station c.1989
(not to scale)

possible. Indeed on wet days when the rails might be slippery and adhesion poor, or there is a particularly heavily-loaded train, the guard will in any case partly apply the screw-down brake in the van to assist in stopping the train at the platform. If it should fail to do so the train would proceed through the buffers and to the BR Cambrian coast line beyond. That has never happened to a passenger train, but in 1894 some slate wagons did breakaway and end up across the Cambrian sidings, fouling the main line. Fortunately they were cleared before the coast-line passenger train arrived twenty minutes later. The Cambrian management wrote a strongly worded letter to the Talyllyn. The latter, following its normal custom in such circumstances, failed to reply.

As our train pulls slowly into the single platform at Wharf Sarah screws the brake down hard. Once this is done, John, who by now is on the platform at the front of the engine, can remove the engine couplings. Locomotives on the Talyllyn almost invariably face up the line, because they are supposed to work better that way round. On the down trips the main function of the engine, once the train has been started, is to act as a brake to stop it running away with itself. There is no turn-table on the line, so once the engines are put facing one way that is how they remain, until a large crane is hired to lift them round. Similarly the guard's van is always at the rear of the train on the journey up the line, and next to the loco on the down trip.

Having put the screw coupling back on the front of the engine, John signals Dai to take the engine back clear of the loop point right up to the buffers. The train has been stopped short, so that the engine could pull clear, and then run round the train on the loop. John pulls over the point lever and the engine goes ahead into the loop. However it does not immediately go to the front of the train. John pulls over another point, and Dai takes the loco back on to the coaling point. Here, he and John fill metal containers with coal, which they then empty into bunkers on the side of the engine. It is obviously more sensible to coal at Wharf where the coal dump is, than to carry the coal up to Pendre. Until BR withdrew freight facilities from Tywyn the coal always came by rail to the adjacent siding where the slate was once loaded. Now it comes by road, but still from South

Wales. For a considerable period it came from the Lady Wind-sor pit until it closed. During the 1984 miners' strike coal from Nottinghamshire had been used, but it produced vast amounts of smoke and dirt, and tended to clinker. Some coal is stored at Pendre for emergency use, but the crews are expected to coal at Wharf. They also take water there between trips.

Sarah meanwhile has taken the red tail lamp from the back of the train, and placed it on its hook at the end of the guard's van, now at the rear of the train. Safety rules are strict, and all volunteer and paid staff are given intensive training both on and off-the-job. They are not allowed to perform responsible duties until they have proved their competence. The railway has never had a serious accident, and since 1953 its safety record has been almost impeccable.

The engine pulls forward under the road bridge, and then, after the station supervisor has worked the ground frame con-trolling the points, sets back on to its train. The guard waves the train back a few yards so all the carriages are in the platform. The train is now ready for the off. Sarah has collected her box of tickets, her waybill, a float of loose change, and some leaflets on forestry walks, from Phil Care, a permanent member of staff, booking and general clerk, replaced by a volunteer on his days off. The guard requires tickets, for only the booking office at Wharf is permanently staffed. That at Abergynolwyn is manned for five days a week in the season by volunteer Jim Callaway, who lives in the village close by. He also acts as stationmaster, porter and cleaner. The other booking offices at Nant Gwernol, Dolgoch and Rhydyronen are only staffed in the height of the season, when there is heavy traffic and volunteers are available. The guard also issues tickets, against additional payment, to passengers occupying the limited first-class accommodation. Sarah has already checked she has her whistle, that the fire extinguishers, emergency telephone hand-set, tools and flags are in their place in the van, and that once the engine has been connected up, the train alarm system is working. She has also packed away in the van the milk and other stores for the refreshment room at Abergynolwyn.

The railway's staff and volunteers have excellent, friendly relations with their passengers, who constantly comment on the courteous yet informal service. Considerable amusement has been derived from some of these comments.

One person from across the Atlantic was heard to remark: 'Gee, ain't it real cute? Gotta hev a postcard for ma girlfriend. Gimme six of each, bud!'

Another passenger: 'Is "that" the train? Do you sell insurance tickets?'

And another to the guard: 'What are you? Guard or ticket collector? Oh, I see, a non-union man!' (that was in the early fifties. How things have changed on BR since then!)

Passenger: (at a time the Talyllyn railway carried a third child in a family group free): 'Two adult and three half returns to Nant Gwernol, please.'
Booking clerk: 'You get one free child for that journey, sir.'
Passenger: 'Oh no! Not another child! I can't cope with the three I've got already!'

Booking clerk: 'You will need a ticket for the dog, sir'
Passenger: 'But it's only a little dog.'
Booking clerk: 'That's all right, sir. It's only a little ticket!'

Passenger: 'How much are children?'
Booking clerk: 'We don't sell them here, madam. Try the shop.'

Another passenger: 'Three returns, please.'
Booking clerk: 'Yes, sir, where to?'
Passenger: 'Why? Back here, of course!'

Wharf station has undergone almost a complete transformation since the Society took over. The old office building has been largely re-built and in 1988 consist of a booking office with entrance porch, leading into an open shop space, with a small cafe behind. In the rear was a guard's room and toilet, and a storeroom at the side. In the booking office sits the clerk and the controller for the day, with the block instruments, and telephones to the outside world, first fitted before the 1952 running season. There is also a completely separate internal telephone system linking all stations and the emergency plug-in points situated at quarter-mile intervals all the way up the line. The first internal phone had been a field telephone linking Wharf and Pendre, laid by Charles Uren in 1952, and later extended by him to Brynglas. This was the one that had the distinctive feature of relaying the BBC Home Service from the nearby Tywyn transmitter. In 1989 the station entrance was remodelled to give direct access to the platform at times of peak demand, and to provide two booking windows. One is for tickets and information for the TR and the other for BR, the TR having acquired an agency. The refreshment area was also remodelled and carpeted to give the atmosphere of a country tea-room.

The general manager and his secretary had, like the chief engineer at Pendre, been driven out into a Portakabin. The main building also had a canopy over the platform, erected in 1965. In early Society days, even after a short platform and run-round loop had been built in 1952, passengers still had to cross the rails of a branch siding to join their train. This siding led to the old fenced-in yard, where wagons with goods aboard were sometimes stored, together with the coal, to prevent pilfering. This had been replaced with a hanger-like building housing the Narrow-Gauge Railway Museum.

The track layout, like the buildings, had changed in fits and starts, over the previous thirty five years or so. Gone with the slate trade were all except one of the turntables for the wagons. In 1965, when the old ticket office had been converted into a passenger terminal, all the old trackwork, together with the weighbridge and other 'unnecessary obstructions,' was removed. Then a low-level siding had been built so that trucks could be loaded by gravity, by being run beneath a platform on to which lorries had loaded ballast brought from a nearby quarry; that used in the past from the quarry siding having proved very unsatisfactory. The line along the wharf edge was a facility no longer needed once BR had lifted its siding on the other side, after withdrawing its coal and other freight services from Tywyn. The locomotive coal store had then been re-arranged to cope with lorry transport, and an inspection pit and water facilities provided for servicing the locos between trips. When a two or three train service is in operation there is, after the first train of the day, a spare loco standing in the loop. This then moves up the line to back on to the rake. The down train engine pulls right up to the buffers so all the stock on a normal length train is in the platform. That loco is then trapped. When the train had departed the now untrapped engine pulls on to the loop, and then back into the servicing bay to get ready for its next duty turn. This method of working ensures a rapid turn round of trains, and gives the crews and locos a rest between turns.

10.19 am on a fine summer's day at Wharf station! *Talyllyn's* brasswork gleams and her green paint shines. The coaches too present a fine sight, with their mahogany bodywork relieved by the brightly polished door handles and freshly cleaned windows. Dai and John are ready on the footplate waiting for Sarah to give the signal to depart. Sarah in turn is waiting for the station staff to give her the signal for the train to leave, after they have checked that there are no last minute customers rushing down the slope, and that the line ahead is clear.

The station supervisor for the day, Eric Nicholass, on holiday from his senior managerial position with London Underground, emerges from the booking office accompanied by the railway's general manager, David Woodhouse. David is one of the four longest serving members active on the railway; the other three being Dai, John Slater and Peter Bold, later chairman of the Company. David was putting up station signs along the railway on 14 May 1951, the very first day a passenger train was operated under Society management. A traffic clerk with the Midland Red Bus Company, in his home town of Smethwick in the Black Country, for many years David organised the volunteer working parties. He was co-opted on to the Society's publicity committee in January 1954 and to the main committee in May. He was a protegé of Ken Cope, one of his bosses at the Midland Red. In 1952, David, then aged 18, was proposed by Ken Cope for election to the committee against a candidate put up by the Rolt faction, but both were defeated. In 1966 he became a member of the small permanent paid staff as traffic manager, becoming general manager in 1982. He was awarded the MBE in the 1989 birthday honours list 'for services to Welsh tourism'.

Peter, a retired electrical engineer from Gatley, in Cheshire, first visited the TR on 18 May 1951, and immediately became involved in work on the track which remained his principal occupation on the railway for many years. He was closely involved with James Boyd in setting up the North West area group and organised its trail-breaking working parties. A senior volunteer fireman, he has held many of the leading posts in the Society and Company including that of chairman of the board, and also of the TRPS.

Eric gives Sarah a hand signal. She blows her whistle, waves her green flag, and as Dai opens the regulator and the train slowly pulls out of the platform, she steps nimbly into her van. The engine and carriages disappear under the road bridge, and the wonderful sound of a steam engine working hard up a gradient gradually fades away as the train climbs up the cutting towards Pendre.

The road bridge immediately by Wharf station was somewhat reluctantly rebuilt by the County Council in 1955. In his inspection of the railway in 1954 Lt Col McMullen pointed out that with heavier road traffic the bridge was becoming unsafe. The Railways Inspectorate of the Ministry of Transport persuaded their colleagues in its highway department to put pressure on the Merioneth County Council. It in turn informed the railway that it would have to undertake the necessary works as it had built the bridge in the first place, and was therefore responsible. The secretary replied that the Talyllyn railway owned the bridge, but its contribution would be 'limited to the cost of putting the decking into a safe condition to carry the loads for which it was originally designed. If the Council wishes the bridge to carry heavier loads than those envisaged in 1865 then it would have to be responsible for the additional strengthening required.' After some huffing and puffing the Council had to agree.

This principle has since been applied to the repair of all the bridges and a level crossing. New housing beyond Pendre meant the crossing gates that had proved satisfactory for almost 120 years became inadequate in 1983. (In 1954 the four gates had become two as each pair was welded together to form a single gate.) The County Council hired the Talyllyn's engineering department to prepare drawings so that the job could be put out to tender. The Talyllyn then submitted a tender of its own and was awarded the contract. The gates were fabricated in the railway's workshops, within a few yards of their eventual location, and nearly everyone was happy. The County Council had its nice new wide gates so the traffic could proceed much more quickly. The only ones to have some doubts were a few members of the Society who had a nagging thought that the TRPS was supposed to be a railway preservation society.

As the train approaches the blockpost at Pendre, Janet Cox, the volunteer blockman, a school meals supervisor from Coventry, training officer of the Society for many years, is already at the open window of the box with the token for the next section of the line up to Brynglas. Dai holds out his left hand with the token he has been given by the station supervisor before leaving Wharf, and his right hand ready for the new token. The train slows for the exchange. If Janet had wished to give Dai any special instructions she would have held out a red flag, and he would have stopped. Pendre, Rhydyronen and Brynglas, like the farm halts, are all now request stops. Passengers wishing to alight give notice to the guard before leaving Wharf station on the up trips, and before leaving Dolgoch on the down. Passengers wishing to join the train give a clear hand signal to the driver.

Today there are two passengers on Pendre platform: the chief engineer, John Bate, and his colleague, the signals and telegraph engineer, Don Southgate, who are going up the line to inspect some new works required at Abergynolwyn. John Bate first came to Tywyn as a volunteer in 1951. Over the course of the next five years he completed a survey of the line and amongst many other jobs produced accurate gradient diagrams. As a civil and mechanical engineer with John Laing & Son, he was welcome indeed. He was offered and accepted the post of chief engineer on the Talyllyn in 1963, even though it meant a drop in salary, and he and his wife, Olwen, moved to Aberdovey.

John Bate was an extremely versatile engineer and commanded great respect. He designed and built brake systems and various kinds of artefacts for other railways, standard as well as narrow gauge, and all kinds of equipment for local mining, manufacturing, agricultural, and other firms, as well as doing almost everything needed in the civil and mechanical engineering line for the TR itself. In 1985 the farmers in the valley above Rhydyronen station were anxious to take advantage of EEC subsidies on liming their upland pastures. The lime came in seventeen ton lorries. The bridges were designed to carry five tons, and there was obviously a risk of damage to the lorries and the railway. So the chief engineer informed the County engineer's department which promptly slapped on a weight restriction. The farmers protested bitterly. They were in danger of losing their subsidy payment. Plans were quickly made to strengthen the bridge. The County Council supplied the cement and the labour, and the Talyllyn the steel girders to replace the original supporting timbers. The bridge was made safe for the heavier lorries within a few months, and the farmers were able to get their lime, and their subsidies.

The signals engineer, Don Southgate, was also a former volunteer, first coming to the railway in 1952 with Yorkshire area working parties for general labouring duties. It was then discovered that he was by trade an electrical engineer, so he was re-assigned to areas where his specialist skills were urgently needed. Always interested in telephones and electronics, in 1971 he became a member of the permanent staff in charge of this area of work, under the general direction of the chief engineer. He and his wife Doris moved to Tywyn, where they ran a small boarding house at the end of the High Street close by the BR station. Over the years Don had been largely responsible for the build-up of the block and signalling system, and a complete automatic internal telephone network, to which was later added a secondary independent alarm system. Guards could then plug into this at points only 440 yards apart along the line, and so were never more than 220 yards from a contact point: more than could be said for much of BR. Don was also responsible for the introduction of flashing light warning signals at Forestry Crossing and numerous other small but important improvements.

John Robinson, having been given a wave of the green flag from Sarah, the guard, passes the message on to his driver – 'Right Away'. Dai opens the regulator to get up speed ready for the sharp little bank up under Ty Mawr bridge and on to Hendy.

As the train clears the crossing gates, it passes on the left hand side of the track a new industrial estate with units built with government subsidy by the Mid-Wales Development Board. The Board had helped the railway, as a major employer in the area, over the years in a variety of ways. In the late seventies the Board offered to lease the railway Company a site on the new estate when it was still at the planning stage. The TRPS Council was very interested in the offer as Pendre is cramped for space, and the building of a new locomotive shed with room for additional sidings and extensive workshops seemed a most attractive proposition at a time when traffic still seemed to be growing and activity expanding. But there was a major legal impediment. On 5 July 1865, when Her Majesty Queen Victoria gave her Royal Assent to: 'An Act for making a railway from near the Aberystwyth and Welsh Coast Railway in the parish of Towyn in the County of Merioneth to the township of Maestrefnant in the direction of Talyllyn to be called "The Talyllyn Railway" and for other purposes', it limited the powers of the promoters of the new railway 'to incorporating themselves as a limited company; to taking lands by compulsory purchase for the purpose of making a railway in accordance with plans already laid before Parliament; and to charge fares to persons travelling on the railway'. In a 'Local and Personal' Act of this kind 'what is not permitted is prohibited'.

The Development Board would only lease the land, and then with the stipulation it be used solely for the purpose of carrying on a manufacturing business. Mere maintenance of locomotives was insufficient. So the Talyllyn Railway Company could neither take a lease, nor carry on a manufacturing business. Nor could the Company simply take shares in another Company it set up. But the solution was readily at hand in the form of Talyllyn Holdings Ltd so thoughtfully incorporated on 3 October 1952. Specifically incorporated to hold shares in the Talyllyn Railway Company, it could also hold shares in a new company, Talyllyn Railway Engineering Co Ltd. This latter Company was incorporated under the Companies Acts 1948 to 1976 on 9 July 1980, and its Memorandum and Articles of Association, unlike those of its sister Company, meant it could almost anything it liked in the field of engineering. Jeremy Wilkinson, the Company and Society's solicitor, himself an active volunteer, entertainingly set all this out, quoting the appropriate legal precedents, in Talyllyn News No 109 of March 1981. But as traffic and receipts fell, the TR could no longer afford to expand its estate, and the Company was eventually dissolved on 3 October 1985.

One of the new units was occupied by a precision engineering unit established in 1985 by 'Chips' Harrison. He was one of the earliest volunteers, while stationed during his National Service at the Royal Artillery Firing Camp, long since closed, at Tonfanau. This is only a couple of miles from Tywyn as the crow flies, but seven by road. It was much less then, just over two, because there was a Bailey bridge at the end of the beach road across the estuary of the Dysynni river. After the closure of the camp the bridge remained in use, until it began to be used by heavy lorries from a nearby quarry, and becoming unsafe, had to be closed. It was rebuilt in 1972 when the Tonfanau camp was re-opened as a resettlement centre for refugees from Uganda. One of the Society's members, seconded to the Home Office at the time for service with the Uganda Resettlement Board, was able to put his local knowledge to good use. He made sure that the refugees came by train; and for the six months or so the camp was in use, Tonfanau Halt was one of the busiest stations on the Cambrian Coast line. The improved traffic figures may even have been a contributory cause in helping to keep it open at a time when it was under threat. He was able to clear the way for army engineers to repair the bridge to facilitate rapid access for the fire and ambulance services, but after the camp was closed again, the lorries once more damaged the bridge, so it was partially dismantled.

Pat Garland remarked that the railway was very lucky to have had 'Chips' services for he was a skilled shipwright. There appeared to be no objection to Gunner Harrison spending as much time at Pendre as he wished, for there was nothing for him to do at Tonfanau. So he did an enormous amount of work on getting the coaching stock ready and numerous other jobs. After being demobilised he worked in the port of London for the next thirty years before returning to Tywyn on his retirement to open a workshop making models, but increasingly moving into precision engineering. He employed two TRPS members, Mandy Daines

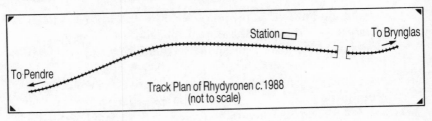

Track Plan of Rhydyronen c.1988
(not to scale)

who previously worked in the TR's Pendre works under a Manpower Services Commission Scheme where she learned at least some of her trade, and David Jones, Dai and June's only son.

As the train pulls up towards Ty-Mawr bridge, Sarah keeps a particularly close look-out along the train to ensure no passenger leans out the window too far and so risks decapitation. The sides of the bridges are very close to the carriage sides. Working hard, its exhaust beat reverberating across the countryside *Talyllyn* pulls its train up past Hendy farm and on past Fach Goch halt. Approaching Cynfal halt, John Robinson, like the engine itself, is working hard. He has to keep the fire burning well, and water in the boiler, to keep up the steam pressure. If too much coal is put on the fire, or too much cold water put through the injectors, then heat will be lost and so therefore no steam! It requires skill and experience to get the balance right.

The engine and crew have to work hardest along this stretch of the line between Pendre and Rhydyronen, for the steepest gradients are to be found rather surprisingly in this wider lower part of the valley. Once under the road bridge, and past Cynfal halt – a few slates set into the bank to make the briefest of platforms – John pulls the string of the engine's whistle to warn any passengers at Rhydyronen of the train's impending arrival. The train crew keep a good look-out to see if there are passengers wishing to board, Sarah having already reported there are none wishing to alight. As soon as she is sure there are no passengers on the platform, she gives John a wave of the green flag which he acknowledges. It is a great help to the driver if the train does not have to stop at Rhydyronen and can keep moving, as beyond there is a steep bank where the track curves sharply under the road bridge and across the stream. It can also be slippery if there has been a fine drizzle, especially when compounded with autumn leaves. On the offside front plate of *Talyllyn* is an oblong metal box, looking rather like a jewel case, with its moulded fitting lid and round ball on top. It contains sand for use when the rails are slippery. The fireman has to jump off the engine, run round the front, take off the lid, and grab handfuls of sand to deposit on the rails ahead. Most of the other locos have automatic sanding equipment, but it does not always work and over the years several trains have failed to make the bank at the first attempt. Their drivers have rather shamefacedly had to back and go for a fresh run at the short steep gradient.

Rhydyronen station was opened in 1867, and remains largely unaltered. It has a slate platform built on a curve, with an open-fronted slate shelter towards the western end. From the platform a carriage way leads off through the woodland surrounding the station to join the road from Bryncrug. This crosses the line by a bridge at the far end of the station, and goes on past Plas Goch, Hugh's railway cottage, another half mile or so up the valley to a small quarry from which slate was brought down to the station for loading on to railway wagons. A small siding left the running line just before the platform and what is now a pleasant wooded glade was then the yard where the slates were stored prior to loading. The siding was used to turn round the first Society passenger train in 1951, but was lifted in 1957. There was once talk of developing Rhydyronen as a spa, as there are

Rhydyronen Station.

chalybeate springs nearby, and for a time it was possible to buy bottles of Rhydyronen mineral water. But as so often happens in this particular area nothing came of it. Rhydyronen incidentally translates into English as 'Ash ford,' as the road crosses a stream at that point.

Dai keeps a good look-out as the train approached Tynllwyn-Hen halt, another name-board in the hedge. In 1982 a special departure took place from this wayside halt, a mere gap in the hedgerow, an hour and a half after midnight. The daughter of the nearby farm was getting married. The ceremony was to take place in a church a few miles to the north, and the reception, a grand affair, in the farmhouse. The only approach to the farm was a narrow track, which would soon become a quagmire with any degree of traffic. The problem was solved by the guests parking at the hotel near Dolgoch station, and taking a special train to Tyllwyn-Hen, returning early the following morning. It must have been quite a sight to see them descend in their evening clothes, but shod in green wellies. The train consisted of TR bogie coaches equipped with electric light, hauled by No 3 driven by Roy Smith and fired by M.J. Davis. Additional floodlighting was provided at Tynllwyn-Hen and Dolgoch.

Our train now makes the steep climb up to the small girder bridge across the Nant Braich-y-Rhiaw, with ease. Then there follows the only falling gradient between Pendre and the end of the line at Nant Gwernol. A short descent, where the parties who had hired slate-wagons for the run-back home, would have had to get out and push, unless they had worked up sufficient speed to clear the small incline, gives John Robinson a chance for a breather from firing.

Having had a brief respite, John has to put on more coal

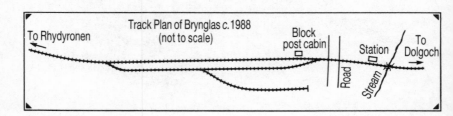

Brynglas Station.

as the train once again begins to climb. Now the fields to the
north fall away more sharply, and those to the south rise more
steeply, as the line begins to run along a more clearly defined
ledge cut into the hillside. Still pulling steadily up the valley,
our train approaches Brynglas station. Before reaching the station, there is a long passing loop, the first since Pendre, almost
three miles back down the line. Dai and John keep a careful
look-out, as if they did not see the blockman waving a green or
yellow flag, they would have had to come to a halt at the 'stop
board', well short of the loop. To give the driver ample warning, the blockman walks down to the end of the loop from his
blockpost, a small wooden shed erected in 1972 by Midland area
volunteers. It is sited next to an ungated road crossing, beyond
which is Brynglas Station: a structure very similar to those at
Rhydyronen and Dolgoch, with a simple waiting shelter built of
slate, on a slate-edged platform. In 1953 the existing siding was
converted into a passing loop. Together with the introduction of
the internal telephone system in 1954, linking Wharf, Pendre and
Abergynolwyn and intermediate stations, the new loop enabled
the introduction that year of more trains. It became possible to
run an advertised 'two-train' service. The loop was extended in
1961 to cope with ever longer trains. A short siding was added in
1975 to accommodate wagons, and in emergency, carriages that
have to be taken out of service; for example running a 'hot-box'
The points are controlled from the blockpost.

There were no scheduled time-table crossings at Brynglas until 1959, but extra trains had been worked before this. A volunteer would be sent up to Brynglas as 'stationmaster' to supervise the crossings. In those days there was not even a ground-frame, so crossing trains meant a lot of rushing up and down from one end of the loop to the other, unlocking and re-locking the padlocks which stopped the points being moved. The engine crews were responsible for changing the single-line working staffs. The volunteer then cranked the phone handle madly to obtain contact with control at Wharf to report 'trains crossed'. In the fifties guards had to remember to place the meat being delivered to Brynglas high up on a ledge in the station waiting shelter so it could not be got at by the farm dogs. Woe betide any guard who got the different boxes of groceries and meat rations muddled up. There were regular deliveries, especially on Fridays to Rhydyronen and Brynglas, and often to Cynfal and Tynllwyn-Hen as well. In the early days of the Society Tom Rolt derived immense pleasure from the use of the railway, albeit at infrequent intervals, to transport consignments of wool between Brynglas mill and Wharf.

On our particular day the blockman is Peter Dray, who like several other Society members, in what is becoming an increasing trend, has retired to Tywyn. Peter, after twenty years service with the Southern Electricity Board in Southampton, bought a house in National Street. Here his wife, Kathleen, with Peter's help, ran a small, select boarding house, with three bedrooms, catering for Talyllyn members working on the railway, and/or attending meetings. Peter serves as a volunteer blockman when needed, otherwise as a volunteer painter and carpenter; outside when the weather suits, and in the paint shop when inclement. Single-handed he has made a great impression in clearing a back-log of maintenance work on the carriage stock. Not only have other members made their permanent homes locally but others have second homes, making it likely there will be a resurgence of volunteer influence on the railway's operations and policy.

Having got the yellow flag, Dai draws the train up to the blockpost, and John hands to Peter the token he had received from Janet at Pendre. Peter then goes into his blockpost, presses the release button to get clearance from Pendre blockpost, puts the token in the machine and informs Janet with 'two bells' that the train is out of that section. The section between Pendre and Brynglas is then clear for another train to enter at either end: the 11.25 from Wharf. Peter then checks with the next blockpost at Quarry Siding that the line ahead is clear, and having obtained a release, extracts the Brynglas-Quarry token from its machine. He hands this to John the fireman. Sarah the guard having noted this and checked that all is clear, then in turn gives a green flag to John, who acknowledges, passing on the 'right away', to Dai. The train pulls forward and immediately John looks back to see if they are required to stop at the station platform. There are no passengers on the platform, and none have given notice of wishing to alight, so Sarah gives another green flag, which John acknowledges.

Both men keep a careful look-out as the train approaches the road-crossing at Brynglas. This settlement had been called Pandy in the early days of the line. The small wooden mill has closed and now just three farms remain by the picturesque stream flowing through a wooded glade just beyond the platform. There had been crossing gates when the railway was first built, and even signals protecting them. But it was only a short time before the signals on the line were all dismantled and sold off, as were the gates at Pandy.

The train then passed the platform without stopping, and heads up the valley towards Dolgoch.

Dolgoch Station .

CHAPTER 13

Further Up The Line

After Brynglas the country became wilder, and the pastures rougher, soon degenerating into scrub woodland. On this stretch the sheep tended to find the grass much greener along the track than in the rough pastures on either side, and often broke through on to the railway. Quite apart from the aesthetics of the matter, for passengers do not like seeing gory remains scattered along the track, it is quite expensive in compensation if one is run down. Sir Haydn Jones in the old days became mightily displeased if he had to pay out, in accordance with inflexible local custom, for a sheep killed or severely damaged on the railway. Sheep also have the disconcerting habit of running ahead of the engine instead of waiting meekly at the side until the train has passed. Unfortunately few sheep can manage 12 mph for more than a few yards, and so the engines have to reduce speed, getting gradually slower and slower as the sheep tire. Generally they either get back to their field through the hole in the fence by which they left it, or disappear into the woodland further up the line. The one thing they are reluctant to do is to run across the viaduct, so they eventually disappear at that point. If they stand in the track and refuse to budge, the fireman or guard is detailed off to remove the obstruction: usually causing much amusement.

Dai begins to shut off the regulator as the train runs through a series of short cuttings through rocky outcrops, and slows on the approach to Dolgoch station. Just before the station, the train suddenly emerges on to a lofty three arch-viaduct across Dolgoch ravine. The stream waters of Nant Dolgoch can be seen over fifty feet below, and up to the right, just out of sight up the tree clad

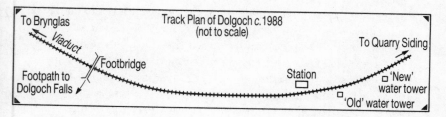

Track Plan of Dolgoch c.1988
(not to scale)

To Brynglas
Viaduct
Footbridge
Footpath to
Dolgoch Falls
Station
To Quarry Siding
'New' water tower
'Old' water tower

ravine, the Dolgoch Falls themselves. The viaduct remained virtually untouched from 1865 until the spring of 1968 when, because
of bulging spandrel walls, strengthening tie-rods were affixed as
a temporary measure. In late 1969 contractors were employed to
make the somewhat overdue repairs. The work was far too big a
job to be left to volunteers and in any case it had to be completed
for the first train of the season on Good Friday 27 March 1970. The
railings, coping stones, and brickwork down to the arches, were
removed. They were replaced with new brickwork and railings,
but the old coping stones were restored. Whilst the scaffolding
was in place, defective bricks in the arches were replaced, and
some re-pointing done. Some twenty thousand bricks and two
hundred tons of sand and stone were delivered to Wharf station
yard, and conveyed to the site by rail. The preliminary work of
removing the track and ballast was done by the railway's own
staff and volunteers. They also put in two temporary sidings, for
tipping the old ballast and filling, and handling the contractor's
building materials.

The viaduct was the cause of the unmasking of the Talyllyn
ghost train. In 1982 rumours were circulating up the Fathew valley, between Tywyn and Abergynolwyn, that late at night a train
could be heard rumbling along the line. These rumours reached
the ears of general manager, David Woodhouse, who dismissed
them as nonsense. At the times stated all the engines and most
of the coaches were safely locked away in their sheds at Pendre.
But he was wrong. There was indeed some unauthorised traffic
on the lines at midnight.

One dark autumn night, members of a management training
course based at a nearby village, were engaged in a night exercise
in the hills around Dolgoch, which included abseiling down the

side of the railway viaduct into the gorge below. They had fastened their ropes to the steel rails, and had descended. Suddenly there was the sound of wheels coming down the track, a terrific bump, some cries of alarm, and whatever it was disappeared down the line towards Tywyn. The mystery was solved. Some persons unknown were emulating the picnic parties of old. Late at night they were putting a trolley, which they had hidden away somewhere, on to the rails, and riding it down the line: whether simply for fun, or to get somewhere is still unknown. The rumour is they had a small motor to take them back up again. They must have got the shock of their lives when they hit the ropes around the rails, and were very lucky not to have been derailed or thrown off. The 'ghost' train has not been seen since.

The engine rounds the sharp curve and slowly draws under the footbridge, and into the platform. The bridge had been erected by the railway in 1957 so that passengers could more easily get from the station platform into the gorge. On the right hand far side of the bridge is a small notice board fixed to the main beam: 'Dirty Knickers – H.R.J.' This commemorates one of Herbert Jones' favourite practical jokes. On occasions when he was the driver on a down train going toward Wharf, and the train was

Dolgoch Viaduct.

in Dolgoch station waiting to leave, he would produce five used plastic cups he had picked up from the refreshment room at Abergynolwyn. These he had filled with cylinder oil. He would tell his fireman to put them in the firebox, together with some slack coal. Then off would go the train. Just as the funnel of the engine was under the bridge, lined with mini-skirted girls watching the train pass underneath, he would open the regulator. A mass of black oily smoke would shoot out of the funnel straight up the girls' mini-skirts. Hence the 'dirty knickers'.

Another of Herbert's ploys at Dolgoch was to leave behind certain guards who foolishly gave the 'right away' when standing half way down the platform, well away from their vans. Herbert would then accelerate very rapidly, but stop the train on the viaduct twenty yards down the track for the guard to catch up. That unfortunate then had to walk the full length of the train, with the windows of each coach presumably full of grinning passengers, as the brake van is at the front of the train on the down journey. The angry guard would threaten to report Herbert to the general manager, then Harold Parker. Sometimes the guard was furious enough to do so, and Harold would solemnly agree to speak to the driver: but he never did. But all that was nearly thirty years ago when life was less serious.

Dolgoch is the third most important station on the line after Wharf and Abergynolwyn. Like Brynglas, it was opened in 1873, and consists of a slate platform and open waiting shed. It is a beautiful spot, especially when the rhododendrons are in full bloom. This station is popular with visitors, for close by are the Dolgoch Falls, only a few yards away, and the station makes an excellent base for a day's walking. It is manned during the height of the season, as considerable numbers of visitors break their journey here, either just to visit the waterfalls as part of a round trip up and down the line, or as the starting point for long walks into the hills. The locomotives take water here, from a new tank on a steel tower erected in 1961. However the old tank on its slate pillar still stands for all to see. The water supply comes down a pipe, leading from a small dam across a mountain stream further up the hillside: simple but effective.

There is another test of driving skill here. The object is to bring the loco to a halt exactly by the water column. In the old days the fireman would jump out as soon as the engine came to a halt, and run round the front of the engine, climb up the other side, and lift the hinged lid of the locomotive's water tank. Turning round he would drag a wooden chute out of a recess in the stone column supporting the wooden water tank. The driver then pulled on a wire, which by means of a pivoted lever released a primitive wooden flap, resulting in a flood of water only a small part of which went into the loco's water tank. Most of it watered the rest of the engine, any unwary passengers, and the surrounding countryside. It would have watered the fireman too, had he not skipped nimbly out of the way.

The old slate waiting shelter remains unaltered. The platform was widened in 1963 to accommodate the increasing number of passengers. In 1987 new fencing was erected, and the platform and paths resurfaced, using labour from a Manpower Services Commission scheme. The station was 'Highly Commended' in the 1987 'Ian Allan' Heritage Awards for successful preservation.

Sarah gets the last of the passengers aboard our train; she has previously emptied the waste-paper bins on the platform into a plastic bag for disposal at Abergynolwyn. She has sold a few tickets from the booking office hatch in the van, for with the hotel and car park nearby, some passengers board at Dolgoch for a round trip. Checking all doors are properly shut, and the highly-polished brass handles are in the correct position, she waves her green flag, gets an acknowledgement from the fireman, John, who again says 'right away' to Dai. The train resumes its climb along its hillside ledge, with the narrowing Fathew valley below. At this point the main road is close to the line and some excellent views of the railway can be obtained from it. Motorists look up when they hear what sounds like a main-line whistle in such a remote spot, particularly if they are unaware of the railway's presence.

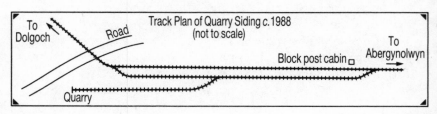

Track Plan of Quarry Siding c.1988
(not to scale)

To Dolgoch

Road

Block post cabin

To Abergynolwyn

Quarry

Having cleared Dolgoch the train passes along the open hillside, interspersed with woodland dells through which small streams make their way to the valley below. Soon it draws to a stop at another passing loop called Quarry Siding, where there is a small blockpost with an ungated farm crossing adjacent. This means the blockman can use his car to come on duty. Today the blockman is Tony Randall, who manages to have two daily jobs. He works for London Transport, near Victoria station, during the day, but drives a Green & Grey commuter coach to and from his home at Billericay, thus getting paid for travelling to and from work. His varied railway duties on the Talyllyn include on occasions deputising as controller for the general manager. At Quarry there is also a small siding off the loop, hence its name, serving a tiny shale quarry from which ballast for the tracks was obtained until the mid-1960s. This shale ballast was fairly acceptable in dry conditions but it was no good in wet places as it contained fine silt and clay which softened easily. For a few years, until about 1967, 'second hand' ballast was obtained from B.R. Since then new stone ballast has been bought from local quarries. The old shale quarry is today used for storing spare track materials, and the siding is useful if a carriage or other stock has to be taken out of service for some reason.

Tony exchanges tokens with John, for the train has by then left the Brynglas/Quarry Siding section, and is entering the next shorter section to Abergynolwyn. The blockman gives the guard the 'ready to go' clearance by means of his green flag, and she in turn waves her green flag to signal 'right away' to the engine crew. The train then passes through open country on its ledge high up on the hill side, giving a clear view of the Cader range to the north. Suddenly the train runs into forest. A trackside yellow disk, bearing the outline of a tree in black, shows that the line has entered Forestry Commission land. The driver has to take special care to try and avoid emitting sparks from the engine, especially as there has been a rare dry spell. The rails in this section came from the Channel Tunnel project aborted in 1975.

Dai glances across the narrowing valley at the high mass of Cader Idris, rising to 2927 feet, away to the north. There is a way up to the summit from the head of the valley, from Minnfford,

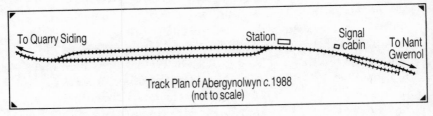

To Quarry Siding

Station

Signal cabin

To Nant Gwernol

Track Plan of Abergynolwyn c.1988
(not to scale)

beyond the Talyllyn Lake, from which the valley got its name. The path starts by the Idris spring, a source of pure sparkling water, used as a trade-name for soft drinks.

Dai pulls the cord and the whistle sounded to announce the train's arrival at Abergynolwyn station, always in the past labelled as being the station 'for Cader Idris (6miles) and Tal-y-llyn Lake (3¾ miles)'. The train swings round the curve out of the woods, left across the points, and proceeds at a sedate pace along one of the longest (620 feet) narrow-gauge railway platforms in the country. It comes to a halt by the signal box and station building at the top end. This was a very different station from the one that Dai's father knew in the nineteen thirties. In fact the station building is the third on the site. The original was a simple wooden shelter with a small booking office, just like the one at Pendre. In 1940 it was in a bad state of repair, and was, or so it is alleged, replaced by a 'pill-box' to replace the expected German invasion. It followed an unusual pattern in that it was built of slate instead of brick, and whilst it had the usual loopholes, it was open on one side so that it could double as a shelter for railway passengers. In appearance it was like the other TR station buildings such as the one at Brynglas, but smaller: perhaps to deceive the enemy!

As the traffic increased, these facilities became hopelessly congested. The former booking office was inadequate for serving refreshments. So as has already been told from 1964 until 1968, No 7 van, converted into a mobile tea-bar, or 'take-away,' was brought up each day and parked in a specially built short siding at the east end of the station. But it soon proved inadequate to meet the demand. Early in 1967 a committee was set up to recommend what should be done. In spite of the proposed extension of the railway for another three-quarters of a mile, along the route of the old mineral extension to the foot of the incline at Nant Gwernol, Abergynolwyn would still remain the major traffic point at the head of the line. This was because it was the last station up the line with road access; Nant Gwernol itself being served only by a narrow footpath. The Forestry Commission had already provided a car park and picnic site by the access road to Abergynolwyn station, and the National Park Authority was going to extend these facilities by constructing public toilets.

The committee recommended that a new station be built during the winter of 1968-9. In spite of some opposition at the AGM, the plans drawn up by TRPS member Douglas Thorpe of Aberdovey, were approved. Being situated in the National Park, the structure had to be appropriate to its environment. The building is of cavity wall construction with an outer shell of local slate, a roof of Welsh slate, and a wooden framed canopy. The accommodation consists of a waiting room cum cafe with a servery, two staff lavatories, and a store and booking office, with a canopy over the platform out front. The job was put out to tender, as it had to be done quickly between running seasons, and cost £7000. The old building was demolished by railway staff and volunteers in September 1968 to clear the site for the contractors, Wilnor Estates of Tywyn. They had the new building ready in time for the railway staff and volunteers to complete the fitting out before the start of the following season. The station was

Abergynolwyn Station.

re-opened officially on 28 May 1969 by the National Hostess for Wales, Miss Stella Mair Owen. The seven cast-iron pillars used to support the canopy came from Towyn BR station where the awning had been removed from the up platform. In 1986 doors were fitted to the west end of the station building, and the canopy extended, in order to provide a far larger area for the consumption of refreshments when the weather is fine.

Some amusing stories are told of interchanges between passengers and guards up the line.

A passenger asked the guard at Abergynolwyn one day: 'Do you take cheques.?'
'Certainly, sir. We take any nationality.'

Another guard: 'The first class supplement is 1s single.'
Passenger: 'What if I'm married?'

Passenger to booking clerk: 'Are you running to-day?'
'Not personally, sir, but the train leaves at 3 pm'

Scene: Down train ready to depart from Abergynolwyn behind No 3 engine *Sir Haydn*; the injector is 'on'.
Passenger: 'That's a modern engine you have there.'
Fireman: 'What do you mean, modern?'
Passenger: 'It's got a toilet'
Fireman: 'A what?'
Passenger: 'A toilet – I can hear the cistern filling'.

John hands over the token to the blockman, Roger Whitehouse, a lecturer at Keele University, a member of the TRPS since 1958, of council from 1973 – 1981 and again from 1983. Members do get voted off the truly democratic council and on again. Roger's wife, Sue, was the daughter of Graham Vincent, a retired senior insurance company executive, a Society member since 1952, on council since 1972 and its chairman 1982-5. He was chairman of the council's marketing and museum committees, associated with the latter since the Narrow Gauge museum at Wharf was but a gleam in someone's eye. Unlike the blockposts at Pendre, Brynglas and Quarry, that at Abergynolwyn actually had signals, needed because the line is set right up against the hillside and the sight-lines are poor. The fourteen levers controlling the points, and the switches for the colour light signals are, we can see on our imaginary journey, housed in what was a relatively large signal box. In May 1976, with the opening of the extension to Nant Gwernol, it became necessary to enable Abergynolwyn to have enough platform capacity and associated loops to accommodate two trains together, plus a small siding. Hence the relatively complex signalling arrangements.

Sarah, the guard has meanwhile handed over the boxes of supplies and milk to the two ladies, Mrs Thomas and Mrs Marjorie Jones, seasonally employed to run the catering by now well established at Abergynolwyn: not forgetting the guard's important duty of telling the refreshment staff how many teas the train crew would require on the way back. One of the privileges of being a working volunteer on the Talyllyn is the provision by the catering staff of unlimited cups of free tea: all other food and drink is paid for at special rates. The tea order is given on the up journey, for the train would be back from Nant Gwernol twenty four minutes later. It would then spend twenty minutes or more at the station for passengers also to refresh themselves and make purchases from the shop.

Sarah then hands a pouch to Jim Callaway, the five-day a week unpaid volunteer stationmaster at Abergynolwyn throughout the summer season. Retired, he lives in Abergynolwyn and comes up ever day with his dog. Always smartly dressed in his stationmaster's uniform, you can tell his devotion to the railway and his job. In the pouch from the traffic office at Wharf, are railway forms, instructions and letters.

The train only spends a couple of minutes at Abergynolwyn on the up journey, giving just enough time for passengers to alight, and join, for John to exchange the token for the metal staff with Roger, the blockman, and for the guard to deliver the wallet to Jim, and the refreshment stores and tea order to the catering staff. Jim, as stationmaster, having seen all passengers safely aboard, and all the doors shut, indicates to Sarah that she may give the 'right away'. For the last time she waves her green flag, has it acknowledged by John, and the train heads off up the extension.

On leaving the station it clatters across the siding points, and on past the spot where a gate used to mark the end of the 'Statutory Railway', the one authorised in the 1865 Talyllyn Railway Act. This gate appeared as the first picture in Tom Rolt's *Railway Adventure*, with the caption 'The road to adventure' – an even more apt title than he realised, as there was as much adventure beyond the gate as behind it. Continuing through the woods the train soon passes over a tarmac road at Forestry Crossing, ungated but protected by a 'main line' flashing light system, with trains reducing speed to 5 mph. Dai points out to John the small waterfall by the lineside at Ty Dwr, where the original engine shed and water supply for the locomotive were located, prior to the construction of the depot at Pendre. The stone pillar from which projected a length of open wooden trough still stands. One end of the trough was placed on the engine water tank, and the other connected with another length of open trough linking the top of the pillar with an adjacent mountain stream. When all was properly connected the stream ran into the locomotive's water tank. This being filled, the trough was pushed back, and the stream allowed to continue its fall into the valley below. There was no storage tank.

The line, on its mountain ledge, swings southward into the Nant Gwernol ravine in a series of reverse curves. The remnants of a large drum are all that remains of the winding house at the top of the Abergynolwyn incline. The caption to a picture of the winding house taken at Easter 1969, which appeared in the *Talyllyn News* the following September, read 'Not only is this building squarely in the path of the Nant Gwernol extension, it is also unsafe, and is now being demolished. The slate slabs recovered from the walls will be used for the new station at Abergynolwyn.' The preservationists were outraged! With hindsight, it is probable, even from a commercial angle in the longer term, that its destruction was perhaps an error. (See Postscript). But there was little choice at the time. Finance was limited, and to have moved the line clear of the old winding house would have involved going outside the TR land boundary and purchasing land from the Forestry Commission. An additional one thousand cubic yards of rock would have needed to be blasted out – right above Abergynolwyn village.

This last section is the most scenic. The line curves into the narrow defile of the Nant Gwernol ravine, perched on a narrow ledge 150 feet above the roaring torrent. The crashing white waters can fleetingly be glimpsed far below, through occasional gaps in the dense woodland. On sharp curves on narrow ledges, the extension claws its way into the mountain side.

John leans out of the cab, and looks down the steep cliff side through the trees to the fast flowing stream far below. While still close to the edge, the track is by no means as close as in the days when it was just a mineral line. The Ministry of Transport required most of the old curves to be eased considerably before they could be used by passengers. This involved much blasting, both literally and metaphorically, by the staff and volunteer gangs, the 'Gwerns', who re-built the extension between 1970 and 1976.

Suddenly the line rounds yet another sharp curve and emerges on to an enlarged shelf in the valley side. With trees above and trees below, the roar of a waterfall only a few yards away up the defile, its sides constantly dripping with water, it can be a rather eerie and inhospitable place in the half light of early morning, or as darkness begins to close in at the end of a winter's afternoon.

Dai brings the train to a halt by the platform at the terminus, laid out with a loop and a siding. Sarah screws down the brake in her van; absolutely essential this, as otherwise, once the engine was uncoupled, the train would roll away back down the line. She removes the tail lamp, and walks off down the platform to the little office at the end of the waiting shelter to report the train's arrival by telephone to control back at Wharf: everywhere else it was done by the blockman or fireman when exchanging tokens. John meanwhile has uncoupled the engine, and back on the footplate, taken the engine forward over the points into the head shunt. Dai jumps down, and operates the point lever. John takes

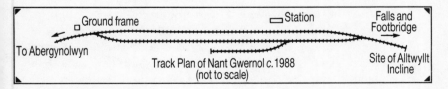

Track Plan of Nant Gwernol c.1988 (not to scale)

the engine back along the loop, over the points at the other end, and on to the main line again. Dai swings over another point, the loco backs on to its train, and is coupled up ready for the down trip. About seven minutes were allowed for this, giving time for passengers to walk thirty yards or so beyond the platform to view the rushing torrent from the bridge across the ravine, and then re-board the train.

On one occasion during the wait at Nant Gwernol the engine driver was approached by a young woman holding a tin of baby food. 'Excuse me,' she said, 'would you mind heating up the baby's feed?' Overcoming his surprise the driver, who as it happened, was Bill Faulkner, the railway's volunteer managing director, took the tin, placed it on the fireman's shovel, and carefully inserted it into the fire. After a few minutes he then removed it and passed the now heated tin to the passenger. Steam railways are nothing if not versatile.

It is now almost time to go. Sarah, the guard, blows her whistle most vigorously three times. She then walks off the end of the Nant Gwernol station platform, and down the path a few yards towards the footbridge. When she had a clear view, she discovered there are two laggard passengers, quickly making their way back towards the train, the whistle having awakened them from their reverie. Holding open the door of an empty compartment, Sarah ushers them aboard, and checking that all the door handles are horizontal, she makes her way to the front, waved John the driver off and steps smartly into her van.

Dai opens the regulator only a fraction, for the main function of the locomotive on the down journey was to act as a brake. Soon they are back at Abergynolwyn. The passengers alight, most of them heading straight into the refreshment room. The train has stopped at the far end of the platform, to allow the next up train to pull into the east end of the platform on its way to Nant Gwernol. John the fireman has handed in the staff and ticket to Roger, the blockman. Now a fifteen minute wait there, and as there are not many passengers, Sarah places the tray with the four teas ordered on the way up on a spare table on the platform. The crew are joined by John Bate and Don Southgate who has finished checking the signalling, point levers and connections.

Shortly the next up train, headed by No 2 *Dolgoch*, creeps across the points into the platform. Once safely at rest, the driver, Graham White, a British Rail clerical officer, gives the party a wave from his cab. His fireman, Ian Evans, who also works for British Rail, disappears into the signal box to hand over the token and receive the train staff and ticket, while the guard, Sara Eade, a senior youth worker with Shropshire County Council in Shrewsbury, disappears into the refreshment room to give the tea order. Ian is soon back on his footplate, Jim the stationmaster having checked all is in order, gives Sara the 'all clear', and she waved her flag. A brief whistle, a puff of steam, and *Dolgoch* and train disappears round the bend. No 1 *Talyllyn* continues to hiss gently by the platform edge.

Now it is time for us to go. John has collected the token, and shown it to Dai. Jim comes down the platform, and seeing everything is in order, gives a wave of the arm to Sarah, who says 'right away' to John and shows him the green flag. A touch on the regulator, a hiss of steam, and No 1 heads off back down the valley, and peace descended for the moment on Abergynolwyn station.

Nant Gwernol Station.

Postscript:
Preserving The Preservation
– A Living Museum

Tom Rolt recognised the tension in himself between that side of him 'fighting to save something of the beauties of England and the English Tradition from the barbarity and philistinism of science and technology', and his penchant for the latter. He loved the landscape and the rural heritage in which he was brought up, but became an engineer, fascinated with machines. This tension is reflected in the continuing saga of the railway he saved. How to preserve the spirit of the past without destroying it.

In September 1959 he wrote in *Talyllyn News* that 'when the Society was formed the Talyllyn was at the end of its tether, and it was our aim, not to preserve it in that state by a feat of brinkmanship, but to make it an example of what such a railway was like in the days of narrow-gauge prosperity'. He went on to say the two major temptations were to introduce too many elements of main line practice, 'never used on the narrow gauge even in its palmiest days', and to make the railway too tidy, saying he would rather see Wharf looking like a scrap yard than a suburban garden'. He did admit there could be some tidying up, but his comments taken together reveal the conflict in his own mind. And this is the conflict most members face. Just how is the spirit of the past to be preserved whilst still coping with traffic, safety and other demands?

In May 1960 Tom quoted Rule 3 of the Society's constitution and rules: 'The Society may not recommend any alteration to the gauge of the railway, abandon steam haulage or effect any other change calculated permanently to alter or destroy the original and historic character of the Talyllyn Railway', and went on to say: 'Ever since the Society was founded the committee has observed this rule so far as it was consonant with the needs of safe and efficient working and the handling of a rapidly increasing volume of traffic. Inevitably this had entailed compromise and the necessity for difficult decisions on policy questions where it was obviously impossible to please everybody.' The committee emphasised this policy in *Talyllyn News* in September 1960.

In the first place, any anxiety that we are no longer a preservation Society must be speedily and emphatically allayed. When it was formed in 1950 the Society pledged itself to preserve the historic character of the railway, and the committee still stands by this pledge. This is not just antiquarian sentiment, but sound business, for it is this historic character which is chiefly responsible for attracting members to the Society and passengers to the railway. Inevitably, there must be certain compromises so that an increasing volume of traffic can be handled with safety. In just the same way, modern road conditions may compel the proud owner of a vintage car to modify the brakes or lighting system, but he does not, on this count, destroy the character of the car. He knows that to attempt to ape modern practice except in safety essentials would not only be fruitless and absurd, but would also debase an historic piece of machinery to the value of its weight in scrap metal. Exactly the same conditions apply to the Talyllyn railway.

At its next meeting after the 1960 AGM a majority of the new council (as the committee re-named itself) stated their belief 'that the continued pursuit of new traffic records is not consonant with the basic aim of the Society, which is the preservation of the Talyllyn Railway.'

Tom's wife, Sonia, upset by the destruction of the winding house and the old Abergynolwyn station (although Tom is reported to have gone along with this particular plan reportedly saying in council that 'there was nothing special about it'), reacted passionately in a thought-provoking article in the March 1969 edition of the

News. She headed her piece 'Abergynolwyn, the Winding House and Rule 3 – or preserving the preservation.' She wrote:

> Your railway, they said at frequent intervals over a number of years. To me, as a member of the TRPS, the democratic principle never seemed to mean anything like this: it could not belong to me or anyone. Rather, the railway belonged to Wales, to the place, to time, to itself. The democratic principle seemed more to mean – having respect for that which one had the power to change. Respect arises from love, love from understanding, and understanding involved everything to do with this unique form of life. Not any old railway this one. Why it was there, the men who brought it about, the hard fact of the slate in that one mountain and the men who got it out, worked it, built a village with it and all the artefacts belonging to the line: who had lives intimately linked with it and whose efforts and the acretions of whose lives we inherited in this extraordinary way. Such feelings, and I've always believed that many others shared them, could never be satisfied by simply running a railway, however successfully. We had to do honour to the past, to celebrate it by our success and by the understanding we brought to it.
>
> Every ounce of effort in the early years was devoted to renewal, to existing as well as we could, until we came to 1963 when, in the hideous reality of falling traffic receipts, we had to change or die. That effort, the redevelopment at Wharf station . . . was an evolution rather than a destruction and alteration, a spontaneous growth change inherited from within all levels of the Society and as such it is a success. It dishonours nothing. The office building is still there for anyone who wants to recognise it: the old wagon compound is there imaginatively incorporated in a building and an idea, the museum, which must enhance the railway experience, educative and assuming the best of the railway visitor, his desire to know and to understand, and by its presence implacably stating a greater duty than profit making.

Mrs Rolt went on to bewail that the council seemed to be stalling on an offer to design a new station at Nant Gwernol made by Clough Williams-Ellis 'the greatest Welsh architect', whose monument is the Italianate marvel of the settlement of Portmeiron, a few miles up the coast.

The one man imbued with the history of Wales and inspired with the sense of place to be able to give us something which would be nationally recognised and visited and which could become a little Wonder of Wales: reached by train only as the crown and end of the pilgrimage into the heart of the mountain. Clough Williams is 86. This is not an offer we can keep in abeyance until we think we might take advantage of it. We should be overwhelmed with the opportunity and be doing everything to bring it about.

The Winding-House has gone. It should have been kept, the ingenuity and effort required to keep it a challenge to our engineers, to provide one of the visual pleasures of the journey, and, for those who can look further, evocative evidence of the old crucial links between village, railway and mountain.

We have a wonderfully devoted and skilled permanent staff at Towyn. The very best that could be found: but by the very nature of things their skills are in running a railway and making a profit out of it. Not one of them is a preservationist as such, nor should be. It should be the duty of the Council to see the wood for the trees and hold the overall view as a preservationist Society. This, in the matter of Abergynolwyn and the Winding House, it has signally failed to do. Neither the latter nor Abergynolwyn station, were discussed at any time with particular reference to Rule 3. There will be more and more danger of this as the Board of the Company and the Council move closer and closer to problems at Towyn and difficulties connected with day-to-day running, handling crowds and financial profits.

In the last resort the application of the Council's policy at the present time depends on it being only able to insist on those things being done which the permanent staff at Towyn will do. Thus the policy of the Society can become precisely as large, or as small, as the permanent staff. The demolition of the winding house and the destruction of Aber. station are ideas which have originated at Towyn, the understandable expression of people concerned with day-to-day successful running and handling of crowds. No one will deplore the existence of a comfortable new station, lavatories, refreshments and shop when it is there, but the vast investment and the effort involved to achieve success for it will be at the expense and in the place of, for many years to come, Nant Gwernol. What a lost opportunity! What a choice of expediency in the place of inspiration!

Mrs Rolt went on to point out that the Society is a preservation Society and that its policy should be 'to preserve the railway in its full meaning, not just . . . a train and a journey'. Members 'should try to ensure that we have preservationists as well as railway enthusiasts on our Council'. She added emphatically: 'We don't have to make money for anyone, only enough so that we should be able to do what is right in a preservation Society and go on preserving.'

The Talyllyn can incorporate, with sufficient imagination, the spirit of the narrow-gauge railway in its heyday nearly a century ago, whilst at the same time providing its public with a reasonably comfortable and safe journey in an historic atmosphere.

If the public wants fast, warm, comfortable travel with meals laid on, and extensive refreshment and shopping facilities, it doesn't have to travel miles to the remote west of Wales. What it seeks there is a reminder of a different way of life, to see something of its roots. Something unique! This is what now sells the railway for most of its operating season. The crowds seeking the sun have gone to Spain. The new tourist developments in the area are now recreating industrial archeology: the gold mine, the slate quarry. On the Talyllyn, moves are afoot to restore the winding house on the Alltwylt incline, perhaps the incline itself, and to put together old quarry artefacts at Bryn Eglwys. It is now recognised by some, in retrospect, that the destruction of the Abergynolwyn winding house was possibly a mistake.

But perhaps the Talyllyn was ahead of its time. Think what a tourist attraction a Clough-Ellis building attuned to the grandeur and beauty of Nant Gwernol might have been in the new climate of the affluent visitor to Wales, seeking something different and prepared to pay for it. Ironically in the long run, the preservationists, albeit unconsciously, had the true commercial instinct. Quality, combined with prudence and integrity, pays.

References

The Tal-y-llyn Railway, Lewis Cozens. TRPS
The Talyllyn Handbook, TR
Railway Adventure, L.T.C. Rolt, David & Charles
Talyllyn Century, ed Rolt, David & Charles
Tom Rolt and the Cressy Years, Ian Mackersey, M. & M. Baldwin
Landscape with Machines, L.T.C. Rolt, Reprinted Ian Sutton
Slates from Abergynolwyn, Alan Holmes, Gwynedd Archives
Great Preserved Locomotives No 6, Johnson & Weaver, Ian Allan
The Little Wonder, John Winton, Michael Joseph
Talyllyn Railway Extension, Chris White, TRPS
The Island of Sodor, Rev. W. Awdry, Kaye & Ward
The Talyllyn Railway, H. Fayle (article in *Railway Magazine* October 1904)
Corris Conservation, Richard Greenhough, article in *Railway Magazine*, March 1988)
Also the Talyllyn's Operating Rule Book, various issues of *Talyllyn News* and *John Slater's Newsletters*.

ACKNOWLEDGEMENTS

With grateful thanks I acknowledge the gracious help of all those who gave of their time, either in checking drafts, or in reminiscing about the past, or both; and also the authors of the sources named in the references. Especial thanks go to John Bate, Peter Bold, Sara Eade, Pat Garland, Richard Hope, Dai Jones, Anne Jaggers, Jean Potter, Owen Prosser, Gordon Rhodes, Sonia Rolt, John Slater, Roy Smith, John Snell, Bill Trinder, Graham Vincent, Pat Whitehouse, David Woodhouse; to the staff of the County of Gwynedd Archives Service at Dolgellau for their patience and courtesy in retrieving numerous Talyllyn Railway papers; and not least to my editor and publisher, David St John Thomas.

None of the above, nor the Talyllyn Railway Company, nor the Preservation Society, has any responsibility for errors of commission or omission, or for the views expressed, all of which lie at the feet of the author.

Index